Jim Smith

The Autobiography

IT'S ONLY A GAME

Dedication

To my wife Yvonne and my daughters Alison, Suzanne and Fiona for their love, patience, understanding and support through many crazy years.

Jim Smith

The Autobiography

IT'S ONLY A GAME

Jim Smith with Bob Cass

André Deutsch

First published in Great Britain in 2000

by André Deutsch Ltd
76 Dean Street
London W1R 5HA

www.vci.co.uk

A catalogue record for this book is available from the British
Library.

ISBN: 0 233 99803 9

Typset by Derek Doyle & Associates, Liverpool

Printed and bound Great Britain by
Mackays of Chatham PLC

CONTENTS

FOREWORD

by Howard Wilkinson, FA Technical Director

Jimmy Smith was in his first management job at Boston United when he phoned me in Sheffield. Two weeks later I was working with him in my first professional coaching job. One successful year later, just to underline how well we had done together, he left! I picked up the reins and benefited enormously from his legacy. Jimmy left to take over his first league club at Colchester United and so began his incredible journey through over a thousand games in professional football management. It would be neither accurate nor fair to pretend the marathon had left him unscarred; he remains however totally unbowed. Come match-day, the eye of the tiger – or in Jim's case the eye of the 'Eagle' – shines just as bright and sharp as ever.

But Boston was not our first meeting. I ran into him – or should I say he ran into me – some forty years ago. A school pal and I had been invited as fifteen-year-olds to train at Sheffield United on Tuesday and Thursday evenings . . . bit players in a cast of thousands. In those days clubs like United and their city rivals Sheffield Wednesday would turn out five teams every Saturday – first team, reserves, Yorkshire League, Northern Intermediate and 'A' team. A large proportion of that lot would be part-time or what were euphemistically referred to as 'amateurs'. Jim was a Wednesdayite – so was I. He had just finished at Firth Park Grammar School and I was concluding my excursion into academia at another local grammar school, Abbeydale. Training in those days was all about running laps around the football and cricket pitch at Bramall Lane as quickly as possible. Interspersed with the running would be exercises such as sit-ups, push-ups and the like. These were performed without question, on command from the trainer Harry Latham, himself an ex-United player. This process made you fit to play properly and other benefits were you got to breathe the life-threatening amounts of smog which hung over Sheffield from November through to February. At the same time you dehydrated yourself in a fashion akin to walking in the Sahara. We were all told, and therefore believed, that sweating and the misleading resultant loss of weight accurately indicated the benefits of training. To that end we covered ourselves in enough sweaters and tops to do justice to an Antarctic crossing.

This was the exhausting and boring preamble to the carrot with which every training night was concluded. Bramall Lane cricket pavilion had a gym and on a Tuesday and Thursday night that gym was no place for the faint-hearted. Come to think of it, it may have been the birthplace of kick boxing as a sport. There was a ball in there somewhere but, given half a chance, the ball tried to stay out of harm's way. When I eventually played my first game in the Yorkshire League I quickly realized the benefit of those kicking matches in the gym. Jimmy started to learn his trade in that league at places like Frickley Colliery, Stocksbridge Works and Swillington Miners' Welfare. Overnight success then was getting into a Football League team's reserves as twelfth man before your twenty-first birthday.

Jimmy has made a few bob now. He's nicely comfortable and not averse to the odd glass of half-decent red wine, preferably quaffed in an up-market eating establishment serving Michelin-starred grub. Nevertheless you do not have to scratch too deeply to find the real Jimmy Smith, a man who has maintained all the real, worthwhile and genuine values he developed during those early years. His old friends, and I would like to count myself as one, still get their Christmas and New Year phone call: 'Hello, Jimmy here, compliments of the season and a happy New Year.' And it is always welcome.

Mere survival in football is an achievement and he is the ultimate survivor. His honesty, pride, enthusiasm, passion and anger still burn as strongly as ever. He has made a few bad decisions which he will admit to, but he made his best one when he married Yvonne. She probably understands football and what it means to people better than he does. It has been my pleasure and privilege to know him most of my life and I wish him luck with this book. If the sales are restricted to only his enemies, nobody will buy it.

INTRODUCTION

I could have ended up as anything but a football manager . . .
steelworker; fishmonger; bookmaker; car body repairer; laboratory assistant; removal man; painter and decorator. I was a
real jack of all trades but unfortunately the master of none.
But it was after dabbling in all those jobs that either fate or
myself decreed that football was the life for which I was
destined. There was always something which contrived to
point me in that direction – usually a painful reminder that
manual dexterity was not one of my strongest assets. I think
my dad, who was also called Jimmy, called it right when he
urged me one day, 'For God's sake, Jimmy, I hope you manage
to do something with your feet because you are bloody
useless with your hands.'

Football was always my passion but, as a teenager leaving
school, it was not my life as much as I dreamed it might be.
My first job was at Tinsleys Wireworks in Sheffield where I
enrolled on a managers' course with the intention of learning
everything to do with the industry. After completing that I
would then be appointed a departmental manager, a nice
steady career which I could probably have combined with
playing part-time. I started just after I left school so was still
wet behind the ears and therefore a target for all kinds of
practical jokes – the sort which had been played at Tinsleys
from the year dot on green, impressionable kids who did not
know their arm from their elbow. On one occasion one of the

older chaps sent me to the store-room to get a long weight. 'Just stand there and I'll fix you up in a minute,' said the store-room manager. The penny did not drop even when I had been kept standing around for an hour. That was when the manager came back and said, 'Okay son, you can go back now – that's the longest wait anybody has had for a long time.' There were plenty of other opportunities to have a laugh at my expense. One day when I was cutting metal rods, one jumped up as I was getting it out of the vice and smashed me in the mouth, knocking a tooth right back into the gum. Eventually it had to come out but not before I had a couple of days of excruciating toothache which was hardly eased when I had to perform another of my duties – filing down the welded joins on steel girders in a workroom lit by a single light. I said to myself on that day, 'Jimmy, you've got to get out of this place.'

I had signed as an amateur with Sheffield United and played on Saturday mornings in the Northern Intermediate League. At first there was no problem because I was in the maintenance department which finished at 5 p.m. on a Friday and had Saturdays off. Later I was absolutely delighted to be taken on as a part-time professional with United but unfortunately it was around that time that I was switched to the wire netting department at Tinsleys where the hours were different. We finished at 4.30 p.m. every afternoon but had to work Saturday mornings. This forced me into an early decision about my priorities. I pleaded with the foreman to allow me to stick to the work schedule I had in the previous job but he refused so that was the end of Tinsleys. Instead I inflicted myself on my dad, who had had his own wheelwright business for twenty years until horses stopped pulling carts around the streets of Sheffield. Then he switched to repairing damaged bodywork on lorries. He had a small rickety old yard where he worked every hour that God sent. He never made any real dough, although he made sure his family never went short when it came to holidays, clothes and spending money. My dad was from the old-fashioned school; not only was he careful never to swear in my presence, but also he would never allow the chap who worked for him for years to do so either. One day I walked into his workroom at the precise second he hit his thumb with a hammer. I saw my dad in a new light then as he gave vent to the kind of Anglo-Saxon language that would have made a docker blush. It was the chance his mate had been waiting for – quick as a flash he wagged a stern finger at dad and shouted, 'Jimmy, mind your language in front of your lad.'

I was never really cut out to be a manual worker although my dad exercised limitless patience to try and get me to do the job properly. Then one day he finally reached the end of his tether as I botched another simple task and he uttered his exasperated plea to me to concentrate on becoming a footballer. I resolved to try even harder.

In the meantime, he persuaded a pal of his, Ernest Baldock, who had a business in the fish market, to give me a job. The football yearnings were still strong but the top clubs were not exactly milling around the touchlines at United's youth-team matches and I had to do something to supplement the few quid I picked up as a part-timer. My role at Baldocks was a simple one that needed no special tuition in the art of fishmongery. I had to pick up the boxes of fish at the railway station at 4 a.m. and take them to the market where the fish were prepared for sale. Then I had to deliver the fish to the schools which had a contract with Mr Baldock. My vehicle was an aluminium flat-back lorry which, because I was determined to get finished as soon as possible, I drove at a speed which would have done credit to Nigel Mansell. Unfortunately, one morning as I went careering around a sharp bend the boxes shot off the back, smashed on to the road and scattered fish all over the place. I had to pick them all up, take them back to the market and wash them under the tap before resuming the deliveries. I thought I had got away with it until Mr Baldock became inundated with complaints from the schools about the amount of grit in the fish. He was not amused and we agreed that I should find another way of earning a living.

A change of scenery might have provided the solution and the opportunity for that arose when I was given a free transfer from Sheffield United and signed for Aldershot in July 1961. But I stayed in Sheffield that summer, mainly because I had found employment labouring for a local builder but also because I had met my future wife Yvonne and did not want to leave the area. It was back-breaking work, digging foundations for houses and other buildings. The only time the lads really pulled their fingers out was when the foreman offered them incentive bonuses to work faster. That meant they could get into the pub for 4.30 p.m. instead of 6.30 p.m. Thursday was pay day but when it came around I was intrigued to notice that a lot of my fellow workers had hardly any money at all in their packets. This, I was informed, was because they had taken 'subs' – their word for an advance – during the week. It turned out this was a regular occurrence which enabled them to get to the pub and have a bet on the horses. That seemed a bit daft to me so I suggested to a couple of them that if they decreased the amount of their 'subs' and eased off the drinking and gambling, they would have more in the packet at the end of the week. They just would not have that at all although, to be fair, I also contributed to their downfall with a profitable sideline as a bookie's runner. The lads would write out their bets on slips of paper and I would take them to the bookie who kept regular lunchtime hours in a local pub and paid me a small commission. He was obviously not short of a few bob so I wondered, as digging seemed too much like hard work, if bookmaking could be the answer. But you needed money to get started in that and that was in short supply.

My football career was hardly blossoming. The wages at Aldershot were less than astronomical – £18 a week in the first team, £13 in the reserves and £10 in the summer. Part-time employment was a necessity, especially since I was now a husband and father. I earned £5 a week working in the afternoons as a laboratory assistant at Farnborough Technical College. That was a doddle because I spent most of the time playing badminton with the top lecturer. I gave the job up when we went back to Sheffield for the summer where I was taken on by a removals firm. I quickly discovered, rather than simply lugging wardrobes, settees, beds, tables and chairs all over the place, there was an art to the job – for instance, the last article you take out of a house and the first you take into the next one is a kettle. That means the last thing you have at one house and the first thing you have at the next is a pot of tea. And the household item removal men hate the most is a piano because they are so heavy and awkward to handle. Needless to say I always seemed to end up helping to shift them.

We got paid by the hour and did a lot of work for the local council, so consequently we were never in too much of a hurry to finish a job. But you did get to see the other side of life. One day we were moving a family out of a seriously run-down area where their house was in a terrible state – paper peeling off the walls, outside toilets and no bathroom – into a place which, by comparison, seemed like a palace with all mod cons. There were about ten kids who were clearly seeing inside plumbing for the first time. We piled their belongings into the van watched by the man of the house. He wore a dirty vest, beer belly hanging over his scruffy trousers, and never offered a finger to help. As we carried out their tattered bed settee, he pointed to it and shouted, 'Be careful with that – me and the missus have slept on that for fifteen years.' I couldn't resist the dig, 'Looking at all your kids, mate, I don't think you've spent much time off it.' 'Aye – you're bloody right about that, mate,' he laughed. It was a happy day all round because it was a real pleasure seeing the smiles on the children's faces when they got to their new place and surveyed the bathroom and their new bedrooms. I suppose you could call it a moving experience but it was not what I was looking for.

We stayed in Aldershot the following summer and with another player, Peter Chamberlain, I began to do a lot of painting and decorating. Dave Smith was our manager and he agreed to let us decorate the club houses. We were doing them a lot cheaper than if they brought in professionals but it became quite a lucrative sideline for us. We got £13 a house with the club paying for all the materials and we did so well that our reputation grew and the jobs rolled in. I was not rich by any means but I had more money in my pocket than I had ever had before. Sadly it all went pear-shaped, when, not unlike the days when I drove the fish lorry, I tried to cut one corner too many. We were asked to give a quote to paint a school. It wasn't a large one – just four or five classrooms, a hall and a few other rooms – but it was still our biggest undertaking yet and we needed to enlist more help. We also had to stock up on a few more raw materials such as brushes and the like so I went to the local suppliers and put our order in. I was a bit apprehensive when the guy in the shop gave me a nudge, mumbled 'leave it to me' and arranged to meet us in a pub that evening when he would bring the stuff with him. When he arrived he was loaded up with brushes, scissors, rules, scrapers – everything you could name and a lot more than I had asked for. 'Give me a fiver for the lot,' he said. I told him I only had two pounds with me and we agreed that I would give him the rest later. The following week when Peter and I went to the ground to pick up our wages my namesake told us the police wanted to see us – they had been keeping their eye on the bloke at the suppliers and when the game was up for him we found ourselves involved as well. We got done for receiving stolen goods and finished up getting fined £16 each. That was also the end of our spell at Aldershot because we were both given free transfers. I've always suspected the main reason why Smith let me go was because I had been at the club five years and was due a £500 loyalty bonus if he kept me on. But, whatever the real circumstances, by now I had finally got the message – I was never going to be a football superstar – and a life of crime was apparently not the answer either.

As it turned out, as far as playing the game was concerned my feet were only slightly more useful than my hands – but, when it came to recognizing the talent in others, I would like to think I did Jimmy Smith senior proud.

CHAPTER ONE

THE NUT BORE FRUIT

Club chairmen come in all shapes and sizes. I should know – in thirty years as a football club manager I have worked for, with or under fourteen. Their characters and temperament can be just as complicated and different. You learn to cope with moods that can be good, bad or downright ugly; to be diplomatic; to withdraw graciously from a confrontation when what you really want to do is tell them to do the other thing. And I have to confess there has been the odd occasion when I have failed miserably to resist the temptation. There have been chairmen I wouldn't have changed for the world but they are as rare as pit heaps in my native Yorkshire. I have come across the odd diamond but more often than not the jewel might sparkle but close scrutiny reveals nothing but paste. Their personalities have changed over the years. Invariably they used to be local businessmen who often had to dip into their own pocket just to keep their club afloat. That hasn't altered much as far as many of the lower league clubs are concerned but it is a different story in the higher echelons of the game. There the concern is how a result might affect the share price rather than the league table. I sometimes worry that the stockholder has become more important than the season-ticket holder.

It would be difficult to work out a league table based on the various merits of my employers because many were not around long enough for me to tell if they were good or bad. But the top three, without any question, would be the first chairman to give me a job – Ernest Malkinson at Boston United; the man who appointed me at Blackburn Rovers – Bill Bancroft; and the one who believed in me enough to give me probably my last job as a manager, Lionel Pickering at Derby County. The others include some of the game's most notorious personalities – people like Robert Maxwell with whom I worked at Oxford United and Jim Gregory who took me to Queens Park Rangers and later to Portsmouth. I was also associated with Sir John Hall for a brief period at Newcastle United although he was never my chairman.

They say that fortune – good or bad – takes a hand when you least expect it. It was certainly one of the luckiest days of my life when I bumped into the man who put me on the first rung of the managerial ladder. Ernest Malkinson, the chairman of Boston United, was a football nut. He had been something of an entertainment entrepreneur, owning night-clubs, concert halls and roller-skating arenas in Lincolnshire before turning his attention to bingo halls. My not too illustrious playing career was stuttering to a close at Lincoln City who considered me too old at twenty-eight to play for them. The manager Ron Gray called me into his office to give me the news personally. 'You're the first player I've done this with . . . normally I just send letters out,' he told me. He also explained that it wasn't his decision but that it had come down from the boardroom. Ron then told me he wanted me to play my last game the following Saturday in a Lincolnshire Senior Cup game against Scunthorpe United.

Ironically I got a call on the morning of the game from the Scunthorpe manager Ron Ashman who told me, 'It doesn't matter how you play tonight, I want to sign you.' That Saturday evening the local sports paper in Lincoln contained two pages of letters from irate supporters, denouncing the club for giving me a free transfer and saying that it should be withdrawn. We went out and beat Scunthorpe 4–0 and I played well enough for Ray Harford, then a team-mate at City, to remark that the deal could be off because it looked at times as if I was taking the mickey out of the opposition. I certainly impressed one particular City director who came to me after the match and told me, 'You're going nowhere. We'll talk about it on Monday.' We had a chat and it would have suited me to stay at Lincoln but, as they had cancelled my previous contract, to all intents and purposes, I felt I was entitled to a £250 re-signing fee and they wouldn't agree to that. That was when I decided I was going to Scunthorpe. As it turned out, fate decided otherwise. My mate Peter Kearns had also been given a free by Lincoln. He lived near me and the first thing I noticed as I was walking across to tell him I was off to sunny Scunny was the biggest Mercedes I had ever seen in my life parked outside his house. It was gold-coloured and gleaming – and I thought that either Peter had won the pools or he was getting a visit from some Mafia debt collector. I was certainly intrigued when I rang his doorbell and Peter invited me inside. I discovered the car belonged to a distinguished-looking gentleman sitting in an armchair in the lounge. Peter introduced Mr Malkinson, who was apparently trying to persuade him to sign for Boston. You couldn't fail to be instantly impressed by the chap. He was a tall man, superbly suited with silver hair and thick horn-rimmed glasses, who chain-smoked Manikin cigars. And he didn't mess about. After a few token words of introduction he turned to me, smiled and said: 'Why don't you come and play for us as well.' I had to think fast – part-time football was not part of my plans, my wife Yvonne and I had a young family, we had just moved into our first house and we needed every penny I earned. But, because I knew he had just sacked his manager, I decided to jump in with both feet. 'I won't come just as a player but I'll be your player-manager,' I told him. To my surprise he seemed delighted with the idea, so we arranged that I would go down the following Monday night to watch them play their final match of the season. I sat on a fold-up chair behind the goal in what could loosely have been described as a directors' box. It wasn't how I had envisaged the route down which I wanted to travel; but there was something about the place that I liked.

Nor was I put off when I went into a little private room afterwards to have a chat. My eyes were drawn to a desk on which £400 in crisp, newly minted notes were neatly stacked. It was more money than I had ever seen, let alone earned, and the sight of it certainly pre-empted any prolonged discussion. I just picked it up, shook hands with the chairman and told him he had got himself a new manager. That's how it all started ... through a chance meeting when I thought I was going to see out my playing career with Scunthorpe. Ironically after all that Peter didn't sign for Boston although I would have loved to have taken him with me. He wanted to go south and he eventually went to play for Weymouth. But I'm certainly glad Mr Malkinson made the effort to travel up to Lincoln to see him. I wonder what would have happened and where I would be today if he hadn't.

I found out later he only used the Merc on special occasions and that his normal mode of transport was a little nondescript number that shuttled him around the town. But the gold limo came out again when he drove me down to Chelmsford for the Eastern Counties Cup final which we won. When we got back to Boston at about 1 a.m. I said to him, 'Oh, by the way, Mr Malkinson, I want £250 to sign George McLean from Barrow tomorrow.' Without blinking – and certainly without a questioning word or glance – he reached over towards the glove compartment and pulled open the door to reveal a pile of cash strewn all over the place. He counted out the readies and the deal was done the next day. It was typical of the way he operated. He was forever digging into his pocket, sparing no expense to get me the players I wanted and paying them whatever I thought they were worth.

Our friendship lasted long after I left Boston but mine was not the only career that Mr Malkinson followed enthusiastically. There was another young coach who would thank him for being the instigator of a change of direction that would take him to the very top in the game. Howard Wilkinson will be the first to admit that the day he agreed to sign for me turned out to be the most momentous of his football life. One thing is certain, I doubt whether he would have gone on to the magnificent career he has enjoyed in football management had he not been given his first start as a coach at Boston. I knew about him because he was a Sheffield-born lad like myself who had played for Wednesday as a kid, something I had always wanted to do. I knew he had gone to Brighton where things hadn't worked out and that he intended to pack up playing full-time, go back home to Yorkshire to enrol at Teacher Training college and become a PE teacher. I was looking for someone to play on the left side and he seemed just what I wanted. I persuaded him to play for me part-time. He was quite happy with the arrangement because the £20 a week he got from us was good money at the time and helped to fund him through college.

I was doing a lot of wheeling and dealing, experiencing for the first time the pleasures and pitfalls of the transfer business. The players we took to Boston came from all over the place, signed mostly on 'frees' from league clubs, usually with the little friendly financial persuasion necessary to do the business. When I first took over I had a playing staff of sixteen. There were lads I wanted to bring in but I also decided to offer new deals to eight or nine who were already at the club and whose contracts had run out at the end of the previous season. Howard was one of the newcomers. He travelled from Sheffield to train and play in the matches. Football was not his biggest priority at the time because he was more interested in teaching as a career, but playing for Boston provided the link with the game that was to develop into greater things. In fairness, one of the things that attracted him to Boston was my promise to let him do a little coaching and he got involved in the two-nights-a-week training sessions. The qualities that were to make him a top-class coach, a championship-winning manager and now FA Director of Football were plainly evident in those days. So much so that when I left Boston to manage Colchester United, he was my recommendation to take over. But Mr Malkinson disagreed. 'He's too young,' he insisted, but made him coach with a lad called Keith Jobling becoming manager. 'Fair enough,' I said. 'But take it from me, Howard's your man.' And that's how it eventually worked out with Howard assuming control and Keith taking a more administrative role.

And so an illustrious career was launched. Under his guidance the team won the Northern Premier League title that eluded me and he went on to become assistant and then manager of Notts County and boss at Sheffield Wednesday and Leeds United, where he joined the select band of managers who have won the league title. He now has the crucial role of spearheading the development of the game from grassroots level upwards to the international team and I feel very proud of the part I played in his career. I am sure, like me, he values the experience he gained from starting in football's basement. Sometimes I wonder how some of the other top managers in the game would have enjoyed learning their lessons in the school of hard knocks. I have experienced the thrill of leading a team out in a final at Wembley but every August or September I always spare a thought for the managers of the non-leaguers setting out on their long FA Cup journey because that's what we used to do at Boston United, playing preliminary round after preliminary round at places like Louth and Spalding. These games were always a hard slog, played on poor pitches against sides that were ready to kick you up a height. But it was vital to the club's finances that we got through and kept alive our hopes of reaching the first round proper and coming up against and hopefully beating a league club.

I'll never forget one such game when we had been paired with Ellesmere Port and I am sure it will live equally long in the memory of Howard. Ellesmere had just been promoted to the Premier League and had done well. The week we were due to play the cup match on their ground, we took them on in a league game at our place and drew 2–2. They had a real hard case at centre-half called Gerry Casey and as we were leaving the field after the first match he went round to our players saying, 'Wait till we get you next week; I am going to kick shit out of you.' I could tell before we went there that half our team were petrified. I have to say I wasn't looking forward to meeting him again too much myself.

The weather on the day of the match was diabolical: gales, freezing cold and sheeting rain blowing horizontally down the pitch. I won the toss and decided to kick with the wind, hoping we'd get far enough in front by half-time to hang on. Howard stood like a drowned rat on the wing for most of the game. In fact his only contribution was to hit a screamer from about thirty yards into the back of the net. I don't know where he got the strength from because he looked totally fed up and probably wished he was in some warm classroom. But that was all we had to show for having the advantage of the conditions and I didn't think it would be enough. Fortunately for us, although it wasn't too clever for our player, Casey decided to make good his threat. He head-butted John Froggatt, away from the ball but not out of sight of a linesman who drew the referee's attention to the incident and Casey got his marching orders. We managed to hang on against the ten men and win 1–0.

I don't think I have ever felt so cold. We could hardly get our kit off in the dressing room afterwards. Mr Malkinson walked in with a bottle of Scotch which was welcomed not only by us but also the match officials who had to use our facilities because there was no hot water in their room. I remarked to the referee that I was terrified he would put the game off because the conditions were so bad. He just shook his head and said, 'No chance of that, you won't catch me coming back here in a hurry.' But the afternoon was far from over. I went into the lounge after the game and was enjoying a chat and a drink with Mr Malkinson and the other Boston and Ellesmere directors when I was suddenly gripped with fear. I looked up and saw Casey staring at me, eyes blazing, from the other side of the bar that separated the two lounges. He pointed at me, snarled 'I'm coming for you – you got me sent off', and started walking around the bar in my direction. Believing he would never dare to do anything in front of both sets of club officials I edged nervously nearer the main group of directors but as I shuffled towards them, they shuffled further away, leaving me and Mr Malkinson to face the wrath of this menacing monster. I have to admit that for a moment I thought of hiding behind my sixty-five-year-old chairman but decided against it and instead braced myself for the onslaught, with a twitching backside.

Fortunately when it came it was all verbal. I learned the art of diplomacy that afternoon – or was it cowardice? – nodding and smiling and generally agreeing with Casey that he had been hard done by. He settled for giving me a few prods and a good ear-bashing. Later I received a letter from Ellesmere apologizing for his behaviour and telling me he had been suspended for a fortnight.

In 1970 we were drawn to play a third round qualifying round tie away against our local rivals Boston FC – the team started as a spin-off from our club by a couple of blokes who upset Mr Malkinson by the way they wrested control of Boston United's lottery, of which more later. For obvious reasons Mr Malkinson hated Boston FC and although we went into the match as strong favourites, there was always the niggling worry that we might come unstuck. I went to the chairman a couple of days before the game and asked what the bonuses were for winning. He replied, 'Let me sleep on it.' I'd been to watch the opposition and came to the conclusion they were useless but I knew how much it meant to the old man that we won the game. To him this was just as big a derby match as Liverpool against Everton or Newcastle against Sunderland. He decided to pay us £20 a man to win the game and £20 for every goal difference. At half-time it was goalless and there were a few nervous twitches in the dressing room. But I scored from the penalty spot early in the second half and that opened the floodgates . . . two, three, four and eventually five. The chairman was happy to fork out the cash even if he did confess later that he appealed for offside every time we went forward after we got to four.

You cannot imagine the thrill and expectancy of playing in the fourth qualifying round of the FA Cup – ninety minutes away from going into the hat with the so-called big boys. That year the team standing in our way was Rickley Colliery Athletic from the Midland Counties League. That league was inferior to ours and although we again faced a tough away match, I fancied our chances and my confidence was borne out with a 3–1 victory. In those days the cup draws were always made on a Monday – a custom now sadly deceased – and around lunchtime I took a call from the local paper and was given the news that we had been drawn away at Southport, who were then a league club doing well in Division Four.

I went to watch them the week before our game. Standing in the boardroom at Haig Avenue I heard some snooty sod say quite loudly, 'Who the devil is that chap over there?' I thought, 'Cheeky sod – have another look because you'll know me next bloody week.' So there was an extra bit of satisfaction when we beat them 2–0. There were a few celebrations after that. We stopped at a hotel owned by Noel White, who was chairman of Altrincham in those days but later became a director at Liverpool, as well as a leading light with the Football Association, and lived it up a little.

Nothing has changed in the game – football has a habit of lifting you up into the clouds one week and bringing you crashing back to earth the next. It did then and it still does. You learn to ride with your emotions, to accept the rough with the smooth. We drew York City at home in the next round and I bet I was the only player on the field counting the receipts from a replay as the game headed towards the final whistle with the score at 1–1. Just as I was thinking, 'This is a right touch for us, picking up a nice few quid from a match at York', all hell let loose. One of our players had belted the ball up the field to waste a few more precious seconds when to my utter astonishment the referee blew his whistle and awarded York a penalty. I didn't see anything but apparently one of our lads, Billy Howells, had swung a punch at Barry Swallow, one of the City players, who is now a club director. They scored from the penalty, we went out of the FA Cup and I suspended Billy for a fortnight.

They never came more colourful than Mr Malkinson. He was his own man with tremendous vision and a passionate devotion to Boston. But his loyalty got him into hot water on more than one occasion, particularly when he was twice suspended *sine die* by the Football Association. The first time was in the 1940s when as a young chairman he tried to stitch up Arsenal. He had a young player at the club that he knew the Gunners were thinking of buying. He was desperate for the deal to go through so he organized a gang of his mates to go and watch the kid and pretend they were scouts from different clubs. They all started shouting the odds about what a good prospect he was and that they were going to recommend that their respective club bought him. It was a real sting. The Arsenal representative at the game fell for it hook, line and sinker and the lad eventually went to Highbury for what was a decent fee in those days. It didn't take Arsenal too long to discover they had bought a pup and that they had been well and truly conned. And they weren't very happy about the mighty Gunners being outsmarted by the chairman of a little non-league club from Lincolnshire. Unfortunately for Mr Malkinson, he made one grave error. It turned out that the lad's age was wrong on the transfer forms; a mistake which enabled Arsenal to challenge the deal with the Football Association and the whole story came out in the subsequent inquiry. The FA cancelled the whole transaction and slapped a lifetime ban on Mr Malkinson. Clearly the powers that be had no sense of humour in those days either but fortunately they relented and the suspension was lifted after a few months.

He was a showman with bingo halls in Cleethorpes and Skegness as well as Boston. His establishment at Boston was the town's big attraction: a huge night-club, concert room and casino where he would put on the big dance bands and top pop groups of the time. It was all very successful until he became worried about the growing drug culture. He was determined that his establishment would not become a centre for drug trafficking. In fact he became so concerned about it that he eventually shut the place down completely and turned it into a bingo hall. Again the venture turned out to be a huge success and that encouraged him to introduce bingo into football, a move that was to change the face of the game.

Before the riches obtained from television, the bingo ticket provided life-saving funds for clubs, especially those existing on the breadline, and it all started at Boston United. Mr Malkinson put two men in charge and the money soon came pouring into the club's coffers. But then things went wrong. A club director reported the chairman to the FA for running a bingo operation without official permission and Mr Malkinson was again suspended *sine die*. His message to the FA at the time was, 'Gentlemen I will accept your decision but mark my words, bingo will be the saviour of football.'

The irony of the whole thing was that the two men running the operation used what remained in the pool – around £18,000 – to start Boston FC. Still Mr Malkinson bounced back. He was reinstated some time later, inaugurated another pool – this time with the FA's blessing – and went on to develop Boston United into one of the top non-league outfits in the country.

I like to think I played a part in that. But being full-time player-manager was only one of my responsibilities. I became the club secretary and handled all the administration, not only spotting and signing players but sorting out their contracts and registering them as well. It was invaluable experience that served me well throughout my career and certainly helped after I moved into my first league job at Colchester United. The people who ran the club were superb but they were quite new to the game, so my knowledge of transfer dealings came in very handy. I think I was good for Boston but equally they were brilliant for me and friendships forged there have not only stayed with me throughout the years but some have come in very useful as far as later dealings with players were concerned.

It was around that time that I first got to know Gordon Milne, who was manager of Wigan Athletic, then probably our greatest Northern Premier League rivals. Along with Macclesfield and Altrincham, we were the big four in the league. Gordon was someone I admired. He had had a wonderful playing career with Liverpool and England and it was a great thrill for me to be competing with him on level terms, both of us attempting to build the profile of our clubs high enough to be elected to the Football League. Like myself, he was a player-manager and we had some cracking games against each other. We shared a common bond because we were the only full-time bosses in the league and we had set out to learn the job the hard way. I'll admit there was more than a little pang of envy when he left Wigan and went straight up the ladder into the First Division as assistant to Joe Mercer at Coventry City, later taking over as manager when Mercer retired. That was the kind of path I was yearning to follow. But there were no short cuts to the top for me – there were a few slides down slippery snakes before I finally got there. Years later after Gordon moved to Turkey and I was with Queens Park Rangers he did himself, me and Les Ferdinand a favour when he took Les, then a young striker, on loan to Besiktas. It was during that spell with Gordon that Les really got his head around his game and began to blossom. I even lumbered Gordon with the role of chief executive of the League Managers' Association when I left to go back into management with Derby County but, like me, he did not feel he was cut out for an administrative job and after only a year he too went back into management.

Gordon is now at Newcastle with Bobby Robson, two wily characters who have forgotten more about the game than most people will ever get to know. It was a typically shrewd move by Bobby to get him on board because it will allow him to concentrate on the coaching, tactics and the other important aspects of management at the sharp end, knowing there is somebody to handle all the rest of the business of shaping a football club. I can reveal now that he beat me to the punch. I was looking to give him a similar role at Derby at the end of the 1999–2000 season. You cannot put a value on his kind of experience. He had that spell at Coventry but spent a lot of his managerial career abroad working at top clubs in Turkey. I suppose it was hard work over there but at least he didn't have to go through the daily routines that were part of the apprenticeship for young managers like me and him at Wigan and Boston – like concreting the car park, digging the drains for the pitch and decorating the boardroom. I used to go back from time to time taking teams for friendly matches and the wallpaper had never changed so I must have done a good job.

At Boston United you did not dare allow yourself the luxury of an ego – even when you became something of a local hero. We made the FA Cup first round proper for the second time in 1971. We had given old Ellesmere Port a good old 3–0 stuffing at their place which had taken us into the dizzy heights of round two and a home match against Len Ashurst's Fourth Division side, Hartlepool United . . . and I had scored the winner. We had been awarded a free-kick on the edge of the Hartlepool penalty area and I could not wait to take it because I noticed their 'keeper take up a position directly behind the wall with his vision clearly impeded. I wish I could say I bent it David Beckham-style but there was a big enough gap even for me not to miss it. And I didn't! Glory be . . . we were in the velvet bag with the big boys. The players, Mr Malkinson and myself clustered around the radio the following Monday lunchtime to hear us drawn at home to Second Division Portsmouth.

The whole town was gripped by FA Cup fever but, for me, the sweat did not end there. I might have been feted as the second-round matchwinner but there were tasks to perform which went beyond preparing the players for the match. Not only was I in charge of the ticket-sales operation but on the Friday evening before the game, I actually went around the ground sticking ticket numbers on seats. It was a job that needed to be done and there was nobody else around but me to do it. Sadly, there was no happy ending. We gave Pompey a run for their money but lost by the only goal of the game. It was one of many great days I enjoyed at Boston – they were not only happy times for me, but for my whole family too. Yvonne mucked in at the club as well, handling all the wages for the players and staff. We also took over the running of the club lottery when, over a period of time, we uncovered more fiddles than you'll find in the London Philharmonic. Yvonne had another job too. She and the trainer's wife opened a little tea bar at the ground which became very popular with the supporters. There were no high horses at Boston United. I suppose everybody took their cue from the chairman.

I felt more than a little remorse when I went behind Mr Malkinson's back to apply for the job as manager of Colchester United. It was the first and only managerial post I have ever applied for. I saw an advert in one of the papers, made contact and was asked to go and watch Colchester play at Peterborough where I was to meet the chairman, Mr Roy Chapman, vice-chairman Mr Robert Jackson, and one of the directors, a Mr Jack Rippingale. The team was struggling in the Fourth Division but they got a very good point in a 2–2 draw and the three board members were really brimming afterwards. Mr Chapman smiled at me and said, 'I thought we played really well – what about you?' And he seemed quite stunned when I replied, 'Well, to be quite truthful, I thought you were crap.' That kind of honesty is not often the best policy but they told me later that it got me the job. I was invited to Layer Road to meet the rest of the directors. It didn't help much when I got a puncture on the way and had to change the wheel. I got to the ground late with dirty hands and in a generally dishevelled state. Fortunately Betty Scott, the club secretary and general factotum, calmed me down and made me presentable. It was the start of a lasting friendship. I discovered after I was appointed just what a vital role she played in the day-to-day running of the club.

That night I left Layer Road with the offer of the job as Colchester's new manager, as long as I could start straight away. They had a game that Saturday against Mansfield Town, who were top of the league, and they wanted me in place by then. I drove back to Boston with mixed feelings – excited and enthusiastic that, at thirty-two, I was going to be one of the youngest managers in the league, albeit in charge of a club that at the time were holding up the rest of the ninety-two, but fearful and apprehensive about having to deliver the news to the man who had treated me like a son. I should not have worried because in telling Mr Malkinson, I experienced again the stature, principles and fairness of the man. I had decided there was no point in beating about the bush. 'I've got the Colchester job,' I told him. 'I'd like to go there but I have to go this week.' He just shook me by the hand and gave me his blessing. 'Go and give it your best, Jimmy,' he said. 'It will be hard here without you but you have deserved this opportunity.' And then he smiled and said by way of a parting shot, 'If you don't like it you can always come back here.'

We stayed in touch. I signed two players from Boston for Colchester, Bobby Svarc and John Froggatt, and took a few teams back there to play in friendlies and his welcome was never less than wholesome and friendly. He always knew how well or badly my teams were doing and told me mine was the first result he looked for on a Saturday afternoon. His wife told me a few years later that his great wish was to live long enough to see me lead a team out in a Cup final at Wembley. I achieved that distinction in the 1986 Milk Cup final when I was manager at Queens Park Rangers. Ernest Malkinson died twenty minutes after the game finished. For me he was a founder member of the league of gentlemen – an absolute diamond. I always said he should have taken over a league club because I think he would have been a great success. But he was happy to do what he did for Boston and I could never thank him enough for what he did for me.

CHAPTER TWO

THE FIRST LAYER

I wouldn't say that I found being in charge at a league club easy but I did win the manager of the month award in my first month at Colchester. I was young and a bit cocky because I'd had the run of things at Boston and done well. In my four years there we were never out of the top three and enjoyed some excellent FA Cup runs. When I left they were five points clear at the top of the Northern Premier League and, eventually under Howard, won the title at the end of that season. Colchester were rock bottom of the Fourth Division when I took over towards the end of October 1972 but that didn't stop me announcing confidently, 'If I don't get my team out of the Fourth Division in two years I will consider myself a failure.' Brave talk which sounded even more like hot air when the club was forced to apply for re-election to the league the following May, having risen to the dizzy heights of third from bottom. In fact I was more worried about getting the sack – it certainly was not how I had planned things. We drew that first game against Mansfield Town and followed that with a couple of good results, including a goalless draw in the second round of the FA Cup at Bournemouth, who were doing well in the Third Division under John Bond.

I was made up, especially when it came to the presentation of the award – a gallon bottle of whisky – before the replay at Layer Road. That's when I came to an early conclusion about that manager of the month award and nothing that has happened during my years as a manager has made me change my mind – it is nothing but a jinx, the proverbial kiss of death. We lost 2–0 and struggled to get none. It was the start of my first really bad spell as a manager and I have to admit that after a few weeks I felt mentally shattered. Looking back, I have won the Manager of the Month award about thirteen times and lost every match that followed the presentation. I promised myself some time ago never to receive it on the pitch again before a game. The only trouble is I haven't been able to put my theory to the test by winning it since.

My ideals at the time were clear and really haven't changed throughout the years I've been in the game. I have always been a great believer in getting the physical side right, making sure my players lack nothing in the way of fitness and condition. One of the first things I did when I went to Boston was to appoint a fitness coach, John Hall – a PE teacher from Grimsby. I employed him to do the fitness training with the part-timers. It might have been the first time anybody in football had a job like that. I had certainly never come across one as a player. I was persuaded to do it because I only had the players for training on Tuesday and Thursday nights and I needed quality time with them. I realized there would be a tremendous advantage if we managed to get them as fit as possible. John introduced weights into the training and he structured the whole fitness programme for the season. The effect on the players was almost immediately obvious and for me it was the key factor in our success. These days people might consider me to be one of the game's traditionalists but I was forward-thinking enough to see the value of a specialist fitness coach long before it became an automatic feature at football clubs.

In addition to Svarc, my first signings included Barry
Dyson from Orient and Mike Walker, a goalkeeper from
Watford, who went on to manage Norwich City and Everton.
Mike had been a bit erratic at Watford but we were desperate; we needed a goalkeeper and he was available on a free
transfer. He came to Colchester and did a brilliant job for us.
What I remember most about Mike was his dedication. He
was an exceptional trainer, forever working out on the
weights and the other equipment I had installed at the club.
We bought the weights second-hand for £100 from Ipswich
Town after I heard they were having a new multi-gym put in
and we built a little weights room under the stand. Mike was
never out of it. Like Howard, I would have forecast that he
would go on to become a manager, although unfortunately he
has not been quite as successful. There have been many players I have worked with who have aspired to a successful
career in management and coaching, people like Graham
Taylor, Trevor Francis, Ray Harford, Alan Curbishley, Ray
Graydon, to mention just a few.

It wasn't too difficult to spot the leadership qualities in
Graham Taylor, who was a team-mate of mine at Lincoln. When
we played together I was around twenty-eight and he was
twenty-two going on thirty-two. Lincoln's manager Ron Gray
came from the old school of sweat and liniment – what we today
would recognize as standard coaching techniques were not
exactly his forte. But Graham more than made up the leeway.
One season, Lincoln were going for promotion but we had had
a bad result on the Saturday. Graham gathered the rest of the
players together in the middle of the pitch at the start of our
Monday training session and went through certain players like
a dose of salts, accusing them of not doing their jobs properly
and generally giving them a right old rollicking. I couldn't help
thinking at the time, 'Well son, you certainly have balls'. It took
a lot of courage to do what he did and I admired him for it even
if there were one or two who thought otherwise.

Later, after I had gone to Boston, I got a phone call from

Graham and he asked me if I was interested in the manager's job at Lincoln. I didn't hesitate in saying that I would love it. 'You'll have to make me your coach,' Graham insisted. That was no problem either and I told him so. That was the last I heard from him about it and I had to have a little smile to myself a week later when the announcement came that Graham himself had been given the job. There were no prizes for guessing why my face didn't fit. Some time earlier just before I left Lincoln I had a bust-up with the chairman, one Mr Henage Dove, after I dropped a clanger in a crucial match, ironically at Colchester. It was a big game as both teams were going for promotion. I had the ball on the edge of the penalty box facing our goal and, rather than give away a corner, I attempted to back-heel to one of my team-mates. Unfortunately one of the Colchester lads came steaming in and smashed the ball into the net from twenty yards and we lost 1–0. I felt rotten about it anyway but Mr Dove charged into the dressing room straight after the game ranting and raving and calling me all the useless sods in the world. My reply was to tell him to go away, although maybe in not such polite terms. Ron Gray told me later that was the real reason why I was given a free transfer. Certainly when it came to the popularity stakes Graham was Mr Dove's blue-eyed boy and I was the villain. But it has not prevented us being great friends over the years and I have enormous respect for what he has achieved at Watford, Aston Villa and as a much and wrongfully maligned manager of England.

Graham certainly justified his appointment. He took the club into the Third Division and it was at Lincoln that he sowed the seeds of a still thriving career. But I think I proved by my record at Colchester that I would not have let anybody down either. The financial resources were limited to say the least and every penny counted. This made me feel all the worse when I persuaded the board to push the boat out to sign Stan Brown, a midfield player from Fulham. He came on a 'free' but we had to pay him a £10,000 signing-on fee – a fortune to a club like ours. He had done well at Fulham but I wasn't impressed when he used to turn up for training on cold days wearing gloves. He didn't perform for us at all. I realized I had made a mistake and decided to let him go for nothing at the end of the season. The chairman Mr Chapman was disappointed but backed my decision. In fact he said he admired me for having the courage to admit I had been wrong about the lad but at the same time it made me realize the importance of good judgement. It was a lesson well learned. I got on well with Mr Chapman. He was another gentleman but if he had a fault it was his indecision – everything had to go through the board and be voted on. And that applied to every decision, big and small. For example, after agreeing to install an industrial laundry unit at the club, I'm sure they had a discussion about which was the best washing powder.

But I loved the job. I quickly adapted to the routine of working with the players on a daily basis instead of just two nights a week. That's what I'd always wanted to do. We trained on land that belonged to the Army and although we couldn't afford a full-time fitness coach, I brought in John Hall from time to time, especially during our pre-season preparation. I changed things around a bit by getting rid of around a dozen players and bringing my own lads in. I was also blessed with an inheritance of several good young players thanks to the efforts of my predecessor Dick Graham, who had quit on health grounds. And we started winning matches to such an effect that by the turn of 1974 we were top of the Fourth Division table. I was still officially player-manager when I went to Layer Road and although I did turn out on a couple of occasions, I quickly realized that by trying to do both jobs I was not doing justice to either. If I had been a player only I could have gone on because I was still very fit. But there was too much responsibility involved for me to treat management as a part-time occupation. I found it impossible to think about playing and at the same time handle all the other things that get thrown at you, such as scouting, training, forward planning, board meetings, team selection and tactics.

I know others have tried to do both and at much bigger clubs than Colchester but, except in rare cases like when Kenny Dalglish had the support of Peter Robinson, Roy Evans and Ronnie Moran – people so strong in their football knowledge – to rely on when he won titles and cups at Liverpool, it just does not work. The issue cropped up again later when I was leaving Queens Park Rangers to take over at Newcastle United. The young chairman Richard Thompson asked me about a possible successor and I suggested he put Peter Shreeves in charge. He replied, 'What about Trevor Francis?' Trevor was thirty-four at the time but I still felt he was our best player and I told Mr Thompson, 'If you move him into management he will become your worst player and you will have lost his value.' Peter held the job briefly before Trevor took over and he became his assistant. Trevor's official title was indeed player-manager but he only played a handful of games after he was appointed. He wasn't pleased when I recommended Peter instead of him but I still stand by what I said and I'm glad to say we're the best of friends again. I think he accepted that you cannot marry the two roles – the pity was that QPR lost arguably their best player.

Hanging up my boots was easy because I enjoyed all the trappings of being a boss, such as meeting fellow managers like Bobby Robson who was then flying at Ipswich Town. I used to go to Portman Road a lot to watch midweek reserve matches and I got to know Bobby really well. I remember the day he offered to drive me to Lilleshall where we were both attending a managers' course. I think he wanted to show off in his brand-new car. The first thing that struck me when he turned up in his huge Jaguar was the colour – a pinky lilac number which would not have been exactly my cup of tea but it was a superbly comfortable ride nonetheless. All the way there and back we played Frank Sinatra on his music system and before he dropped me off back at home he suddenly announced, 'Jimmy, I'm changing the car. I don't like the colour.' A couple of days later he rang me to say he now had a white Jaguar. All I thought was that's the kind of manager I want to be – one who gets a brand-new Jag one week and changes it the next because he isn't suited by the colour.

There was another Portman Road occasion when I went to watch their kids play in the second leg of an FA Youth Cup semi-final. Ipswich won and that gave their wonderful chairman John Cobbold an excuse for a celebration, not that he ever needed one. 'Right, Jim, come on, we're having a glass now. Bobby's on his way up,' he said, beckoning me into the boardroom. I went in expecting to find the usual abundance of champagne but there was not a bottle to be seen. 'Don't worry,' said Mr Cobbold. 'There's champagne here somewhere and I'll find it if I have to turn this place upside down.' And he did before locating a case of the finest hidden deep in some broom cupboard. It was cold enough to demand our serious attention until about 3 a.m. Bobby left to take over England shortly after that and I did not see much of him for a few years. We did bump into each other, however, in Rome before the 1990 World Cup final, barely a few days after the disappointment of the semi-final penalty shoot-out against West Germany. Yvonne and I were walking into our hotel as Bobby was walking out. I commiserated with him and then inquired about his future plans. Bobby smiled and said: 'Jimmy, now I am going to make some real money.'

I had more to do with Bobby than John Bond who was my other near football neighbour at Norwich City. Bondy has always been a larger-than-life character who loved being a big-time Charlie. But he was good company and Yvonne and I enjoyed many social occasions with him and his wife. But he was a different character when it came to football matters. When I was at Birmingham we went to Norwich and they stuffed us 4–0. We had more than half our side out

31

injured and things got worse when Jimmy Calderwood slipped in the toilet before the game and I had to give a young player called Mark Dennis his first-team debut. I went into Bondy's office after the match and he had the champagne out. He was naturally happy and very hospitable. 'Unlucky, Jim, but you had a few problems,' he said as we shook hands. The next day the papers attributed some comments to Bond, that called us a disgrace and accused us of being unprofessional. I remember looking for the date of the return match at St Andrews and thinking, 'Right pal, wait until we get you at our place.' Revenge was indeed sweet when we hammered them by a similar score. Later after he moved to Burnley I bought Billy Hamilton from him for Oxford United for £80,000. He told me, 'Look he can't play – but he'll get you twenty goals a season.' I thought if he got me twenty goals I wouldn't be worried whether he could play or not – and he did.

But a lot of water had passed under the bridge between that time and those early days at Colchester. I have great memories of the people I worked with and the characters I met – like the goalkeeper who was half-blind. I found out about him one night when I was watching a reserve-team game and the club doctor Peter Snell turned up to tell me they had slipped over the medical for Des Kelly, a 'keeper we had signed on a free transfer from Norwich City. 'He's blind in one eye,' said the doc. I was more than a little surprised and resolved to sort out the problem as soon as possible. But the situation became more acute when I was forced to put Des in the side. We had a very good young 'keeper at the time called Barry Smith but unfortunately he picked up a serious wrist injury in training on the day before we were due to play at Bradford City and had to go to hospital. I called Des over and told him to get his kit because he would be playing at Bradford if young Smith couldn't make it. Des was overcome with excitement: 'Oh Bejasus, boss – if God's kind we'll be all right,' he said, shaking my hand until it almost came off. Poor

Barry didn't play and in fact he never played again. Des, who I gathered by now was a devout Roman Catholic, doused himself with holy water before the match, went out and had a nightmare. An ex-goalkeeper team-mate of mine called John Kennedy was scouting for Lincoln City at the game and he called me the next day and pleaded: 'Jim, you have to get rid of that 'keeper or you'll be in serious trouble.' That was the first and only time Des played – we signed a lad from Lincoln on John's recommendation called John McNally and he did well for us.

Apart from a spell halfway through the season when we lost six games out of eight before getting the show back on the road, things could not have gone better in that first full season at Colchester. Joe Hooley had joined us as coach but he left after a short while and I brought in Bobby Roberts, who came from Coventry City, to replace him. Bobby did a tremendous job and it's no exaggeration to say that some of the football we played as a team was as good as any club's I have ever been connected with. It might not have been typical of the fare in the Fourth Division but there was no place for kick-and-rush tactics in my promotion plan. Friday evening under the lights at Colchester was certainly a good place to watch football.

The promotion excitement and anticipation grew as we headed towards the final weeks of the season. We went to Lincoln on a Wednesday night towards the end of March and won 1–0 which pleased me no end for obvious reasons. It also pleased Svarc who scored the goal and Ray Harford who had both been team-mates of mine at Sincil Bank. After the game we went straight to Lilleshall to prepare for Saturday's match at Workington. Lilleshall can be a bit of a morgue at times so the next night I decided to take the lads out for a bit of a knees-up at one of the local pubs. I have to say we all ended up very merry and not in the kind of state players should be in two days before a match. But we still stuffed Workington 4–1 to bring that promotion prize ever closer.

The strange thing was when we did eventually get there, it was all a bit of an anti-climax.

We were actually promoted on Easter Monday 1974 without kicking a ball. We were due to play the following day at Brentford but the teams who could have caught us all lost. And instead of the celebrations and congratulations, all the players got from me was an ear-bashing because we only drew 0–0 at Brentford, giving what I thought was a poor performance. Ray came up afterwards and told me I was out of order. Maybe I should have been thankful for what we had achieved, albeit in half the time I had given myself when I made that reckless boast after I got the job, but I would have loved to have gone up as champions, especially after leading the table for various periods during the season. As it was we had to settle for finishing third behind Peterborough United and Gillingham.

Bury, who finished one place below us, were also promoted, and going up together meant there was a bit of needle involved when we went to Gigg Lane to play Bury early in the 1974–75 season. Both teams were desperate to win because maximum points would take the winner to the top of the Third Division. It was a very tight match with no holds barred but we got the breakthrough when Bobby Svarc cracked one in ten minutes from the end. Me and Bobby were off the bench punching the air when I caught sight of the linesman on the far side with his flag aloft. Then Steve Leslie, one of our young players, started walking off. I couldn't believe it. There had been an incident involving our skipper Stuart Morgan and Bury's Derek Spence but Steve was not involved and I was baffled about why the officials should mix them up because Stuart was about six inches taller and looked nothing like the other lad. My instant reaction was it had been a clear case of mistaken identity and young Leslie would be exonerated. But then, to make matters worse, the referee decided to rule out the goal.

I lost my rag a bit and the headlines the next day were all

about me and Bobby Smith, the Bury manager coming to blows. In fact we never got within ten yards of one another. I think I did question the legitimacy of his birth and I mentioned to Bury's physio Les Hart, who had a lifetime in the game and who was a really good friend of mine, that I felt fair play had not won out that day. I even refused to accept the usual boardroom hospitality after the game. But I was amazed when we got back to our hotel to be confronted by our chairman Robert Jackson, who had taken over after Roy Chapman resigned due to pressure of work. 'I want Stuart Morgan fined and suspended – or even sacked,' he stormed. 'He caused the problem that cost us a goal and stopped us going to the top of the table.' He took a bit of calming down but we compromised by taking the captaincy away from Stuart. He was devastated when I told him and I don't think he was the same player afterwards. In fact I still maintain the whole episode soured our season and we finished halfway up the table when I felt we should have done a lot better.

We certainly had mixed fortunes in the Cup competitions that season. The highlights were probably our performances in the League Cup in 1973–74. We had a great result in the third round when we beat Carlisle United who were then in the First Division 2–1 and then we followed that up by knocking out Lawrie McMenemy's Southampton in a fourth-round replay. The Saints came marching in to Colchester on a night when the pitch was ankle deep in mud and neither side was able to string more than a couple of passes together. It was a case of hit and hope and I think we were both happy with the goalless draw. Nobody gave us much of a chance in the replay the following week and certainly the Southampton players seemed to think it was just a matter of turning up. I couldn't help noticing that at 7 p.m. – half an hour before the kick-off – they were laughing and joking and still wearing their club blazers and ties. That was all the encouragement I needed. I walked into our dressing room and told the players: 'I think we have a great chance if we get among them because they think they're Jack the lads. They think this is a walkover for them.' And we did get stuck in and won the game 1–0 to set up a quarter-final tie against Aston Villa. Lawrie took the defeat on the chin but I could tell he was sick. We played well against Villa too before losing 2–1 in front of a capacity crowd at Layer Road. Our consolation was we could always say we were knocked out by the eventual winners but that was after I discovered what could be on the flipside of good fortune.

The FA Cup was a different story altogether. We had stayed in Bournemouth to celebrate after beating Lawrie's team and on the way back to Colchester I stopped off to watch an FA Cup first-round replay at Leatherhead because we were due to meet the winners of their match against Bishop's Stortford in the second round. Leatherhead won 2–0 but I thought they were poor. In fact I said to Bobby Roberts the next day, 'I daren't tell the players how bad that side is because they could become too complacent.' What we tried to do instead was build our lads up by kidding them that Leatherhead were the best non-league side I'd seen. It was poetic justice because on the day nothing went right for us and we lost by the only goal of the match.

It was one of my worst moments in football. I had been on the other side of the fence a few times when I was at Boston and now I knew what a league manager felt like after being on the receiving end of a giant-killing act. It made me appreciate a little more just how Lawrie had felt a couple of weeks earlier. I thought I would take a leaf out of Lawrie's book and accept defeat gracefully – even to the extent of congratulating a loud-mouthed character who played for Leatherhead called Chris Kelly. He later became known as 'Chris the lip' because of the way he talked up matches and boasted about what Leatherhead were going to do to the opposition. This game had been no different and it hardly eased the agony of defeat when he turned out to be right. Ironically he did not play against us but watched the game from a communal bench with their lot at one end and us at the other. I offered my hand and said – 'Well done' but he brushed me aside with some derogatory remark about my team before racing on to the pitch. I was furious and chased after him threatening all sorts of violence if I got hold of him. Fortunately for both of us he was too quick and I settled for having a few verbal volleys at the players instead.

Colchester taught me the value of success. They were a smashing club but there was a limit to what you could do and because of that I began to get restless. Frustration set in when I was told there was not enough money to sign Brian Talbot, who was playing in the Ipswich reserve team and I felt was a snip at £12,000. And the same applied to John Gregory, now manager at Aston Villa, who was available from Northampton at £9,000. I was torn between loyalty and ambition. Colchester were a club who always stuck by their managers in those days. Dick had been there for four years before me and Bobby Roberts moved into the boss's office after I left to go to Blackburn Rovers and stayed there for seven. I wanted Bobby to come with me to Ewood Park but he wanted a crack at managing and I couldn't blame him for that. He is back with me now as my chief scout at Derby County but I've often told him that staying at Colchester was the biggest mistake he made in his life. Together I believe we could have been a partnership that could have done great things in the game, maybe becoming as well known as Clough and Taylor – we'll never know.

At Colchester it was the chairman who was more likely to change. I had been appointed by Mr Chapman, but he was not really a football man and was only chairman on sufferance. I think he took it on as a short-term measure to help the club out and did not enjoy the pressures of the role. He eventually resigned and was succeeded by Robert Jackson, who was and still is my solicitor. Robert would be the first to admit that he was another whose character was affected by the responsibility of running a football club and he also turned it in after a few short months. The next in line was Jack Rippingale, the third of the directors I had met on that first interview night at Peterborough. That was appropriate in a way because, having been in at the start, Jack was the first director I told when I got the approach from Blackburn. He did not want me to go and threatened to make it difficult for me. But this was an opportunity I did not want to pass up and I told him in no uncertain terms that I was going to talk to Blackburn. The parting was not exactly the amicable affair I had enjoyed when leaving Boston United but again I felt I had earned the chance to manage at a higher level and I was determined to take it.

CHAPTER THREE

NO BREAD IN THE HOUSE

Blackburn Rovers pre-Jack Walker was hardly the million-aire's playground it became when the steel magnate opened his chequebook and invited Kenny Dalglish to set the transfer fees. But, even on that day towards the end of June 1975 when I arrived at Ewood Park as the new manager, I knew I was at a football stadium; you sensed the great tradition of the place. This was a club that had housed League Championship trophies and FA Cups, albeit in the dim and distant past, and even though times had changed for the worse, I felt that I had made it to the big time. I found out later that I arrived eighteen months too late. One of the Blackburn directors, Derek Keighley, also happened to be chairman of Great Harwood who were one of Boston's rivals in the Northern Premier League, and knew me from my days at Boston. He instigated the Rovers approach, inviting me to discuss the possibility of taking over as manager with the chairman Bill Bancroft. Everything went smoothly but some time after I was appointed Derek told me that he had put my name forward eighteen months earlier but Mr Bancroft turned me down because he thought I didn't have enough experience and gave the job to Gordon Lee.

The circumstances behind my appointment were unusual to say the least. Normally a manager takes over after the chap before him has been sacked because of bad results. But I was inheriting a team which had just been promoted to the Second Division and my predecessor Gordon, regarded as the greatest thing since sliced bread by the fans, had landed a nice touch by moving to First Division Newcastle United. People blamed the chairman for Gordon leaving but I couldn't see that although Bill did tell me he had had one ruck with Gordon over a player not wearing a tie. That might sound a bit petty but that was Bill. He was a stickler for detail. He liked everything to be in its place and well organized – and he decreed that the players should wear club blazers, ties and flannels on match-days. I wasn't unhappy with that because I'm a firm believer that employees should uphold the standards of the football club. It's been my policy at all my clubs.

Bill proved himself to be my kind of chairman very early on in my time at Blackburn. He called me to one side before I was due to attend my second board meeting and said quietly, 'Look, there's a director called Mr Pickering who will come in and give you a report on last week's reserve-team game.' In those days, at least one director was required to attend a Central League game and the club had a rota. Apparently it had been Mr Pickering's turn at the last match. 'When you get it,' Bill added, 'just say "thank you very much", put it in your briefcase and then throw it in the bin. For God's sake, don't do what Gordon used to do.' It seemed that Lee would look at the report, tell the director in no uncertain terms that he didn't know what he was talking about and they would end up having a blazing row in the boardroom. I did as he requested then and whenever the occasion arose so I never knew if they knew what they were talking about or not. It was typical of the way Bill operated – he would always mark your card about anything you needed to know so you were always able to handle the situation.

We became great friends as well as having a superb working relationship. He enjoyed the football we played and had a tremendous attitude towards the players. His regular habit was to pop his head around the dressing-room door before a match to wish the lads luck and he would be the first by the door afterwards – win, lose or draw – to welcome the players in. And he always had a cigarette ready to give to David Wagstaffe who couldn't wait to light up. Bill was Blackburn through and through; the club was his life and he was a great traditionalist. He once told me that our kit manufacturers Umbro had offered him a lot of money to change the club's famous blue-and-white halves strip for some new-fangled affair. 'Not as long as I am able to draw breath,' declared Bill. And they didn't succeed – and I love that. As a fan himself he knew what made Rovers' supporters tick; nobody was more aware of their fickleness. He accepted their adulation philosophically when we were doing well and, when we weren't, he gave as good as he got when they hurled abuse towards him in the directors' box. His attitude is summed up in the story he told me about the FA Cup semi-final against Sheffield Wednesday at Maine Road in 1960. 'There were 75,000 spectators in that ground to see us beat Sheffield Wednesday 2–1 to reach the final,' he said. 'Maybe we had around 35,000 there but how many turned up at Ewood Park three days later to see us play Chelsea? About 30,000. So don't tell me about fans.'

It was a pity we did not part on the best of terms. We've sorted it out now but he could not forgive me for leaving Blackburn to join Birmingham. We had some great times together – not the least of which was when, through him, I was introduced to Margaret Thatcher when she was leader of the Opposition. Bill had met her at an FA Cup final at Wembley and invited her to become honorary president of Rovers. To his astonishment she accepted and, not only that, while on a tour of the area, she made it her business to make an official visit to Ewood Park. It was a Tuesday night and we were due to play Stockport County in the League Cup. Bill insisted that we trained that afternoon so Mrs Thatcher could meet the players afterwards. I went along with the arrangement but I was not happy about it. The club gave it the full treatment. A reception was laid on in the boardroom, there was the maximum turnout of directors and their wives dressed up to the nines, all wearing blue carnations and all lined up in the entrance hall ready to greet the lady. And they were not happy when she rushed past them with hardly a glance and came up to me saying, 'You're the man I want to meet because you are the manager and I am the manager.' We must have chatted for eight or nine minutes which did not go down too well with the assembled gathering. Then she went on to the pitch to meet the players. She was scheduled to return to the boardroom for tea and sandwiches but got straight into her car instead and was driven away. The atmosphere in the boardroom was hardly lifted when, on top of everything, we were knocked out of the cup that night.

We had better luck when Ewood Park staged the farewell to English football of the late, great Bobby Moore on 14 May 1977. The England team he captained to win the World Cup in 1966 was one of the finest ever so to be part of such a wonderful occasion was a pleasure and a privilege. Bobby was playing for Fulham and not only was it his last-ever league match, it was also his 1,000th senior game. Both teams acted as guards of honour when Bobby came on to the pitch and afterwards we presented him with a cut-glass liqueur decanter. But there our courtesy ended, I'm afraid, because we did not allow Bobby to go out on a winning note. We had another player with a famous name, Bobby Mitchell, and he scored the only goal of the game.

It was a great day in the history of football and important too for Blackburn. But tradition was not the only thing I sensed when I took over. Once I got into pre-season training, I also became aware of a certain hostility on the part of some of the players to the way I wanted to do things. As I saw it, Gordon had concentrated solely on the first team to the exclusion of the reserves and youths and he had forged a closely-knit élitist clique that I found difficult to break. You would hear one or the other say something like 'That's not the way Gordon would have done it' or 'Gordon did this and Gordon did that'. I soon let them know that in future they would do it my way and like it or the door was there – as it happened some of them did go through. But there were one or two who realized what I was trying to do and supported me, particularly Tony Parkes, who became an important dressing-room influence for me. I appreciated Tony's loyalty then and I know a lot of Blackburn managers have done the same since. He has been a tremendous asset to the club as a player, coach, caretaker-manager and finally manager.

Strangely enough it worked in my favour when we started badly in that first season in the Second Division. We had good pre-season results, winning an Anglo-Scottish tournament by beating Blackpool 3–2 in the final. We thought we were on our way but the league results brought us back to earth. We were not in the healthiest of league positions around the transfer deadline in March 1976 and for that reason, and also because I felt I needed to impose my own identity on the dressing room, I took a chance and bought Gordon Taylor from Birmingham City for about £5,000 and Dave Wagstaffe from Wolves for £3,000. Not a lot of money, less than a day's pay for some of the players that have since gone to Blackburn, but what tremendous value. Gordon, a hard worker these days as Chief Executive of the Professional Footballers' Association, was just as much of a grafter on the wing for me – positive, strong and a tremendous crosser of the ball.

Pound for pound 'Waggy' has to be one of the best players I ever signed. He was a wonderful talent and the fans loved him. They believed he was Bryan Douglas reincarnated. He was getting to the end of his career when he came but he still had a tremendous left foot. The only trouble was there were times when he left you wondering when he was going to use it! 'Waggy' had a bit of a nervous problem; he suffered from bouts of agoraphobia and occasionally he couldn't even come out of his house. He moved to Blackpool where he and his wife bought a boarding house and that's how I managed to get him to sign for us. Sometimes it could be hard work getting him into training – we used to send a driver to his house to pick him up – but when he did come in he was the best trainer I had ever seen. Apart from the normal routine he would practise his skills constantly and if he crossed a hundred balls, ninety-nine would be exactly where you wanted them. But he had you as nervous as he was wondering whether he would turn up.

Any football fan from Lancashire will tell you there is no love lost between the folk of Blackburn and Burnley. In fact they positively hate each other. I've known rivalry in my time – the two Sheffields; the Midland clubs; Newcastle and Sunderland – but nowhere is the animosity stronger than it is between those two sets of supporters. So naturally whenever we met Burnley, our fans were desperate for us to win the game. There was one occasion when this was especially true as we were doing reasonably well and Burnley were struggling at the time. You can imagine how I felt when 'Waggy' walked into the dressing room before the match and announced, 'Boss, I can't play. I'm finished.' I could not believe what I was hearing. 'Can't play,' I shouted, almost bursting a blood vessel with anger, 'you've played in big matches all over the place and you can't play in this one.' Our coach Norman Bodell, who knew 'Waggy' from their days at Wolves together, tried to calm me down. 'Leave him – I'll look after him,' he said and he and the club doctor took him into the toilet. After a few minutes they all came out and 'Waggy' announced, 'I'm all right now, I want to play.' They had given him what he thought was a tranquillizer but was in fact no more than an aspirin.

He went out and played on the left side of midfield and gave one of his best performances in a Blackburn shirt. We were 3–0 up at the interval and our supporters were delirious. Then back in the dressing room at half-time he said he didn't want to go out again. Out came the aspirin and it worked the magic again and how we needed it. We missed a penalty that would have put us four up but then Burnley came back at us and scored twice, one a dodgy penalty. It was a real nail-biting finish made even worse by referee Kevin McNally playing seven minutes' injury time. But we managed to hang on and give the fans the win they wanted.

There was all-round strength, character and skill in that team. We consolidated our Second Division status in the first season back with some degree of comfort and built on that in the following two years to such an extent that we were in the running for promotion to the First Division when I left to go to Birmingham in March 1978. And I was proud of them. I went to a Tony Bennett concert in Manchester and the following day did an interview with James Mossop of the *Sunday Express*. He asked me how I wanted my team to play and I answered, 'Just like Tony Bennett sings – professionally and in perfect harmony.' Two weeks later I received a letter with a Los Angeles postmark from the great man himself. He thanked me for my kind words and invited me to go and meet him any time he was back in England and he signed it 'Tony'. My first reaction was that it was a wind-up because the lads knew I was a big fan. But I made inquiries and discovered that his London agent was instructed to send him every newspaper article that mentioned his name. He had read Mossop's feature and the letter was genuine.

I must have been one of the first managers to play with wing-backs – I had Kevin Hird on one side and John Bailey on the other. They were both wingers who I thought would do better playing deeper. John was a great lad, as keen as mustard. He did not have a decent contract when I took over and I told him he would have to work hard and impress me enough to get into the team if he wanted one. To be fair to the lad he did just that. But there was one game in which he pulled out of a tackle so I got him in the dressing room afterwards, grabbed his curly perm and told him if he ever did it again he would be out of the team. I never saw him do it again and he went on to have a great career with Everton. Graham Hawkins and Derek Fazackerley were safe and reliable at the centre of defence. 'Faz' has since made a name for himself as a coach. I made him a member of my back-room staff at Newcastle and he stayed on to work with Kevin Keegan before Ray Harford took him back to Blackburn. Kevin thought enough of him to give him a job with the international team but I thought he had the potential to be an England player. He was a classy individual, unflustered and seemingly always in control. I thought 'Faz' underachieved; he was far too laid back when he should have been more forceful and imposing.

The midfielders were Tony Parkes and Stuart Metcalfe, as good a pair as I have ever had, and Taylor and Wagstaffe played on opposite flanks. The big weakness was up front. I could never get a front pair to match the rest of the team. I tried various people at different times without getting it right. I even brought the old reliable Bobby Svarc from Colchester but by then Bobby was past his best. He had been a bit of a scallywag in his younger days but then found religion and became a Jehovah's Witness. It might have done wonders for him as a human being but it took away his sense of humour and his spark as a player. He used to have everybody in stitches impersonating me or Bobby Roberts and telling jokes. And he would kill his granny to score a goal. I wished he was three-quarters of the player he had been but the edge had gone.

The subject of goals was always high on the agenda at the annual shareholders' meetings which Blackburn used to hold in the local council offices. There would be the usual comments from the floor and there was one chap who asked more than most. He was tall with wavy ginger hair and he would bellow questions like, 'Are you going to play with wingers, Mister manager?' and 'Are you going to put the right numbers on the shirts because it's bloody confusing at the moment?' Then one day I heard we were getting a new director and when I went into the board meeting, he was sitting there. He introduced himself as Bill Fox, who later not only became club chairman but also president of the Football League. I thought to myself there would be fun and games with this one but he was a great character. I mentioned at one of his first meetings that I wanted to sign a centre-forward called Jack Lewis from Grimsby Town. I told the directors that his wages would be £175 a week. We had an old farmer on the board called Arthur Fryatt and he piped up, 'Eh, Mister manager, if we pay him that much we'll go bloody bankrupt.' But Bill, who had a wholesale potato business in the town, laughed and said, 'Arthur, I pay my bloody drivers as much as that.' That's how we got Lewis but unfortunately he did not quite fill the bill either.

It was a really frustrating time for me because I knew we were so close to a side that could go up. I went to the chairman again and told him I wanted £75,000 to sign Steve Kindon from Wolves. I know he tried persuading the banks to let us have the cash but in the end he came back to me and said, 'I'm sorry Jim – we can't do it.' I took John Radford, the former Arsenal striker, on a free transfer from West Ham instead but again he was coming to the end of his career and was not the success I was hoping for. I felt even worse when Burnley, who had been bottom of the league, bought Kindon back and he scored twelve goals in sixteen games. If he had scored two-thirds of that total for us it would have taken us up. The whole episode left me with the distinct feeling that my opportunities and ambitions would be strictly limited at Blackburn and I began to get itchy feet again.

I had already turned down the chance to go to West Bromwich Albion, which, looking back, might have been one of the biggest mistakes of my career. Around the turn of the year I took a phone call from a pal of mine, Graham Smith, who was the top man with adidas, asking me if I fancied going to West Brom. He arranged for me to speak to Albion director Mr Tommy Silk, who was later killed when his own airplane crashed. Mr Silk wanted me to operate without a contract. 'We're a big club and this is a great opportunity,' he said. I told him Blackburn were a big club too and could be bigger than West Brom, even though Albion were in the First Division. I didn't fancy taking the job under those circumstances and I found out later that Graham Taylor had knocked it back as well. My loss turned out to be Ron Atkinson's gain. He took over while I went to Birmingham and struggled.

It was not just the fact that he did not offer me a contract – I just did not get the buzz about the job and I have always been led by my instincts. If I'd followed them I might not have gone to Newcastle United when I did a few years later. I don't regret going there but if I had looked in more detail at what the job entailed I would not have taken it. If I had delved a bit more into what could be done at Albion I would probably have gone there instead of Birmingham. As it was, the timing of the Birmingham offer was unfortunate as far as my relationship with Mr Bancroft was concerned. I had told him about the West Brom offer and he was the happiest man in the world when I turned it down. In fact I signed an improved contract at Blackburn that should have committed me to the club until the following June. The chairman issued a statement saying I had done so 'to end speculation which has linked Mr Smith with West Bromwich' and that he was pleased to announce that I did not intend to break my contract. But then I took another call from Graham Smith – this time telling me that Birmingham wanted to talk to me.

Informing Bill of my decision was the hardest thing I have ever done. He started by pleading with me to stay and then told me straight that he was not going to let me go. I said I was going no matter what he did and walked out. Birmingham were an established First Division outfit with the kind of prospects that could never have been within my scope had I stayed at Blackburn. It was a bitter break-up and an unfortunate end to what had been a brilliant relationship. The following week the two clubs sorted out a compensation deal but it was eight years before Bill and I spoke again. We met at a dinner and he came up to me and said, 'Come on, I'll buy you a gin and tonic, you old bugger.' I told him I had to do what I did and he accepted it. I am glad we managed to sort things out because he was a great chairman and I wish we could have been really successful together. But the Kindon business was a watershed for me. I still believe if we had been able to buy him it would have made all the difference because he would have got us promotion and then I would have stayed.

CHAPTER FOUR

CROSS AT ST ANDREWS

For a former footballer who was never any more than a lower league jobber, I reckoned I was doing well as a team manager and I had no reason to believe my successes at Boston United, Colchester United and Blackburn Rovers would not be repeated at Birmingham City. After all, the City chairman Keith Coombs, acting unilaterally and without consultation with any of his directors, had targeted me because – as he told me at my interview – I had a better points-per-game ratio than any other manager. Unfortunately, nothing I had achieved was adequate preparation for what was to happen at Birmingham. I had scrimped and scrapped in the Northern Premier League and Fourth and Third Divisions and wheeled and dealed in the Second but it was only after I made it to the First that I discovered what management was all about: how to follow a legend; how to deal with superstar footballers; how to negotiate with top managers; how to get involved in million-pound transfer business; how to handle difficult directors; how to accept relegation; how to face up to the sack.

Maybe at the outset I should have heeded the portents of Birmingham – even the circumstances behind my interview were difficult. A pal of mine, Brian Turnbull, who had links with Bolton Wanderers and later Manchester City, had to act as chauffeur when I went to see Mr Coombs because I was banned from driving at the time. After he offered me the job, I wasn't sure and I voiced my concern to Brian on the way back to Lancashire. He urged me to take it – in fact, he said to me, 'If you don't I will never speak to you again.' So I did – but I have to say the £20,000 a year, at the time a fortune to me and almost twice what I was getting at Blackburn, was more than a little consideration. Birmingham were in dire straits when I went – bottom of the league with twelve games left. Their previous manager Willie Bell had been sacked and Sir Alf Ramsey, with the rather grandiose title of consultant director, had been keeping the seat warm. I wouldn't have minded in the least had Sir Alf stayed on in some advisory capacity because I thought he was one of the greatest and I would have looked forward to working with him. But a rift had developed between him and the Coombs brothers and he had left the club. When I was asked recently to nominate my top three managers I put Sir Alf third behind Sir Alex Ferguson and Bob Paisley. His World Cup achievement in 1966 entitled him to the highest respect. I thought that England side and the one that went to Mexico four years later were among the best I had ever seen.

I don't know if it was because I was taking over from Sir Alf but I was not exactly Mr Popular with a section of the City following. Within hours of my arrival a protest group who had been campaigning for control of the club criticized my appointment and threatened a mass walk-out at my first home game in charge, against Arsenal the following Saturday. In the event only a few hundred did actually get up and leave and anyway the chairman was quite forthright in his backing for me, going so far as to be quoted as saying, 'There is a new generation of young managers emerging from the lower divisions and Jim Smith is one of them. They are hungry, confident and imaginative and before long some of the established names in the game might begin to look like grandads.'

51

It's strange recalling those words today now that I am a grandad several times over, and recognizing that there is a new breed of younger boss, many of whom I have helped to get started. But I believe I am as hungry and imaginative now as I was when Mr Coombs backed his judgement against the hotheads. To me it was just a lot of people making a bit of noise and the Coombs family had so much power in terms of shares and money that nobody could touch them. They were desperate to make Birmingham one of the biggest clubs in the country. They talked big time but at times they did not act it. For example, when I was trying to sign Brian Little from Aston Villa I flew him out to Portugal, where I was on holiday, to discuss terms and they gave me a lot of stick because they thought I had been too extravagant.

My first match in charge was at Newcastle and I came to two immediate conclusions. One – it was not too difficult to understand the team's plight at the foot of the table; two – in Trevor Francis, Birmingham had a brilliant young player who could be the club's salvation. Trevor had asked for a transfer just before I took over and I resolved there and then to try and persuade him to stay. Not that my behaviour on that first night would have endeared me to him or the club. He scored a goal to put us in front and we held the lead until five minutes from the end but then sloppy defending let Newcastle in for the equalizer. I thought I might as well start as I meant to go on and stormed into the dressing room afterwards, swept a load of plastic cups off the table and called the players all the useless so-and-sos I could lay my tongue to. I was way over the top and it was probably something they had not been used to, but I did it for a purpose. I wanted them to know straight away what kind of manager I was. And it must have had some effect because we lost only one game between then and the end of the season and finished in a comfortable halfway position.

Francis was magnificent in that final part of the season. He scored nine goals and most of them were crucial in helping us either win or draw a match. I had sat down with him a few times and talked over his situation and he had agreed to wait and see how things went. When we came to discussing a new contract again nearer the end of the season, the vital sticking point was whether or not we would allow him to go and play in America that summer. Freddie Goodwin, a former City manager but then coach at Minnesota Kicks, had been tapping him up. I explained the situation to Mr Coombs, who told me that the Kicks had already made an offer for £600,000 to sign Francis and had been turned down. Freddie and I went out for a Chinese meal and it was decided they would pay Birmingham £30,000 for the loan of Francis and £35,000 to the player himself to play for them that summer and then he would return to us for the start of the new season. That set off a remarkable chain of events that ultimately ended in Trevor leaving the club.

We got ourselves involved in an incredible cloak-and-dagger operation that would have done justice to a John le Carré spy novel when Freddie and I agreed to keep the lid on the arrangement until everything was sorted out. I was more than a little surprised when the full story appeared in the *People* the following Sunday. I don't know who had leaked it but if it had anything to do with Goodwin it certainly rebounded on him and his club big style. I had hardly finished reading the article when the phone rang and on the other end of the line was Jimmy Hill, who was then managing director of Coventry City as well as having a substantial financial interest in another American club, Detroit Express. 'Is this story true about Trevor Francis?' he inquired. I told him it was. Straight away Jimmy asked us to put everything on hold because he wanted Trevor at Detroit Express. I just said that if he agreed to pay Birmingham £30,000 he could talk to the player as well.

Jimmy and his representatives then spoke to Trevor and the net result was they agreed to double the amount he would have received from Minnesota Kicks to an astonishing

£70,000. It was arranged that we should all meet at Jimmy's house in the Cotswolds – Trevor, Jimmy and me as well as his coach Ken Furphy and two directors who had flown over from America to tie up the details. But the plot was only just beginning to thicken. The day before the meeting I took a call from the manager of Charlton Athletic, Andy Nelson. He was ringing on behalf of his chairman Michael Gliksten, who was also connected with yet another American club, Boston Tea Men – and they wanted Trevor as well. I advised him the deal was all but signed and sealed and that we were going to Jimmy Hill's house the following afternoon just to complete the formalities. But Mr Gliksten refused to give up and we responded to Andy's pleadings to let his chairman talk to Trevor before he signed anything. Conveniently Mr Gliksten also had a house in the Cotswolds and we agreed to see him in the morning before moving on to visit Jimmy in the afternoon. These were the days before agents got involved in transfer deals and it was down to me, not only to drive Trevor around the Cotswolds but also to act as his adviser.

So we set off that morning, heading first to the Gliksten residence, a huge spread of a place that would put Southfork to shame. In we went and the upshot was that Trevor would receive an even more astonishing £75,000 for twelve weeks of football with Boston Tea Men. Andy underlined Mr Gliksten's desperation to sign him when he took me to one side and said, 'Look, if you get Francis to sign for Boston, I can promise you a month's holiday with your family anywhere in the world.' I told him that a fortnight in Spain would do very nicely. And that was that. On our way to Jimmy's house, Trevor asked me what he should do. I just mentioned that of the two places, Detroit was a bit of a nightmare city but Boston was a superb place in a beautiful part of America – and I was convinced that by the time we arrived at the Hill home, the Tea Men were favourites to sign him.

Jimmy had the champagne on ice and he and Furphy and the two directors greeted us with smiles of expectancy –

which soon disappeared. 'We've got a bit of a problem, Jim,' I told him. 'What's that?' he asked. I told him about Boston's offer of £75,000. He explained that he had pushed the boat out as far as it would go to come up with £70,000 and there was no more in the pot. They left the room for a confab and when they returned Jimmy said, 'I'll tell you what I will do, Trevor. I'll pay you the £70,000 and on top of that you will also receive a percentage of the franchise.' Trevor looked at me and muttered, 'What do you think?' I told him the franchise offer could be a gold-mine if the American thing took off and, even if it didn't, it was only going to cost him £5,000. And that decided it – Trevor signed to play for Detroit Express for that summer and out came the champagne at last. He also agreed a new deal with Birmingham which tied him to the club for a further two years, which had been my main priority all along. The irony was Birmingham never did receive the £30,000 that was due. The closest we came to getting paid was some time later when Gordon Milne was the Coventry manager and I offered to take Gary Bannister on a free transfer to wipe out the debt. Then a few days later Gordon rang me up to tell me they had sold him to Sheffield Wednesday for £75,000.

But having Trevor signed up was a major plus for me and I could not have approached the 1978–79 season – my first full one in charge at Birmingham – with more hope, enthusiasm and optimism. We had finished the previous campaign in fine style, so much so that I did not see any reason to tinker with the team, apart from buying a young goalkeeper to back up Jimmy Montgomery, signing Alan Ainscow and Don Givens and swapping Terry Hibbitt and John Connolly for Stewart Barrowclough. And we had an unbelievable pre-season, culminating in a win over Ajax in our last build-up match. As it turned out I might have been kidding myself that we were better than we really were. Trevor arrived back from America but I thought he looked tired and in need of a rest so I made him sub for our first game at Manchester

United. That upset him because he wanted to play but I thought the other lads had done well enough. We were beaten 1–0 at Old Trafford and 3–1 at home to Middlesbrough the following Tuesday and it all went downhill after that. We drew three and lost ten – most of them by the odd goal – of our first thirteen games and the problems with Trevor compounded the situation.

I still thought he looked a bit physically done in – although, in fairness, he did play well – and I wanted him to have a couple of days' rest before our match against Liverpool. But he insisted on coming in to train and that's when disaster struck. He snapped his Achilles tendon during one workout and that was him out until December. To make matters worse, the other half of the combination which had scored thirty-six goals the previous season, Keith Bertschin, suffered two stress fractures and he was also unavailable for long periods. We were never able to replace that strike power and it affected us for the whole season. There were rumblings about Trevor's future and strong newspaper speculation that Brian Clough wanted him at Nottingham Forest. I discussed the situation with the chairman and his view was that we would have to sell him and use the money to strengthen the team because it looked like we were going to get relegated.

I went over to Nottingham in the middle of December to watch Forest play in a League Cup quarter-final against Brighton which they won 3–1 and I hung about afterwards hoping to see Cloughie. After a decent while I got fed up and decided to leave, but, as I was heading towards the door, there he was coming towards me wearing that familiar green top. He slapped a big kiss on my cheek, gave me an outrageous hug and invited me to go as his guest to the semi-final. 'Get here at five o'clock and we'll have a good chat,' he said. The match against Watford was on 17 January. I got to the City Ground at 5.30 p.m. and was greeted by Cloughie's sidekick Peter Taylor. He sat me down and then said, 'Right, about Trevor Francis. How much do you want?' I told him I wanted £1 million or £825,000 plus their young 'keeper Chris Woods and a winger called Steve Burke, both of whom were in the England Under-18 side at the time. Taylor hummed and hawed about that and clearly did not fancy doing the players-plus-cash deal. We talked about and around it until about 7 p.m. when Cloughie came in, sat down on the floor and demanded, 'Right, young man, what are we going to do?' I went through it all again with the same non-agreement until it got to about 7.20 p.m. – ten minutes before the semi-final kicked off – when I began to wonder if they should be giving their team-talk.

'Haven't you two got something to do?' I said. 'Don't worry about them – we'll sort it out,' said Cloughie. When the pair of them eventually left they must have had only about a minute with the team before they went out – but Forest still won 3–1. Nothing had been decided before I left. I had agreed to see two pressmen afterwards, Joe Melling of the *Daily Express* and Jeff Farmer of the *Daily Mail*, and they were waiting in a car outside the ground. They followed me to East Midlands Airport where we had a cup of tea and I told them about the situation. Jeff was a good pal of Peter Taylor and he said he would have a word and make it plain that the deal was £1 million or it was off. The next day in the papers Clough and Taylor started making all sorts of noises like there would be no deal and they could not negotiate with me – and that's how it was left.

Then on 7 February 1979 – the day England played Northern Ireland at Wembley – I took a call from Peter Taylor at home. 'All right – we'll take Francis,' he said. 'But we're not paying £1 million because we don't want him to get big-headed about it – we'll give you £999,999 instead.' I told him he'd got a deal but then he suddenly asked me, 'Who do you fancy tonight?' Funnily enough I fancied Northern Ireland so that's what I told him. 'How much do you want on it?' he asked. I said, 'A score.' 'Right, you're on,' he laughed. England won 4–0 so I must be the only chap to have sold a player for a near-million pound and it cost me £20. Taylor did not let me get away with it either. Our last game of the season was against Forest and he chased me all over the ground for the money.

So that was the end, temporarily, of my association with Trevor Francis, although we were to meet up again at Queens Park Rangers. I don't think Trevor endeared himself to the Birmingham supporters by going on loan to America. He had been king in their eyes but it was never the same after he came back. I detected an unease about him after that first home match against Middlesbrough. He came out on to the pitch and there was almost a negative reaction from the crowd. I believe he was so disappointed that he decided it was the beginning of the end for him at Birmingham. Even though we got a record amount of money I would still have preferred to have kept him. The whole Francis episode was a tremendous education for me. I learned that when you're in the big league you have top players and top players need to be looked after differently because they are a special breed who are important to you as a team boss. As a young manager I had made it my business to persuade him to stay and there was no sense of satisfaction when he left. He was on a fantastic wage – something around £40,000 a year. In fact, I remember being at an England match when Trevor was playing and Bobby Robson, who was still at Ipswich, tapped me on the shoulder and said, 'Jim, that boy is some player. How much is he earning.' When I told him, Bobby's sharp intake of breath could have been heard a hundred yards away. 'Christ, I hope he doesn't tell any of my players that,' he said grimly.

Trevor was never a prima donna but he knew he was special. We've had our ups and downs but I'm pleased to say that my relationship with him has developed into a true friendship over the years. His wife Helen and mine Yvonne are very close. We meet on holiday and dine together regularly. He had a wonderful playing career in England, Italy,

America and Scotland, achieving the highest honours before making the natural progression into management. He is now in the hot seat at Birmingham, having cut his managerial teeth at Queens Park Rangers and Sheffield Wednesday. He's had his disappointments but, like me, he has learned from them. He has changed a lot from those early days as a precocious young player but that's what age and experience does for you. We've had a few laughs and a lot of nostalgic reminiscences about the days when I chauffeured him all over the Cotswolds and the dealings with Clough and Taylor. In all the years I have been a manager he was as good a player as I have come across.

It was while I was at Birmingham that I really got to know Ron Atkinson. I had played against him a few times when I was with Aldershot and he was at Oxford United but I could never have guessed then we would become such friends. Ron had taken over at West Brom after I and a couple of others had turned it down, and been an instant success. They were great days at the Albion; the team was doing well and it was always party time in the Europa Hotel near the ground after matches. The room would be full of football people and Ron would get the champagne out and the crack was always good with a fair bit of mickey-taking going on, and, in that season that turned out to be a bit of a disaster for us, plenty of it at my expense. There was never a shortage of bubbly but Ron himself hardly touched a drop. He would get everybody talking and not miss a trick.

That was the year of the big freeze when we went weeks without playing a match. Ron and I decided to take our teams to Guernsey to play a friendly which became known as the Arctic Cup. We flew from East Midlands with my team at the front of the plane and the West Brom players sitting behind us. Suddenly there were a few bumps and one of the Albion players, Len Cantello, shouted out, 'Nothing to worry about everybody – Birmingham can't go down twice in the same year.' Everybody had a good laugh about that. It turned out to be a great social occasion and the match gave us valuable practice. The night before the game Ron and I and the back-room staffs as well as a few of the pressmen were having a drink when I turned round to Ron and said, 'Right, Ron, how seriously are you taking this match?' He replied, 'Well, what's your team?' I started reeling off the names . . . Montgomery, Calderwood, Pendrey . . . 'Just a minute,' interrupted Ron, 'what about Berto?' He meant Alberto Tarantini, the Argentinian international I had signed five months earlier. I told him I was resting him and had left him back in Birmingham. Ron immediately put down his glass, and announced – 'Right, I'm going to bed. This is going to be more difficult than I thought.' Again it brought the place down. The next day I had a bit of a hangover as I watched the match from one of the makeshift dug-outs. I had a go at Keith Bertschin for missing a chance in the first minute. He said something back and I snapped, leapt off my seat and put my head straight through the dug-out roof. But I still had the last laugh on Mr Atkinson. We had agreed that, if the match ended in a draw, he and I would take penalties to decide who won. It finished 2–2 but Ron bottled the penalty shoot-out.

The Tarantini saga became a legend in the Midlands. I signed him for a club record £259,000 in September 1978 at a time when I was trying to pull rabbits out of a hat because everything seemed to be going wrong. I got a phone call from an agent who told me Tarantini was available from Boca Juniors. He trained with us and as he looked very good, and being aware of the success that Tottenham Hotspur had had with Ossie Ardiles and Ricky Villa, I decided to go ahead with the deal. Tarantini had an impressive international pedigree and had been a world star since he was sixteen. They did not come any more colourful than Berto with his flamboyant style and huge mop of curly hair. He was a bit of a playboy but he was a lovely lad who I thought would give us a bit of star quality. The problem at the start was it took us ages to get a work permit for him and when it came we were further down the league and the pressure on everybody was tremendous.

The circumstances were not ideal when he did get to play and maybe because of his image and the fact that he had a poor disciplinary record in Argentina the press were not very kind to him. We had to wait until 11 November for our first league win of the season but we ended the famine with a goal feast, beating Manchester United 5–1. During the game Brian Greenhoff got carried off and there was a suggestion that Tarantini had whacked him with his elbow. When he asked about it, he smiled and said in a heavy foreign accent, 'No, I think him very tired. I think he go to sleep.' The press did not like that but I thought by and large Tarantini got a raw deal from them and from us at the club. We did not provide him with the platform he deserved to show what he was worth. Once after we played Coventry, the great Joe Mercer, who was then a club director, came in to see me and was asked to be introduced to Berto because, he said, he had given the best performance he had seen from a number six for many a year.

At the end of the season we had to face up to relegation and it was clear that Tarantini would be leaving. His private life was a mess. There were reports from Buenos Aires that the former husband of his wife Maria, who was an actress, was threatening legal action to obtain more access to their two-year-old daughter. It seemed the lad was getting stick from every angle. Another Argentinian club, Cordoba, came in and offered to give us what we had paid for him to take him back to South America. Mr Coombs and myself both wanted him to stay but we were overruled by the board who insisted that we take the money. Tarantini came to see me to plead that he be allowed to stay. 'Boss, you tell them I don't want to go. Tell them you are not selling me.' I explained to him that the board had made the decision but if he announced that he was staying, everything would be all right.

He said he could not do that because the Cordoba president was also a prominent figure in the Argentina FA and if he came out against his club it would be the end of his international career. So he was sold and we got our money back. But the story had a postscript a year later when Tarantini played for Argentina against England at Wembley. I was a lot happier then because we had just been promoted back to the First Division and I booked into the Royal Lancaster Hotel without knowing that the Argentinians were staying there as well. Berto spotted me in the hotel lobby. 'Boss, why . . . why?' he said gesticulating with open hands. 'Me in Birmingham – bad team; now good team.' The other classic story involved Tarantini's international team-mates Ardiles and Villa when we played Spurs at home. It was a great game that we won 1–0 but it could have gone 7–6 either way. Before the game the three of them were chatting together when a small boy went up to them for autographs without a pen and so he asked if any of them had one he could borrow. 'Alberto, what does this boy want?' said Ossie. 'He wants a pen,' replied Berto, producing one from his inside pocket and signing a piece of paper for the kid. Tarantini then came to me and said, 'Boss, why in the paper, always me the donkey – not Ardiles or Villa? But they do not know what it is, a pen.'

But Tarantini was an easy target for the leg-pullers, especially when we were fighting a losing battle to stay in the First Division. In those days Birmingham City were considered fair game. An occasion at the opening of Andy Gray's nightclub in Birmingham, an establishment which rejoiced in the name of Holy City Zoo, springs to mind. Ron, myself and our wives went there after attending a Three Degrees concert. While we were having a drink, Ron spotted Billy Connolly who had also been appearing locally and introduced me to him. Billy started talking about what he was doing and said what a good night he had had. 'But I always do well here,' he said. 'I love playing Birmingham.' Quick as a flash Ron jumped in and quipped, 'Yeah – everybody does!' Even

Connolly nearly burst a gut at that one. It was Ron who gave me the nickname of Bald Eagle which has stuck ever since. I rang him up one day when we were bouncing back from relegation and were near the top of the Second Division table, and his assistant Colin Addison picked up the phone. 'The eagle's on; the eagle's flying,' he shouted. Ron added, 'It must be the bald eagle,' and that was it.

The irony of his move to Manchester United was that I finished up buying the house he was having built in Solihull. We lived nearby and when Ron decided to take the United job, he obviously did not want to go ahead with the purchase. But Yvonne liked the place and we decided to buy it instead. It did not turn out to be the luckiest of moves for me either.

CHAPTER FIVE

DOWN – AND THEN OUT

One of the recommendations put to me after Birmingham City were relegated in 1979 was that I take on Ronnie Allen as my assistant. Allen was something of a football legend in the Midlands after a tremendous record as a striker both with West Brom and England. He had been briefly caretaker manager at The Hawthorns before Ron Atkinson took over and later he had a spell in charge after Ron left. I had travelled down to London to talk to Keith Coombs's brother Derek, a fellow director but also a local MP. He suggested Allen should be taken on because he thought I needed help. I rejected the option out of hand and told him I was unhappy about it. My contention was I could pull the thing round with the back-room staff already at the club. I was more than a little worried that it sounded like the beginning of the end for me but I was determined to stick to my guns and I repeated that to the chairman when I got back to the club. He agreed although I felt he would have preferred it had we taken Allen on board. My alternative was to build slowly, using the excellent young lads we had at the club, such as Nigel Winterburn, Mark Dennis, Pat Van Den Hauwe, Kevin Dillon and Kevin Broadhurst, as a nucleus. 'Let's not panic, Mr Chairman,' I urged. 'We might not get straight back up but in two years we will have a very good side.' But he decided he could not wait that long. 'You've got the money – you've got to get us back up,' he told me.

The Francis money had cleared our £400,000 overdraft and with what was left and the Tarantini money I bought eight players, including four internationals, from three different countries. The players who came in were Alan Curbishley from West Ham for £225,000, Colin Todd from Everton (£250,000), Archie Gemmill from Nottingham Forest (£150,000), Willie Johnston from Vancouver Whitecaps (loan for £15,000), Jeff Wealands from Hull (£55,000), Terry Lees from Dutch club Roda (£55,000), Tony Evans from Cardiff (£120,000) and later Frank Worthington from Bolton (£150,000). Alan and Colin have since gone on to taste success as managers themselves and I have taken a great personal interest in their careers. Alan has said that I have been his role model, which is very kind of him. He did a great job for me in the middle of the park. He was a very intelligent player and a superb passer of the ball. As with Graham Taylor, it was easy to detect the qualities and characteristics that would play an important part in his make-up as a manager. He was very ambitious and forward-thinking and had very strong views about the game.

That was a smashing team – a superb blend of youth and experience. They were also a great bunch of lads and they did what the chairman wanted by getting the club back in the First Division even if it was a close-run thing. If I had to pick out one it would be Gemmill. I have never seen a player on the pitch or even during training who had so much desire to win. He worked himself and those around him, especially the younger ones, to the limit. Lads like Dennis and Dillon used to hate him because he was on their backs all the time. Years later I was talking to Kevin and he admitted to me, 'I should have learned from Archie. He was right and I was wrong but I was young and thought I knew it all.'

Toddy was not far behind him. To me he was a genius as a player but he used to drive me round the bend when he did things like playing the opposition offside without telling any of the other defenders. And when it went wrong he would criticize the offender, telling them they did not understand the offside rule. He was a perfectionist and he expected others to be like him. And he was contemptuous about lesser teams, especially those who relied on long-ball tactics. We would go to places like Shrewsbury and Cambridge, long-ball merchants that we should have beaten but didn't, and we might as well have not played Toddy in those games because he approached them with a total lack of interest. He would just say, 'That's not football', and give less than his normal maximum effort. But when we played Chelsea, who were one of our main promotion rivals, it was a different matter.

Chelsea, who were managed by Geoff Hurst, came to us for a Tuesday night game. They were quite a young side at the time and they stayed at the local hotel where we were having our pre-match rest and team-talk. I could see the expressions on those young faces when they walked in and saw the likes of Gemmill, Todd, Worthington and the others. It was a psychological advantage that we weren't about to throw away and we beat them 5-1 with Toddy hardly giving their strikers a kick. It turned out to be a vital result for us as far as promotion was concerned because we ended up pipping Chelsea to third place on goal difference. The following season back in the First Division I decided I was going to play with a sweeper and I thought Toddy would be perfect for the role. We had perfect wing-backs in David Langan and Mark Dennis and Kevin Broadhurst and Joe Gallagher in the middle. But we went to Holland on a pre-season tour and lost the first game against comparatively weak opposition. I could tell Toddy was not relishing the formation and he came to me and said, 'We can't play with a sweeper – our strength is 4–4–2', which meant it was his strength. So we changed it for the next match against Groningen, a Dutch Premier League side, beat them 4–0, and Toddy was magnificent. He was his own man but at his best he was some player.

Later I took him to Oxford United and the circumstances behind that were bizarre to say the least. Colin had moved on to Nottingham Forest and I took a call from his wife asking whether I wanted him on a free transfer. I thought he could do a good job for me so I told her I was interested. She said, 'Why don't you ring Brian Clough?' I asked her what had gone wrong between Colin and Cloughie, remembering that they had had a tremendous relationship at Derby County where he helped them to win two league championships. Apparently Clough had taken him to Forest when it was clear Ron Saunders, who took over from me at Birmingham, did not fancy him but unfortunately Todd picked up an injury which put him out for a few weeks. He was having a run-out in a private practice match against Mansfield Town when, as he was liable to do, he played offside. Cloughie always hated that sort of thing and he stood up and shouted, 'Young man, do that once more and you're off.' But he played the offside card again and straight away, in front of a crowd consisting of one man and his dog, Clough took Todd off. He knew then that he was on his way and that's when I got the phone call from his missus.

So I rang the mercurial Mr Clough one Thursday afternoon and asked whether Todd was available. 'Will you look after him?' he asked and I said I would. 'Ring me at half-past ten tomorrow morning on this number,' he responded. I did as he asked and we went through the whole routine again. 'Do you want him? Will you look after him? He's still a good player, you know.' He finished by saying: 'Ring me on this number at half-past four this afternoon.' And we had the same conversation again to the point that I was losing it a bit. Cloughie must have sensed that because he said, 'Right, get hold of him, get him down to Oxford, take him on to the pitch and sign him in front of the fans because he will get you promotion.' And he was right. His first three games were all away; we won at Hull, drew at Bradford City and won at Sheffield United and Todd was superb in all three and for the rest of the season. I would have offered him another contract at the end of the season but we could not give him the money he wanted so he went off to America to play for Jacksonville. I'll always value what he did for me at Birmingham and Oxford.

My pal Brian Turnbull played a big part in the Worthington signing. I had first come across Frank years before when I was playing for Halifax Town and his brother Bob was one of my team-mates. I got two tickets for the 1966 FA Cup final between Sheffield Wednesday and Everton and Bob asked if I would take his younger brother Frank down with me. I picked him up in Huddersfield, took him down to London and then offered to pick him up after the game. He replied, 'No, it's all right, I'm staying down for the weekend.' It turned out he had no intention of going to the final either. He sold his ticket to pay for his weekend in the big city. He was only an apprentice then so he started early as he meant to go on. When we met at Brian's house and did the deal I said to Turnbull after he had gone, 'Brian, I think Frank drank more Scotch than we did and I've just signed him.' But what a character and what a player he was throughout his career. He arrived at the club the next day typically attired in tight jeans, cowboy boots and a red, silky top with Elvis Presley's World Tour emblazoned all over it. It was hardly the middle of summer, a typically dull November day in fact, but it didn't stop Frank wearing the darkest sunglasses you could imagine. Our coach Norman Bodell tried to make fun of him, grabbing him by the arm and guiding him in as if he was blind and saying things like 'watch that door' and 'mind that chair'. Bertschin mentioned something about Norman taking the mickey but Frank smiled, held out his arms and uttered his first words to his team-mates, 'Don't worry, babies . . . it's just like water off a duck's back.'

I had heard a lot of stories of Frank not liking this or that, and to be fair, he did not like running too much but he would train all day with a ball. To me he could easily have been the best. He was a superb footballer with a quality left foot. I loved having him around and he performed brilliantly on the field in that promotion year and also after we got back into the First Division. I'll never forget one particular game – his best performance in a Birmingham shirt – against Nottingham Forest. Even Brian Clough acknowledged it was one of the best in his time at Forest. We won 4–3 and Frank scored two great goals against Peter Shilton but it was his all-round performance that was worth any supporter's entrance money.

We had some players who went on to earn tasty reputations in the game, people like Mark Dennis and Pat Van Den Hauwe, but they were just babies at the time and I was long gone when Birmingham developed a notoriety for being one of the roughest sides in the league. Dennis was a London boy who was another of Don Dorman's discoveries. Don was the chief scout at City and there was no better spotter of young talent. He demonstrated that when he picked up Trevor Francis when others were put off after he disappointed in an England schoolboys trial. Don believed that London youth football was the best in the country so he used to haunt the youth teams of clubs like Tottenham, Arsenal and Chelsea, and if they discarded any kid that he thought was worth persevering with he stepped in. Dennis was one of them and I thought he had everything necessary to be a top player. Unfortunately he had a temper and he became known more for that than his football in his later career. I know he did some crazy things but he was a lovable rogue and he could play.

But I was always wary of his temperament and because of that it was in my mind to sell him on because we had Nigel Winterburn coming through. Nigel was captain of the youth team and looked to have a good chance of making it. Unfortunately I had gone before I could put my theory into practice and, as a consequence, Nigel's career almost foundered before it got started. I had promised his parents to look out for the lad, telling them that if he ever needed any help they should get in touch wherever I was and I would see what I could do. They did just that when I was at Oxford and Birmingham gave Nigel a free transfer. I had two left-backs but I offered to give him a pre-season trial. I was aghast at the difference between the lad I had left at City and the one who turned up at Oxford. His confidence was so shot that he could not perform at all. He used to be able to throw the ball a mile but he could hardly do that. I just did not know what to do with him but while I was thinking about it, Harry Bassett rang me up from Wimbledon desperate for a left-back.

'I've got one for you,' I told him. I explained that I had Nigel on loan but that I didn't think he was going to get anywhere with us. He agreed to take him and they eventually signed him and the rest, as they say, is history. He just took off and later went to Arsenal for over £400,000 and became as good a left-back as there is in the country. Why he has not had a long and lucrative career with England is beyond me. I spoke to Harry some time later and he admitted that he had serious doubts about Nigel when he first went to Wimbledon. 'When he first came he was hopeless but I was in a right fix needing a left-back and I had no money,' he said. All he needed was somebody to show faith in the lad which is what Harry did and I didn't and once his confidence came back, off he went. Every manager has a few ricks on his record and Nigel Winterburn is certainly one of mine.

Maybe if I had been allowed to stay and finish what I had started at Birmingham, things would have worked out differently although, looking back, I doubt whether Nigel would have done any better. I thought Birmingham acted prematurely and without just cause when they dispensed with my services. The disappointment of relegation in 1979 had been eradicated by the way the team had tackled their responsibilities in the Second Division. And the promotion race provided a nail-biting climax to the season. It came down to five clubs after the Easter programme – Sunderland, Leicester, Luton, Chelsea and ourselves. There was a false dawn when we played at Burnley and we heard that Chelsea had lost at Cardiff City on the same day which meant we were up. Our supporters charged on to the pitch dancing and singing. Then we got the news that Chelsea had scored a last-minute goal which made the celebrations slightly premature. I was asked by the police to try and calm the fans down and get them to disperse without any trouble. It was a real nightmare but I managed it. We now needed to draw against Notts County on the last day of the season. No problem, I thought. The County manager was Jimmy Sirrell, who was my first full-time coach at Aldershot and has remained a close friend ever since. His assistant was none other than Howard Wilkinson, my protégé from our Boston days.

I should have known better; both Jimmy and Howard were determined competitors who would do nobody any favours when it came to winning a game of head tennis, never mind a football match. I had kept in contact with Jimmy simply because he was the kind of person you never lost touch with. He was the main man at Aldershot – secretary, coach, physio, scout, decorator, kit man – you name it, he did it. I remember one pre-season at Aldershot we played in an annual cricket match with a local village team in the most idyllic of settings in Hampshire. We were short of players so we asked Jimmy, a dour Scot who had never previously held a cricket bat in his hand, to make up the numbers. The routine was we would play the match and then repair to the local tavern for afters but the trick was to make the match last until opening time. To that end the local team always batted first and they took their time to knock up a couple of hundred or so and the minutes were ticking away quite promisingly.

Then it was our turn and our wickets began to tumble with such regularity that a distinct time lapse was looming between close of play and opening of pub. It came down to Jimmy's turn to approach the crease with the instruction that he was to stonewall and stay in as long as possible. He got off the mark quite quickly and that instilled a feeling of false confidence that was to prove his and the team's undo-ing. He struck another delivery and this time, instead of just taking the single, he went for a second impossible run. He must have been halfway down the wicket when the fielder returned the ball to rest snugly in the gloves of the wicket-keeper who, as keen to keep the match going as anybody, deliberately missed the stumps with an exaggerated sweep. Jimmy eye-balled the wicket-keeper with a glower that almost turned him to stone and declared, 'Sir, you're not taking the piss out of me. I'm out', and stormed off in the direction of the pavilion. Fortunately the pub landlord opened early and we enjoyed our drinks anyway.

That was Jimmy – a great football man. He used to train us hard but there were always the lighter moments such as when we used to kid him that he was taking penalties for Celtic. He would go off into a world of his own; in his mind he really was at Parkhead taking a crucial spot kick. He would blow his whistle, stick the ball in the back of the net – to my knowledge he never missed – and then do a lap of honour around the pitch. A truly amazing character – and Howard was no less of a competitor. Earlier in the week before the game against Notts County, in order to get the players away from the pressures of the media and well-meaning friends and relations, I had taken them away to play a friendly in Lucerne, Switzerland. It seemed a good idea to me but for some reason it upset one Jimmy Greaves who had a football programme on Central Television in those days. The stick he gave me before we went on the trip was unbelievable and it resulted in a barrage of angry phone calls and letters to the club at the start of that week. I could not wait to jump on the plane and get away from all the controversy that was raging back in Birmingham. We trounced Lucerne and spent a couple of days training and relaxing in the most idyllic of settings . . . clean mountain air, magnificent scenery, comfortable surroundings, so much so that when we came to the Notts County game, the players were bursting out of their skins.

And they hit the ground running. After twenty minutes we were 2–0 up and flying and I was thinking, 'Up yours, Greavsie, getting them away was the best thing I ever did.' And then it began to go wrong. I couldn't believe Jimmy and Howard's behaviour. They began to act as if their lives depended on County getting back into the game, bawling and shouting at their players from the dug-outs. The response was terrific for them and a nightmare for me. They got back to 2–2 and we were beginning to look like Swiss cheeses, all soft and yellow. But suddenly five minutes before half-time Kevin Dillon hit a screamer from thirty yards to put us back in front. I got stuck into them at half-time, particularly the senior players, accusing them of abdicating their responsibility and not showing enough character and determination. But the second half was even more nerve-racking. They equalized again with about twenty minutes to go which prompted Jimmy and Howard to increase the level of their encouragement a few more decibels. I don't think I've ever experienced tension like it. County had a right go and we were hanging on desperately until the final whistle but we got the point we needed.

I was completely drained and numbed by what had happened. I felt no sense of jubilation and I put a real dampener on the dressing-room celebrations when I went through the team like a dose of salts afterwards. The players were not the only ones to get it. The chairman met me as I walked up the big tunnel and made to throw his arms around me in congratulations. I was that uptight, I shrugged him away and told him to take a running jump. He could not believe it either. Somebody asked later why I hadn't brought the sub on for the final quarter of an hour. I just replied that I didn't even know I had a sub – all I did for that last fifteen minutes was pray that County would not score. And Jimmy and

Howard were still at it after the match. They kept their players in the dressing room for an hour – so much for friendship. But it worked for them as they won promotion to the First Division the following season.

I believe the reasons for my eventual dismissal at Birmingham were more to do with the availability of Ron Saunders, who had just quit Aston Villa after leading them to the league championship the previous season, than anything I had done wrong. We stayed up quite comfortably in that first season back and we were all right in the second year without doing enough, especially away from home. There were rumours of talks between Saunders and Jack Wiseman, one of the Birmingham directors, which I have always declined to comment on. I could understand City's interest in Saunders – after all he had proved himself at the highest level in English football. But I was very disappointed in the way it was done. You can always sense when all is not well, and it wasn't. Desperate to break a period without an away win which had lasted fifteen months, I decided to throw a few young kids in at West Ham. We were 2–1 up in the dying minutes when one of their players slung a high ball into our box and there must have been twenty hands up but the referee gave a penalty. The Hammers scored to make it 2–2. Even their chairman admitted afterwards that he thought we had been hard done by.

I sat next to jolly Jack on the coach on the way home, cursing our luck, not knowing that by then I had already been sacked. I found out later that the decision had been taken before the game. I had put myself through all sorts of agonies that afternoon for nothing. The consolation for not getting the win we deserved was in the performance of the kids which augured well for the future. In fact it would not have mattered had we gone to Upton Park and given them a real coating. I was still out on my ear – although I didn't know it. That evening Yvonne and I went out with Ron Atkinson and his wife Maggie for dinner in Stratford. We were joined by

Paul Reeves, who was a director at Oxford United, and his wife, and the six of us enjoyed a really convivial meal which turned out to be a very significant occasion for me. The following day a couple we had met on holiday came to our house for lunch. The chap was an executive with a leading car transporter firm and he called me to one side later and said, 'Don't tell the wife but I have just had the bullet.' Apparently he had criticized a senior's extravagance and paid the price. Of course Yvonne and I felt a great deal of sympathy for him in his situation, not realizing I was in the same boat myself.

I was just beginning to think about the week ahead on the Monday morning when the phone rang. It was the club secretary, who told me the chairman wanted to see me at the ground. My first thoughts were more about whether Mr Coombs was going to resign because I had heard a buzz to that effect. I drove to St Andrews and as I got to the ground I saw the chairman's car in front of me. Normally we would meet in his office but he went straight past it and pulled up in front of the boardroom entrance. That's when I saw it coming. I cannot remember his exact words – it was something about calling it a day – but I immediately went on the offensive. 'Right, if that's your decision I want the compensation sorted out straight away,' I told him. Mr Coombs tried to put me off by saying he was off on a world cruise that week. I went up to his house that day and, to be fair to him, we did a deal that I was happy with and I was compensated without any delay.

Saunders was duly appointed a few days later. I heard it said that he made it clear he would not take the job until I was paid what was due to me. That may or not be true but, in any event, it was largely my initiative which earned me my pay-off. Having said that, Saunders and I had a good relationship when he was at Villa. I dealt with him when I tried to sign Brian Little. I believed Brian would do a great job for us but unfortunately he failed a medical. Saunders and I had agreed not only a £600,000 fee but also that I would take Birmingham to Villa Park for his testimonial match and Villa would come to us to play for Joe Gallagher. And that's what happened. But his appointment did not improve things at Birmingham – in fact the discipline at the club became really terrible. Some time later he admitted to Kevin Broadhurst, 'When I was at Villa I used to read about the antics of Dennis and Dillon at Birmingham and I thought if I ever got the chance I'd sort that lot out within a month. I've been here eighteen and things are worse now than they have ever been.'

There were a lot of people who thought I had a raw deal, including the comedian Jasper Carrott, who had been a director for two years and was a real Blues nut. I had been introduced to him through Trevor Francis and we became great friends, socially and in a business sense when he eventually got on the board. Jasper's New Year's Eve parties were always a howl. They were always fancy dress and his impersonation of Dame Edna Everage at one of them was hilarious. He was a lovely bloke who clearly supported me and I welcomed that. What annoyed Jasper as much as anything was that the decision to sack me was taken when he was out of the country and without consulting him. He felt strongly enough about it to resign, making a statement in which he said that recent events had left him with no alternative. Obviously I was very disappointed about what happened at Birmingham. I took my sacking badly because I had no reason to believe it was coming. They say the only thing a manager can expect when he gets a job is the sack but when it happened to me, and for the first time, I was sick to the pit of my stomach. It was like somebody dying in the family. It wasn't just the act itself, there were also the inevitable inquests and consequences. When I went back into the offices and told the office staff and two or three members of the back-room staff we just sat in my room and got quietly slaughtered. All the players, either individually or in small groups, came to my house to express their regrets and wish me luck, which was nice, but it was an experience I would not want to go through too many times.

But then you have to look at the positive side. I analysed what had gone wrong and the conclusion I reached was whatever I had done wrong I could put right. In hindsight, for all the success I had in buying a team to get us straight back into the First Division, I still believe that my plan to build on the young players at the club would have worked and that the plea for patience that fell on deaf ears would have brought more long-term reward. As it turned out I did not have a lot of time for recriminations because the day after I was fired, Ron Atkinson rang me and asked if I wanted the Oxford job. Paul Reeves, a person I had only just met at the weekend, had been in touch with Robert Maxwell, the United chairman, and put me in the frame to take over from Ian Greaves who had left to take over at Wolves.

So that closed the book on my time at Birmingham, a bittersweet experience in my football career with never a dull moment – but the same could certainly be said for the next port of call among the dreamy spires of Oxford. It was an unlikely place for a steelworker's son from Sheffield to graduate to but the success I had there would go a long way to prove that Birmingham acted hastily in letting me go. I still don't believe Birmingham would have gone down had I stayed as manager but looking back, it was perhaps one of the best things that happened to me. I had fallen into a trap which precious few top-line managers succeed in avoiding. My greatest strength was in working with players but I had become too involved with interviews, dinners and administration. I had followed the pattern of appointing an assistant manager to work closely with the players when I should have been doing that side of the business myself. Management at the highest level can easily turn into a personal ego trip but I am older and a lot wiser now than I was in those days. Keith Coombs told me later that the day he sacked me was the worst of his whole tenure as chairman. It wasn't exactly the best one of mine either but thanks to Bob Maxwell I was able to get over it a lot quicker than I expected.

CHAPTER SIX

THE LORD OF THE MANOR

When I first heard there could be a connection between the Oxford United chairman and myself, I mixed him up with that other publishing baron Rupert Murdoch. My mistake was truly amazing, when you consider the stature, bearing and reputation of the man, but it was not until I met Maxwell that I realized who was who. One meeting was more than enough – you certainly would not make that mistake again. And he continued our association as he began it: pulling the strings, demanding his own way and usually getting it. If there were obstacles in his path, Maxwell just had them removed – it was as simple as that. And yet, having said that, he lost the three major battles he was desperate to win during the four years I was at the Manor Ground: he wanted to move to a new stadium, he wanted an amalgamation with Reading and he wanted to buy Manchester United.

When you consider that the current value of United is over £1 billion it is quite incredible that Maxwell came close to buying it for around £10 million in early 1984. I was made aware of it when he came to me and said, 'Jim, I am going to buy Manchester United', and gave me a wonderful vote of confidence: 'You will not be the manager, I shall be sticking with Ron Atkinson.' He told the story as follows: he went up to see Martin Edwards, having agreed on a price of around £10 million. Within a few seconds of the negotiations, according to Maxwell, the figure went up by £3 million and he told them to stick it. 'I was having none of that,' he told me. He certainly paid heavily for his principles over that deal but that was the kind of man he was – a hard-headed businessman who would not let advantage be taken. He later bought Derby County and I might have taken a short cut to Pride Park because he wanted me to take over there but it was pointed out to him that, in the interests of stability, they should keep Arthur Cox.

My first contact with Maxwell came when the telephone rang at my home and a soon-to-become familiar booming voice thundered down the line, 'Jim Smith, this is Robert Maxwell, chairman of Oxford United Football Club. I would like to discuss with you the possibility of becoming my manager. Could you please come to my home Headington Hall to have a chat about it.' I also discovered that was typical of him too. There was no secretary or personal assistant to make his arrangements – when he wanted a job doing, he did it himself. I told him I was very interested in the job and a meeting was arranged for the following afternoon at the hall which was also the headquarters of his publishing company Pergamon Press. It was the first of many visits I was to make to his imposing residence.

But there were already complications which Maxwell was to remove in his own inimitable style. Shortly after I was sacked by Birmingham and before Maxwell got in touch, I got a call from the Aston Villa chairman Doug Ellis inviting me to use his villa in Son Vida, Majorca, if I wanted to get away for a break. It was a wonderful gesture and I jumped at the chance. Doug arranged the flights himself through his own travel agency and it was all set up for Yvonne and myself to fly from Manchester on the evening of the day of the interview with Maxwell. I had not bothered to tell him about the trip and I thought I had given myself plenty of time to get back home, pick up our luggage and get across to Manchester airport. That, anyway, was the plan but I quickly learned that when you dealt with Maxwell, the rule of thumb was always expect the unexpected.

I arrived at Headington Hall a good hour early, hoping for a quick getaway. No such luck. I was shown into a side office and told he would see me as soon as possible but I had to appreciate that the lord of the Manor was a busy man. I must have waited nearly three hours during which time I had several conversations with his P.A., a lady called Jean Baddeley whom I came to know well and to learn what an important role she had in the Maxwell organization. Eventually he burst through the door, a giant of a man who seemed to tower over me, shaking my hand until I thought it was going to drop off and apologizing profusely for keeping me waiting. He ushered me into his massive, oval-shaped office, plonked himself in his chair behind the biggest desk I had ever seen and sat me down on the opposite side of it.

He did not beat about the bush. He told me he had heard from a director at Birmingham that I liked a drink – somebody had obviously tried to put the knife in already – and I said I did appreciate a glass of wine or a Scotch. I was as honest and straight-talking with him as he was with me and I believe it got us both off on the right foot. We discussed the job and how he saw the relationship between chairman and manager and I liked what I was hearing because it was clear we both had the same ambition. We wanted to take the club as far as it would go but I don't believe either of us imagined just how far that would be. Oxford were a Third Division club, albeit left in a healthy state by the previous manager Ian Greaves, but any suggestion that, within a mere four years, it could finish up rubbing shoulders in the league with the likes of Manchester United, Arsenal, Liverpool and the rest would have been dismissed as fanciful in the extreme.

He then explained that he had to leave to attend an important business meeting but wanted to carry on the discussion later that day. I told him I could not do that because I was flying to Majorca that evening with my wife. 'Oh, well couldn't she go on her own?' he wondered. I said there was no way I would let Yvonne travel by herself. 'Right, I'll sort it,' he said and asked me for my home number, punching his desk telephone as I spoke and switching to his open phone system. I heard the number ring out and then Yvonne's voice as she came on the line. 'Maxwell here,' boomed the chairman. 'Do you want to go to Majorca tonight or wait and travel with Jim tomorrow?' I could imagine she felt as shocked and helpless as I did listening to the conversation. 'I'll just do what Jim wants,' she stuttered. He had come up with a solution that meant us flying from Heathrow the following day. And that's what happened, with the condition that I stayed away for one week instead of two. Ironically, my hope of a non-football break went out of the window when Doug turned up himself after three or four days and football was all we talked about until I came back.

I took the job at Oxford as quickly as I did for the simple reason that I needed to work. I had a wife, three young girls and a big mortgage. In hindsight and in better financial circumstances, although it turned out brilliantly for me, I might have waited until something better came along. It was a gamble because, had I not been successful, my whole managerial career might have gone down the tubes. But I was also confident I could be a good manager. Oxford were in no bad state when I took over – they still had a chance of promotion to the Second Division. That was down to the hard work done by Ian who had left after falling out with Maxwell. Ian was the old-school type of team boss who wanted to be involved with everything at the club and I found out that he went into a board meeting and was thrown out by the chairman after he had lost his rag about something and started effing and blinding. 'I won't have my managers swearing at board meetings,' roared Maxwell. And that was the beginning of the end for Greavsie, who moved on to Wolves much to

Maxwell's annoyance – because he was the kind of person who always had to be in control and wanted to be the one who dictated whether people stayed or left. He did threaten to sue Ian and Wolves for breach of contract but changed his mind, saying at the time: 'They richly deserved to be sued and I would have expected to win but now that we have got Jim, I cannot claim we have been damaged. We have a First Division manager whose record speaks for itself.'

I don't know whether he was that convinced or if I was being damned with faint praise but Maxwell did take the opportunity to mention I was appointed from a short list of three which included Ken Furphy, adding: 'We were impressed with Mr Furphy but felt he had been in America for too long.' The chairman was keen to lay down a few rules which did not bother me in the slightest. No transfers were to be negotiated without his sanction and, following his experience with the previous manager, he apparently felt moved to change the board meeting routine because he told me that I would not be required to attend any at all. The arrangement was that if I wanted anything, I either went to see him or spoke to him on the phone. There was an urgent matter that needed to be cleared up before I had even been in charge for a game. The captain Malcolm Shotton came to me and said Maxwell had promised to put £750 into the players' pool for their end-of-season trip to Spain on the condition that they beat Brighton in an FA Cup fourth round tie.

Oxford had done brilliantly to beat Brighton, who were then in the First Division, 3–0 on their own ground and now the players wanted their money. I went to the chairman expecting him to tell me to take a running jump but he opened up a briefcase which I could not help but notice was full of £50 notes. He started counting out the money and dropped two on the floor in the process. He handed over the £750 and then bent down to pick up the two he had dropped, pushed them into my top pocket and said – 'There, that's for your holidays as well.' But that's the kind of complex character he was – and I have to say that was the first and last time he did anything like that.

One thing that Maxwell and I had in common was our regard for one of the great stalwarts of the Manor Ground, a gentleman by the name of Ken Fish who really deserves some national recognition for his services to football. Ken – or Mr Fish as most people called him – was the club physio when I arrived, a superbly smart sixty-five-year-old still in wonderful physical condition and certainly the longest-serving, most highly respected person at the club. Ken had a lifetime in the game after coming to England from his native South Africa as an eighteen-year-old. He had a brief and unsuccessful spell as a player with Aston Villa before moving on to Port Vale where he spent twenty-one years as a player then coach, then Birmingham, and then to Oxford under Arthur Turner when they were a non-league club known as Headington United. He was even there when Ron Atkinson was a player at the club and used to regale me with tales of the things my mate 'Flash' got up to as a player. Ron thought enough of Ken to bring a Manchester United team to Oxford for a testimonial match for him, which was a nice touch but fully deserved. There may have been more luxurious and better appointed dressing rooms than we had but I would have defied anybody to show me cleaner ones. The young apprentices could not escape for the day until he had inspected all the first-team boots, training gear and changing rooms. And he believed in providing top hospitality for the players and match officials. He would give them all a Mars Bar each, before every match for energy. The day before a match he would make sure the referees' room was spotless with towels laid out neatly. There would also be an abundance of fruit and a bottle of whisky. The match officials never went short of anything while Ken was around.

For me it was like a breath of fresh air to walk into the ground and see him pottering around, busying himself with all manner of jobs. Sadly he did not have much luck with his health after he retired and went to live in Stoke. I'd heard he had a leg removed as a result of illness and Ron and I, together with Jim Barron, who had played in goal at Oxford, and Paul Reeves went to see him in hospital. He was as cheerful as ever and laughed as loudly as the rest of us when Ron, typically, made light of his predicament. He turned round to Barron and said: 'Jim, you've dropped a right bollock; you've brought the wrong slipper – it's his right foot that's off, not his left. I have to apologize, Ken, we've bought you a slipper for Christmas but it's not the right foot.' And then he made a great show of imploring one of the nurses to go round the ward asking if anybody would do a swap. We were all in hysterics to the point of tears but it made Ken's day.

One of Ken's bright young boys at the club had been Mark Wright who went on to have a magnificent playing career with Southampton, Derby County, Liverpool and England. Mark's £80,000 transfer to The Dell had been on the cards before I arrived and it was left to me to supervise the completion of the deal which also involved Oxford taking George Lawrence on loan. George did well for us and I wanted to buy him so I went down to Maxwell's offices in London to try and set the purchase in motion. When I got there he told me he had been trying to get Lawrie McMenemy, the Southampton manager, on the phone, but he was also trying to close down a major business deal with someone in America and as I walked into his office, he mentioned to his P.A. that when this person rang he had to be put through immediately. There were two phones on his desk and he was never off either of them, taking a succession of calls and at the same time trying to speak to Lawrie. After a lot of trying we eventually reached Southampton on his open line. 'Mr McMenemy, my manager wants to buy George Lawrence at the £40,000 we have agreed,' he said. There was a pause and I heard Lawrie reply: 'Mr Maxwell, I thought you were a gentleman – the fee we have agreed is £44,000.' The chairman smiled and said: 'You're absolutely right – the fee was £44,000.' But the smile disappeared when Jean came in and said the American caller had been trying to get through and had eventually hung up. He went absolutely purple with rage and promptly ordered Jean to sack the switchboard operator.

Maxwell did not have either vast knowledge of the game or a close acquaintance with the players at the Manor Ground. I think George was the only one he knew and that was because he was black. He hardly ever went to any away matches – unless they were really something special – and his usual routine for home games was to arrive at bang on 3 p.m., leave half an hour before the end and ring me up five minutes after the match finished to ask about the result. I had to be prepared to take a call at any time and from anywhere in the world. I was woken up in the early hours of one Sunday morning, first to hear a lot of jabbering in a foreign language which turned out to be Chinese, and then his voice on the line demanding to know the previous day's result. When I told him we had drawn 2–2, he exclaimed: 'Oh shit!' and then chortled: 'I bet you have never had anyone calling you from Peking before to ask about the result.'

He was interested in but, in many ways, ignorant about football. But he more than made up for his shortcomings with his mastery of anything to do with the administration of the club, or the buying and selling of players. That was never more evident than when we bought John Aldridge from Newport County just before the transfer deadline in March 1984. Aldridge had played well against us and I really fancied him as a goalscorer but he looked like following Len Ashurst, who had left Newport to take over at Sunderland. Fortunately for us they could not afford his fee. County wanted £75,000 for him but Maxwell was in no mood to pay that much. He rang them up and told them: 'I'll give you £70,000 and I'll organize a motorcycle rider to deliver the cheque today.' And that's how we saved £5,000 when we bought him and what a bargain that turned out to be. He scored on his full debut in a 5–0 win against Bolton

Kids' stuff – that's me (back row, far left) in my first team, Firth Park Grammar School in Sheffield.

A happy dressing room at Aldershot after beating Aston Villa in the FA Cup, I'm on the left with my arm around our 'keeper Dave Jones and a smile for goalscorer Jim Towers.
©Aldershot News

Top left: Two Oxford scholars – myself and my successor at the Manor, Maurice Evans.

Top Right: Les Ferdinand in his early days at Queen's Park Rangers. ©Action Images

Above left: Making my point to Terry Fenwick and Alan McDonald after the semi-final defeat against Liverpool. ©Popperfoto

Left: Here I am with Jim Gregory in St. Tropez.

Wanderers and although by that time promotion was virtually assured his five goals helped us to clinch the Third Division championship. Unfortunately he did not play enough games to get a medal.

We had missed out on promotion at the end of my first season in charge – 1982–83 – largely due to losing our last four matches. One of them was a local derby at Swindon which was played in farcical conditions. Early in the game two smoke bombs landed in our penalty area and they scored a goal when our 'keeper Roy Burton could hardly see his hand in front of him. The referee allowed the goal and was then laid out when the Oxford fans showered the pitch with coins. We lost the game 3–2 and it somehow seemed appropriate that one of our goals came from a penalty scored by David Fogg.

It was a different story at the start of the following year when we won our first four. I wanted to talk to Maxwell about signing Micky Vinter from Wrexham and went to see him at Headington after our opening-day win at Gillingham. I turned up that evening, smoking a small cheroot type of cigar and pressed the front doorbell. He was not short of staff but, as was his wont, he opened the door himself. The first thing he said was, 'Put that shit out.' I thought he was upset because he was a non-smoker but when we went into his lounge he brought out one of the biggest Havanas I had ever seen and handed it to me saying, 'When you're with me, you smoke a real cigar.' Unfortunately there were not many other occasions for celebration although we did have another tremendous spell midway through the season when we won six successive league matches, but generally speaking we lacked real consistency and I was disappointed when we only finished fifth in the table. Still my consolation was I was convinced success was only just around the corner and I was proved to be right.

The only question seemed to be where would I be when it came. Would it be Oxford or riding on another Maxwell flight of fantasy? We were playing at Doncaster Rovers in the middle of April 1983 when I took a call from the chairman, thinking it would be the usual check on how everything was going. But this one was a little different. 'Jim,' he thundered, 'you are now the manager of Thames Valley Royals.' I knew there had been speculation about a merger with Reading but this news was unexpected to say the least. I asked about Maurice Evans who was in charge at Reading and was told he would be working with me. I was convinced enough to tell the players to expect some big news after the game but to go out that day and do it for Oxford . . . they did and we won 1–0 through a Trevor Hebberd goal. I think they were all as mystified and apprehensive as I was about the future. Maxwell held a press conference at the FA headquarters in London that week insisting that opposition to the merger was pointless and that it would definitely go ahead, but it was clear the supporters had other ideas.

The following Saturday we were at home to Wigan Athletic and I took my usual first-half place in the directors' box alongside the chairman. What a nightmare that turned out to be. It was absolute mayhem. The fans hardly watched the game. They looked straight at us, booing Maxwell, showering us with spit and chanting 'Judas, Judas' – and that was one of the milder insults. It seemed the Reading supporters were equally keen on the idea and Maxwell was eventually foiled when they mounted a rival bid which was supported by Maurice Evans. Roger Smee bought the shares that Maxwell had hoped to buy. The merger fell through, much to Maxwell's anger and disgust and he threatened all sorts of retaliatory action, like pulling out of Oxford and threatening to close the club down because the council would not help over a new ground. My job was to keep the players' minds concentrated on the job of playing and winning matches. There were no visible signs of any ill effects but all the publicity and continual backbiting could not have helped us much. A little while after helping to fight the Reading battle,

Evans was rewarded with the sack. I had always valued his judgement of a player so I approached Maxwell and asked him about the possibility of appointing him as chief scout. Knowing the part he had played in the wrecking of the merger, I did not hold out much hope but Maxwell's unpredictability kicked in again. 'What a fine man,' he declared. 'I'll ring him now.' I was dumbfounded when he opened his book, got Maurice's number and offered him the job there and then. It was a double surprise for me – firstly that Maxwell wanted him, second that he had his private number.

Maurice took over as manager after I left and did a tremendous job in keeping the club in the First Division for three seasons as well as, much to my cost as you will read later, leading them to a League Cup success in his first season in charge. I knew I was leaving the club in excellent managerial hands.

I was devastated to hear of Maurice's sudden and tragically premature death just after the 2000–01 season started. He was still actively involved in the game having gone back to Reading, the club which was always closest to his heart, as chief scout. He was one of the unsung heroes of football – a professionals professional who knew the game inside-out. Not only that, he was a great friend and confidant who is sure to be missed by more than just me.

CHAPTER SEVEN

NIGHTS OF GLAMOUR

We had some terrific Cup nights at Oxford – clubs like Newcastle United, Manchester United, Leeds United and Arsenal came, saw and were conquered. We did well in both competitions in the 1983–84 season, reaching the last eight in the Milk (League) Cup and the last sixteen in the FA Cup. But it was in the Milk Cup that little Oxford from the Third Division grabbed all the headlines. Our run started when we went up to Newcastle for the first leg of our second-round tie. On paper it looked a walkover for the Second Division Magpies, who had players like Kevin Keegan, Chris Waddle, Peter Beardsley and Terry McDermott in their line-up, but we held them to a 1–1 draw. All their stars were out for the second leg at the Manor Ground three weeks later but by the end of the night they were seeing different kinds of stars because we knocked them cold. The way we played, particularly in the first half, I think we would have beaten any side in England. It was not just up and at 'em stuff, we played with intent – an intent to wipe them off the pitch with football. We had a lot of ability in that side and that night we proved it. We beat Newcastle 2–1 but the scoreline in no way reflected our supremacy. Neil Whatmore and Andy Thomas scored for us and Keegan came up with one for them but that was their only consolation.

We were drawn at Leeds United, another Second Division side, in the next round and we did well to go there and get a 1–1 draw which meant a replay at our place. In the meantime the draw for the fourth round had taken place and the winners of our match had been rewarded with a visit from Manchester United. We did not need any incentive to beat Leeds but the thought of a game against Ron Atkinson's team certainly whipped up the enthusiasm and expectancy of the Leeds visit. It was a freezing November evening, so cold that the pitch was frozen solid. I took the players on to the surface that afternoon to get them used to the conditions and make sure we had the right footwear for the match. While we were working out, the Leeds manager Eddie Gray and his kit man arrived with all their kit. Eddie took one look at the pitch and started moaning about the conditions, saying, 'We can't play on that – it's far too dangerous.' I muttered something about the decision being up to the referee. And when the official decided the game would go ahead I could sense that Leeds did not fancy it at all. I told the players they had to be positive because the opposition might be beaten before they came out. The result was never in any doubt as we raced about the ice like Olympic skaters and beat them comfortably 4–1. As a matter of fact, Leeds did not do much better when they came back and played in more normal conditions the following season in the league. They had the advantage of the slope in the first half and went 2–0 up but Gary Briggs scored just before half-time and, when it was our turn to go downhill, we put another four past them.

As Birmingham manager I did not have a good record against West Brom when Ron Atkinson was in charge. But I got my own back and a bit more when we faced Ron's Manchester United team in the fourth round. We had been given credit for our earlier round exploits but everybody reckoned, quite rightly, that the game against United would be a different story. Defeat with dignity was the popular presumption but myself and the players and thousands of supporters still harboured the belief we could give Ron's boys something they and the football world weren't expecting. But even I could not have envisaged when and how it happened. We were drawn at home and it was a great thrill to see such a team, which included such fine players as Bryan Robson, Ray Wilkins, Gordon McQueen, Kevin Moran, Norman Whiteside, Frank Stapleton, Remi Moses and a young Welsh boy called Mark Hughes who was making his first-team debut that night. It was also a little frightening when you compared those household names with the players in my team. But the Manor on a Cup night is a great leveller. Not that United played below their best, it was more a case of Oxford lifting their standards to their level. The game finished 1–1, Bobby McDonald scoring for us and Hughes marking his debut with the first of many goals he was to score in a United shirt. Ron was in good form afterwards when he, myself and a group of press lads went to Vicars, a restaurant we always used in Woodstock. What United were not going to do to us in the replay was nobody's business.

And so to Old Trafford a week later with Oxford filling the now familiar role of underdog. Maxwell was again conspicuous by his absence at the game but he did fancy us enough to declare beforehand that, should the match end level after extra-time, we had to toss a coin to decide the venue of the second replay. There had been a suggestion that it would be better for us financially if we agreed to go back to Old Trafford but the chairman would have none of that. There would be a toss-up and he would call it for us. I went along with it, believing it would be something of a miracle if we could even take the match into extra-time, but that is exactly what we did. In fact we scored first when Kevin Brock bent a superb free-kick round their defensive wall and we had them panicking before Stapleton forced the extra period by grabbing an equalizer. And it was not a matter of us hanging on, either; we gave as good as we got in that half-hour and fully deserved to have another bite at the cherry, but where? Ron and Martin Edwards came to me afterwards and begged to play the third match back at Old Trafford. They even offered to put £6,000 into our players' pool which I'm sure would have delighted one or two of them. But I had to tell them that my chairman was determined to leave it to the toss of the coin.

So the next day the scenario was played out at the Football League offices in Lytham St Annes with a league official, in front of witnesses, tossing the coin and Maxwell on the end of a telephone in his office. He called 'heads' and heads it was and we were back at the Manor Ground for what turned out to be one of the best football occasions I experienced as manager there. I don't think you could have squeezed the Thin Man into our ground for the big game just a week before Christmas 1983 and as far as everybody that had anything to do with Oxford United was concerned, Santa Claus came early. Again we played above ourselves and it was the sort of game that could have gone either way. We scored going down the slope through George Lawrence but Arthur Graham equalized and again the issue went right down to the wire. There were not many minutes of extra-time left when Steve Biggins headed the winner. The place went mad then and again when the referee blew the final whistle. We had the usual table booked in Vicars after the game when it was my turn to do the crowing. Ron was naturally disappointed at going out but he took the defeat well.

Then it was Everton at home for a place in the semi-final and a match that their manager Howard Kendall later described as the turning-point of his whole managerial career. Howard and his assistant Mickey Heaton had watched the United match and I knew they did not relish the trip to the Manor because they had not been pulling up any trees in the First Division. The previous weekend they had dropped to eighteenth in the league table and Howard was under a lot of pressure. It was another icy night, which suited us more than Everton, and Bobby McDonald gave us a deserved lead which we were holding comfortably until Kevin Brock made the mistake that changed Howard's life. He tried to be a bit too clever on the ball and Peter Reid, then a hard-nosed midfielder, came in with a crunching tackle. It looked like a foul to me but Brocky panicked and tried a back pass to our 'keeper Steve Hardwick. Adrian Heath intercepted the ball and scored a great equalizer. We still should have won the game in the last minute when Steve Biggins headed over an open goal.

We had a few injuries for the replay but I thought Everton were that poor against us that we went there thinking we could turn them over. I plumped for an attacking 4–4–2 formation but we could not get it together at all and lost 4–1. Howard told me later that if his team had been knocked out at our place he would have been sacked. As it was Everton never looked back after that, winning the league title two out of the next three years. I did not like losing but I am glad some good came out of it because Howard was and still is a great friend.

If our victory night against Manchester United was the best, beating high-flying First Division Arsenal in the Milk Cup the following season ran it pretty close. Don Howe was the Gunners' manager and they had begun the season well, employing a kind of rotation formation which proved so effective against us we could hardly get the ball early on. I thought we would be doing well to get away with a draw and if that happened we would get crucified in the replay. But our lads dug in and twice got level after Arsenal went into the lead. I had been tipped off by a good journalist friend of mine, Reg Drury, that Pat Jennings, the Arsenal goalkeeper, was playing in spite of a wrist injury but I doubt whether a fully fit Jennings would have stopped Langan's winner, a magnificent shot that flew in from thirty yards.

I feel very proud of the fact that we achieved something quite unique when we became the first club to be promoted as champions from the Third Division to the First in successive seasons. After taking the Third Division title in style by amassing ninety-five points, which broke the previous record total by four, I did not want the club to rest on its laurels and, to give Maxwell his due, he was equally ambitious. During the following summer I bought Billy Hamilton from Burnley and he and Aldridge were to strike up a brilliant understanding and score a lot of goals. I also brought Dave Langan from Birmingham but his arrival and subsequent success has more to do with good luck than good management.

I knew Dave well because I had taken him to St Andrews from Derby County. But he developed a bad back after I left and Saunders gave him a free transfer and forecast he would never play again. Dave rang me up and asked if he could come down and perhaps have a trial, so we had him during our pre-season preparation. He played in the reserves one Friday night against one of the local teams and the following day we were due to play Reading in our final build-up match. Dave would not have been considered but our regular right-back Paul Hinshelwood, who had hardly missed a game in the promotion season, went down with flu. Langan came in at the last minute, never put a foot wrong and made the position his.

We went up to Huddersfield Town at the start of the season and hammered them 3–0, Aldo and Hamilton getting the goals between them, and I felt then we had a real chance of doing something in the Second Division. The statistics underlined our strength at home – of twenty-one matches we drew two and lost one and we scored sixty-two goals with only fifteen against. They included a couple of 5–0 wins against Charlton Athletic and Crystal Palace, 4–0s against Barnsley, Cardiff City, Carlisle United and Wimbledon, and a 5–2 against Oldham Athletic. Cynics tried to dismiss us as a freak side who relied on the idiosyncrasies of our pitch to get our results. But, although I admit we rarely lost a half kicking downhill, there was more quality in the team than a lot of those cynics accepted. Ironically, the only league game we lost at the Manor was against my former club Birmingham who beat us 1–0. That was disappointing but it was all forgotten at the end of the season when we went up as champions and they had to settle for runners-up. We made sure of promotion by beating Shrewsbury Town and afterwards I went into the boardroom and there was Maxwell in his shirt-sleeves dispensing unlimited champagne and food. I expected a few congratulatory words for myself and the players and they seemed forthcoming when he banged on the table and called the assembled gathering to order. 'Gentlemen,' he shouted, 'we will not play First Division football at the Manor Ground next year unless we get the promise of a new stadium from the council.' People stood around dumbstruck. He put a real dampener on the celebrations but he thought it was a shrewd political move because the room was full of the local civic dignitaries. As far as I was concerned the whole thing backfired but that was far from the end of the matter.

Our next game was at Leeds and a win would have won us the championship. It seems strange now when you look at the respective positions of both clubs but in those days we were the team on the ascendancy and Leeds were going nowhere. I arrived early because I did a television interview on the Ian St John and Jimmy Greaves programme at noon. St John said that Maxwell had just gone on television and repeated the threat of not playing at the Manor Ground the following season, and asked me for my views on the subject. I just said we would be playing there simply because it was the only ground we had. I explained that I thought Maxwell was playing a political game and was putting pressure on the council to give us a new stadium. Then I went back to the hotel, got changed and returned to Elland Road on the team bus. Everybody was feeling very up – after all it was a big game with a lot at stake – and I was getting things organized when I got a message from one of the secretaries that Maxwell was on the telephone. I picked it up and heard that familiar voice: 'So you are going to pay the wages of our players in the First Division next year, are you?' I asked what he meant and he responded: 'You have gone against your chairman on national television.'

I tried to say that I had been put on the spot a bit because I had not known anything about the statement he was going to make. But he kept going on and on about me defying him and that it was not my place to say what I did. By now it was getting close to 2.30 p.m. with just about half an hour to kick-off and I wanted to be in the dressing room. I said: 'Look, chairman, I have to go and talk to the players.' But, as Vic Reeves might say, he still wouldn't let it lie. Finally I just lost it. I said, 'Look, Mr Maxwell, if that's the way you feel you can stuff your job right up your arse,' and slammed the phone down. He kept tormenting my poor secretary, trying to get back to me, but I refused to go anywhere near the phone. I was not in the best frame of mind and it did not help when we lost the game 1–0 and the title was put on ice.

I thought I had better go and see him and sort the matter out and as soon as we arrived back at Oxford I drove up to Headington. There were a few heated words and then he told me he wanted me to attend an EGM the following Tuesday when the subject of the new ground was the main topic for discussion. I arrived for lunch on the appointed day to find him waiting with his two sons Kevin and Ian. We had a chat about this and that and it was all very friendly and I mentioned the agreement we had with adidas for the following season which we had already discussed. I thought it was a good deal – adidas were going to provide strips for every team, all the boots and balls and they were giving us about £15,000 on top. I asked the chairman what he wanted on the shirts because we had to let adidas know. Up to then we had been sponsored by the *People* newspaper but we had been told that would not be appropriate in the First Division because other papers would not print photographs advertising one of their rivals. 'Is that all we are getting? £15,000?' he said. 'I'm not having that, Liverpool get £250,000.' I ventured to explain that Liverpool sold a million shirts and we managed a couple of hundred but he would not have it. So then I told him I had already signed the agreement because, as I understood it, he had given it his blessing. That only made his temper even worse. 'You're not allowed to sign anything – leave it to me, I'll get a better deal than that.'

He came to me later and announced: 'Jim – I've done a deal with Umbro for £30,000.' I said, 'That's great, what about the boots and the balls?' knowing in those days Umbro produced neither. He had the audacity to suggest we went back to adidas to get those, which was typical of his lack of understanding of the real football world. Of course I could not do that so in the end we ended up with a poorer arrangement as a result of his interference. It was the first time he had really stuck his nose in and I sensed then, as we were getting bigger as a club, he was going to get involved a lot more. He wanted to be the star of the show. He had bought the *Mirror* newspaper and that only added to his delusions of grandeur. For me he was a changed man – and certainly not for the better.

That was reflected in the presentation ceremony after we won the championship. The previous year everything had been great – we were presented with the championship trophy, Maxwell made a brief speech, the players did a lap of honour and everybody enjoyed the day. I anticipated something similar and the players were in a great mood after we hammered Barnsley 4–0 at the Manor to clinch it. I suggested that the players stay in the dressing room until we got the call and then we would go up to the directors' box and receive the trophy and medals. We must have been in there for about twenty minutes and there was still no word about us going up. What had happened was that Maxwell had picked up the public address microphone and was talking to the supporters and he went on and on.

I went to the secretary Jim Hunt and told him that if the presentation ceremony did not take place in the next five minutes, the players and myself were off. Maxwell got the message and then he started introducing the players to the crowd, starting with the skipper Malcolm Shotton. The only trouble was after he got to George Lawrence, he did not know the rest and had to be prompted about the names because he did not have a clue about who they were – it was totally embarrassing. The next day we were due to tour around the city in an open-topped bus but it turned into the Robert Maxwell show. We met at Headington and as I was getting on the bus, he ordered me to ride with him in an open white Rolls Royce which preceded the bus with all the players on the top deck. He held the trophy aloft and waved and cheered to the crowds as if he had won it while I thought about how much of a prat I was sitting next to him. The daft thing was the people in the streets were booing him anyway because he had sacked most of them. Halfway through the tour he suddenly handed me the trophy and said, 'I'll leave it to you now, Jim – I'm off to lunch.' I got out of the car and jumped on the bus and I must say I felt a lot better for being with the players.

The time came round for discussions about a new contract and I made a couple of approaches to the chairman about it. I did not anticipate any problems because the previous year when we went up to the Second Division he was amiability personified. When I saw him then he asked me how much I wanted – I was on about £19,000 – I said £25,000. 'No problem,' he said and the deal was done in ten minutes. This time he asked me down to his office in the *Mirror* building in Holborn, London, saying we could get together at some time before a dinner he was hosting on the night of the European Cup final between Liverpool and

Juventus at the Heysel Stadium in Brussels. He had organized a big screen to watch the match on and also invited
officials of several minority sports to which he had
promised support from his newspaper.

I waited for an hour in the foyer before I was spotted by
the faithful Jean, who apologized and ushered me into a
room where he was entertaining the top writers from the
paper. 'Sorry, Jim, I had completely forgotten about seeing
you,' he smiled, before taking me into his office. He sat me
down and then said, 'Come on then, Jim, how much do you
want?' I told him £50,000 a year. He hummed and hawed
and then offered me £47,000. I told him I thought it was
negotiable. But before there was any more chat, Jean burst
through the door to tell us what had happened in Brussels.
We went straight into the television room to watch the tragic
events of Heysel and never got any further with the contract
negotiations.

It was a few days before he asked me to go and see him
at Headington – in between I had a call from Jim Gregory,
the chairman of Queens Park Rangers, telling me he
wanted me as his new manager. So I felt I was in a strong
bargaining position when I met Maxwell but again the
complexity of the man came through. We never had any
further discussions at all. He did not offer me a penny more
and, in a rather terse, matter-of-fact manner, told me
instead that I could go and talk to any other club chairman
whenever I wanted.

I did eventually move to QPR but there was an ironic
twist in the tail of my relationship with Robert Maxwell.
Things had not gone as well as I had hoped at Rangers and
I let Paul Reeves know about it. After a while he got in
contact and told me Maxwell wanted to see me. I went to see
him one Sunday afternoon and we went for a stroll in his
garden before sitting down together on a grassy bank. He
asked me if I was happy and I said I wasn't. 'How long have
you got to go?' he inquired. I told him I had a year left on my

contract. He leant over, patted me on the arm like a benevolent uncle and said: 'I'll tell you what – see this year out and then come back home.' It was obvious he was just going through the motions and going to see him had been a complete waste of time.

I look back on my association with Maxwell with mixed feelings. He was a megalomaniac – there is no doubt about that. But he brought out the best in me and, apart from the final weeks, he let me get on with the job. I did feel cheated about not managing Oxford in the First Division. It was one of my biggest regrets that I was not at the club to welcome the likes of Arsenal, Manchester, Liverpool and the rest on a 'level' playing field. I don't believe I was treated fairly after everything that had been achieved at the club during my time there. We went from the Third to the First Division all for a total outlay on players of a little over £200,000, which was cheap at the price. In my book that warranted a much better contract than the one he was prepared to offer me. I did hear later that whenever he had a bright young executive or somebody who threatened to steal his thunder, his habit was to create a situation that would force them to leave.

But he was a football visionary who would have become one of the most powerful forces in the game if his inflexibility had not got in the way of his attempted take-over of Manchester United. I did not agree with his plans to merge with Reading but backed him all the way in his efforts to move Oxford to a new stadium. He may have picked the wrong time to air his views on the occasion of our promotion to the First Division and he talked a lot of rubbish about us not going back to the Manor in the First Division if we did not get a new ground. But if he had been given proper backing from the council, Oxford might have gone on to greater things instead of being in the poor state they are now. I sympathized with Maxwell over his continued battle with the council because the Manor, quaint and productive as it was as far as results were concerned, was not equipped for Second Division football, let alone the three seasons the club enjoyed in the First.

I always believed the council prevented us having a really successful club. Under the circumstances the club did well to stay in the top flight as long as it did but it was inevitable that, sooner or later, the team would come back down. Maxwell had a site earmarked at Marston for the new premises – a 25,000-capacity stadium with a supermarket and commercial offices that could have increased our financial turnover to around the £500,000 mark, a lot of money in those days. Oxford could never have been a Manchester United or an Arsenal but it could have been placed on the same level as a Coventry City or a Derby County.

While I have to admit that anyone who walked away from a mega-million pound fortune, as Maxwell did with United, might feel suicidal, even he did not realize what an opportunity it was. Understanding his football frustrations and accepting his business failures, I still find it difficult to accept that he killed himself by taking a walk into the sea off his yacht. I got to know him and the kind of person he was pretty well and for me he was a fighter, shrewd and dirty when he needed to be, but a fighter. He had been in scrapes before but emerged largely due to his business acumen, strength of character and ruthlessness which often meant cutting a few legal corners. In my opinion, whatever mess he was in, he always thought he could get out of it somehow.

So was his death an accident or was it the result of something much more sinister? I believe the latter and my feelings are shared by several other people who worked closely with him. There was no telling what he was mixed up in but some of the people he was dealing with at international levels certainly had the power and capability to make even the murder of somebody as powerful and well known as Robert Maxwell look like suicide. But it was typical that such a controversial, larger-than-life type of man should leave a string of questions about his death. I am sure he would have enjoyed that.

CHAPTER EIGHT

GREGORY'S BOY

If Southampton had been had been a little more forthcoming, they might have been my next port in the storm of bitterness and disappointment that marked my departure from Oxford United. Lawrie McMenemy had left the Saints and later became manager at Sunderland and although his recommendation was to appoint somebody with experience of either working or playing at the club, I knew I was one of the favourites to take over. But they dithered over the appointment and in the meantime Jim Gregory had made a positive move to take me to Queens Park Rangers. Having decided to go to QPR I was then informed by the Southampton secretary Brian Truscott that, had they known I was unhappy enough at Oxford to want to move, they would certainly have offered me the job at The Dell but it was too late for them and me. To be truthful, given the choice I would rather have gone to Southampton.

The Rangers approach came through an intermediary, Dennis Signy, a well-known football journalist, who was an associate of the Rangers chairman. The Maxwell negotiations had not quite reached the point of no return but I told Dennis I could be interested in going to QPR. When Maxwell turned awkward and I realized a move was my best option, the contact was made with Gregory and a meeting arranged to discuss the details of the job. I'd heard a lot about him; that he was a colourful character who could be difficult to deal with but, after my experiences at Oxford, I felt able to cope with any chairman. We chatted and had a laugh before agreeing a contract that bumped me up to the £50,000 a year I was refused at Oxford, and I embarked on what was a regular routine with Gregory and his cohorts . . . champagne at 4.30 p.m. Strangely enough I had gone to the Rangers Stadium in Shepherd's Bush the previous Saturday night to watch Barry McGuigan beat Eusebio Pedroza and win the world featherweight championship and I got a good feeling about the place. It made the decision to take the job the following Monday even easier.

In fact, everything about Rangers was big time: the stadium, training and medical facilities, administration offices and not least the players – top men like Terry Fenwick, Steve Wicks, John Byrne, Michael Robinson, Paul Barron, Gary Bannister and others. What I did not like was the plastic pitch which had been laid down in the days when Terry Venables was in charge. I was to learn the advantages and disadvantages of that surface. The games were so repetitive; they all followed a pattern to a degree that you could almost time incidents by the minute. I would look at my watch and think – right Bannister or Byrne will score any time now and they did. We were one of three clubs who had an artificial surface at one time or another and for the life of me I still do not know how Rangers, Preston North End and Luton Town managed to get away with convincing the authorities that they were good for the game. Obviously we used to spend time training on it and there is no question it gave us a distinct advantage over visiting opposition, and at the same time I don't think we were at any great disadvantage when we played away because we also did a lot of our preparation on a normal training pitch.

The pitch ruse was a typical Gregory move. The excuse was he wanted to create an all-purpose stadium which would cater not only for football but other sports and activities, such as pop concerts. It did stage that McGuigan fight but I cannot remember any concerts being held there. I remember the first time he tried it on with me and it resulted in a row which helped us both to know where we stood with each other. We had played at Luton Town and I had just got my first month's wages slip. It was clearly not enough and I worked out that Rangers had docked the whole of my pension contribution instead of paying a percentage of it themselves, which is normally the case. To be honest, in my negotiations with Gregory it was never stipulated they would pay my pension – I just took it for granted they would. What with the Southampton thing and a few other niggles in my day-to-day dealings with Gregory, who was terribly hard work when it came down to discussing the players I wanted at the club, I was already getting the feeling I had not done the right thing by going to QPR and this just pushed me over the brink. I decided I had to confront the chairman and tell him how I felt and we had a few heated words. In fact my son-in-law, who drove me to and from the meeting, told my wife Yvonne that he didn't think I would be the manager much longer. Gregory claimed the club did not pay any pension contributions – I contended that he should have made me aware of that. I told him he was out of order and I took the opportunity to let him know about a few other things I was not happy about. And we did not part exactly the best of friends. I had no promise that he would put the matter right, so I felt I had won a major victory in the battle for supremacy in our relationship when he rung me two or three days later and told me the club would indeed pay the appropriate contributions.

It was a lesson well learned. It taught me I had to work Gregory as much as he thought he was working me. He was the kind of bloke who, if he felt he could trample all over you he would do just that. Given the opportunity, he would chew you up and spit you out. I discovered the best way to handle him was to stand up to him because deep down that was what he wanted. I respected him for being a football man even if he tried to interfere too much. He was pretty much a hands-on chairman, checking with me two or three times a day, wanting to know the team, who was doing what, what my movements were – he just seemed to be on my case all the time. I had not been used to that and we developed a relationship that was a mixture of confrontation and conciliation. There was never a better example of the latter than whenever I wanted to sign someone. I would give him a list of four players, any one of whom I would have taken, and allowed Jim to pick the one he fancied best. I never minded that because, for all his faults, he did know a player when he saw one. But if I went to him with just one name he would find a reason to get bloody-minded about it and make it difficult. It was a little charade that we went through and it usually ended with both of us getting our own way.

But not always. There was the time when I told him I wanted to sign Ray Houghton from Fulham. I had him with us for a week's trial when we did some pre-season training at Stowe. Ray had not done particularly well but the reason I wanted him was I knew Oxford were in and I had always valued Maurice Evans as one of the game's top judges. He asked how much and I suggested he ring the Fulham chairman Ernie Clay and find out. Jim and Ernie were never the closest of pals, not by any stretch of the imagination, and that gave him an excuse to sound reluctant about doing business at something like £120,000. Towards the end of the session at Stowe we had a friendly against Fulham and Ray actually played for them when I had hoped he would be with us by then. But they also had a young striker playing for them called Leroy Rosenior who really put himself about and I really liked the look of him. I was driving away from Stowe, having made more than a mental note about Rosenior, when my mobile rang and it was Gregory. 'I've got you Houghton,' he announced. 'I've managed to knock that sod Clay down to £60,000 and he's yours.' I was mindful that Ray had not done so well with us and I thought to myself if he turned out to be a flop Gregory would crucify me, so I told him, 'Sorry, chairman, I've changed my mind – I don't want him.' And I added that I wanted Rosenior instead because I thought he would be one for the future. We did that deal instead and Ray turned out to be the one that got away. He eventually went to Oxford for £150,000 and later to Liverpool and Aston Villa in near million pound deals.

Leroy struggled to make an impact and so did we as a team in that second season. But I decided to gamble on playing him in a match against Manchester United at Old Trafford towards the end of November. I remember the game well for lots of reasons, primarily because my mate Ron Atkinson had been sacked by United three weeks earlier and Alex Ferguson had been put in charge. I spoke to Ron at the time and he was not very happy about the way it was done, especially as Fergie was appointed almost immediately. He rang me up in the week before the game and we arranged to meet in the Four Seasons Hotel near Manchester Airport. We were staying there on the Friday night and he was flying out that evening on holiday. Imagine my surprise when we arrived to find that Fergie was staying at the hotel as well. I had first met Alex some time before when he was in charge at Aberdeen and he and I were in a party that went on a football trip to watch the semi-finals of the European Championship in France in 1984. We were two of a group of managers flying on a private jet to watch France play Portugal in one semi-final in Marseilles, which, incidentally, turned out to be one of the greatest games I have ever seen, and then on to Lyon where Spain and Denmark met in the other semi. We got on really well then but we did not have a lot to say on this particular night. It was a really awkward situation because, naturally, my loyalties were to Ron, who was my mate, and he was in no mood to be friendly to the man who had taken his job.

While all this was going on a call came through for me from Gregory, who was back in his office in London getting through a few bottles of champagne in his own inimitable style with a gang of his cronies. 'Oh, you'll be having a party with your pal,' he muttered sarcastically before demanding to know what the team was. I went through it, finishing with the name of Rosenior at number eleven. 'Ah Rosenior,' he guffawed sarcastically. 'I'll be there tomorrow to watch us take a big stride towards the Second Division.' But I stuck to my guns. 'Say what you like, Mr Chairman – but he's playing tomorrow.' And I put the phone down. Ten minutes later he rang again with another moan about Rosenior and received the same reaction from me. And again and again and again at various intervals for most of the night. He never stopped ringing until finally I said I was going to bed and if he had any more to say, he'd better do it face to face the following day. Frank Sibley told me he did the same thing with my predecessor Alan Mullery over a full-back called Gary Chivers, pestering the life out of him until in the end he left the lad out. Sibley reckoned that was one of the reasons why Mullery was eventually shown the door. We lost 1–0 to United – it was Alex's first win as manager – and it did not help that Rosenior was probably our best player on the day.

Jim loved to do things in style. The spread of food and drink in the boardroom at matches could not be bettered anywhere. His favourite food was fish and no expense was spared to get the finest for directors and their guests – everything from caviare to crab, washed down with the best vintage wine or champagne. Not only was he a generous host at Loftus Road but he enjoyed taking me out to the top fish restaurants for lunch and then it would be back to his office for more bubbly and good football chat. I would not get home until about 10 p.m. but I enjoyed those sessions because we had a laugh and the crack was good. It was the same after matches on a Saturday afternoon. You could not leave before he left. He did multi-million pound property deals involving garage sites but socially the club was his life. He kept everybody back drinking and eating, chatting and arguing. Sometimes it would be getting on for midnight when we left the ground and the wife did not always enjoy having to drive back to Oxford but that was the way it was. He was a man of changing moods and he could be as tight and awkward as he was generous. Travelling back from an away match, especially if we had not done well, he would ring me and try and be sarcastic with comments like: 'Have you got Chablis out?' 'Is the red wine going down well?' 'What are the steaks like?' I got so fed up with it that I stopped carrying food on the coach and we used to stop somewhere on the way back and have fish and chips. He was also forever moaning about the cost of staying overnight before a match. You just never knew where you were with him.

Gregory had more personality changes than a library full of Jekyll and Hydes. That was never better illustrated than in his treatment, and I use the word literally, of former Rangers favourite Stan Bowles. Once after a match I found Stan waiting outside the boardroom. I went in and told Jim he was there and he mentioned something about looking after him and went outside. When he came back he explained that every now and then he dropped Stan a few quid. 'He was the best player I have ever had at QPR and to be fair I didn't pay him as well I should have so I am trying to make it up to him now,' he said. And Stan turned up regularly and was never refused.

Rangers had only just managed to avoid relegation in the

season before I joined. We finished in a respectable thirteenth in my first year in charge but the bonus, a rather
bitter-sweet one at that, was in reaching the final of the
Milk Cup. We had beaten Hull City and Watford in the
earlier rounds and then faced Nottingham Forest at home.
It was a match full of incidents, not the least of which was
a floodlight failure before the game which prompted the
Forest manager Brian Clough to accuse Jim Gregory of
deliberate sabotage. Cloughie was not too happy at the end
of the match either because we scored twice in the last two
minutes through John Byrne and Gary Bannister and beat
them 3–1. That took us through to a home quarter-final
against our local rivals Chelsea and it turned out to be a
battle right from the whistle with neither of us taking any
prisoners.

The game ended in a 1–1 draw which meant a replay at
Stamford Bridge and again it was certainly not an occasion
for the squeamish. Chelsea chairman Ken Bates set the
tone for the evening by slamming the Loftus Road pitch in
his programme notes, saying it was a joke and what they
weren't going to do to us now that they had got us on grass.
He might have been right about the plastic but he could not
have been more wrong about the result because we beat
them 2–0 after extra-time with Bobby McDonald scoring
first and then Michael Robinson hitting a magnificent
second from about fifty yards. I really do not know how
gracious or otherwise Mr Bates and his directors and their
friends were in defeat because I never saw any of them
after the match. The only people in the boardroom when I
went in were Jim Gregory and our other directors. 'Help
yourself to a drink, Jim – we're on our own,' shouted the
chairman. It turned out that Bates and his entourage had
been so confident of winning they booked a restaurant for a
celebratory dinner and were too mean to cancel it. The fact
that the game had gone into extra-time meant they could
not hang around afterwards either to perform the usual

niceties. We enjoyed their hospitality without them and I must say it was very generous in their absence.

There was always an undercurrent of bad feeling whenever we met Chelsea and the fact that we had put one over on them in the League Cup clearly jarred with them when we went to Stamford Bridge later that season for a league match. It was business as usual with both sides going at it hammer and tongs and players being booked at regular intervals by the referee Howard Taylor. It did not look good for us when Pat Nevin put Chelsea in front. But then they lost their goalkeeper Eddie Niedzwiecki, who was carried off after a collision with Steve Wicks, and little David Speedie went in goal for the last twenty minutes. He did well enough but he had no chance when David Kerslake smashed in an equalizer from twenty-five yards five minutes from the end.

The Chelsea players were obviously gutted and they started to put themselves about even more. I was furious when their defender Doug Rougvie caught Kerslake in the face with an elbow right in front of our bench and his nose exploded in a mass of blood. I leapt out of my seat to have a go at Rougvie and suddenly there was a bunch of players, back-room staff and officials pushing and shoving and pointing at each other. Mr Taylor came charging up and told me to back off. He had not penalized Rougvie at all so I asked him in a less than diplomatic fashion whether he had something wrong with his eyesight. He did not appear to appreciate that too much and he ordered me to leave the dug-out, telling a police constable to escort me to the dressing room. The final whistle went just after and Kerslake came in with his face a mess and his shirt covered in blood, so I took him into the referee's room and had another go at the official.

I suppose it was inevitable that Mr Taylor would report my behaviour to the FA and I was charged with bringing the game into disrepute. By that time we had beaten

Liverpool in the League Cup semi-final and there was a suggestion I could be banned from the bench at Wembley. I was on the carpet a few days before the final when the referee accused me of using threatening behaviour, saying that he thought I was going on to the pitch to hit him. I was astounded by that accusation and pointed out that I was trying to bring his attention to the elbowing incident which finished with my player sustaining a broken nose. I never think you get much of a chance in these situations but the touchline ban did not materialize. I was fined £750 and warned about my future conduct.

We had made it hard for ourselves in the two-legged semi-final. Kenny Dalglish, who was manager of Liverpool at the time, made no secret of the fact that he too hated our artificial pitch and in the circumstances they did well to keep the score down to what was for them a very acceptable 1–0 defeat, with Fenwick scoring our goal. Howard Kendall allowed us the use of the Everton training facilities before the second leg. After training Howard and I repaired to a favourite Chinese restaurant of his for lunch. Knowing him, I thought it was taking a bit of a chance with the game that evening but I managed to keep my eye on the ball and escaped in plenty of time. We were always up against it at Anfield: Steve McMahon scored and the referee gave them a dodgy penalty which would have put us in even deeper trouble had Paul Barron not saved Jan Molby's kick. Then Craig Johnston did score a second to put Liverpool ahead on aggregate and at that stage, with the Kop going crazy, I didn't fancy our chances of staying in the cup.

But fortune favoured us when we needed it most in the shape of an own goal by Ronnie Whelan which put us level again over the two legs. Extra-time was approaching when I sent on Wayne Fereday, a real speed merchant who I thought would provide us with fresh legs for the extra half-hour. There were only seconds left when he chased a ball into their penalty area and put the Anfield defence under so much pressure that Gary Gillespie scored another own goal. That was us through to the final and we made no attempt to contain our jubilation. Our success was put down to my brilliantly timed substitution but the truth is I had given up any chance of a result in normal time – I was only thinking of the extra half-hour. The celebrations began after the match when Jim Gregory brought the champagne down from the boardroom to the dressing room but Liverpool's generosity ended with the two goals they gifted us – they sent Jim a bill for the bubbly, which he was happy to pay.

I went up into the boardroom later just as one of their directors was coming out. You don't know really what to say in those circumstances but I offered my sympathies, holding out my hand and saying, 'Unlucky.' He pushed by with his face contorted in fury and told me to go away in terms that sounded distinctly Anglo-Saxon. But I could put up with that because we were in the final and I was about to achieve one of my greatest ambitions, which was to lead a team out at Wembley.

I cast more than a glance at the other semi-final which involved none other than the club I had just left after guiding them to the First Division. Oxford had drawn 2–2 at Aston Villa on the same night that we had beaten Liverpool and I knew Villa would have it all to do in the second leg at the Manor Ground. We had made it and I was desperate for my old club to get there with us when their second leg came up a week later. It turned out to be yet another great cup occasion. Les Philips and Jeremy Charles scored the goals in the 2–1 win that made it a Queens Park Rangers–Oxford United final. Not the most glamorous of games for the uncommitted – not one that gripped the imagination of outsiders but to me it meant everything. Rangers were my team and I wanted to win, especially since I was on a £25,000 bonus if we did, but I had a lot of friends at United, not least Maurice Evans, the manager in charge of the team which I had virtually created.

We used the Royal Lancaster Hotel as our base before the

final and on the Friday night I was having dinner with my wife Yvonne, the chairman and his wife and another couple when Jim piped up, 'You know that bonus you're on, Jim – what you should do is have a nice few quid on Oxford to cover yourself.' It occurred to me that it could be dangerous if he had something like that up his sleeve about me. It also made me more aware that with Gregory there was always an extra angle. He was probably just testing me out and I let it go – although I must confess I did check out the odds but felt they were a little too cramped to have a bet.

Getting to Wembley was an education in itself. I found out you have to be there at least a couple of hours before the kick-off and I enjoyed all the trappings of the occasion: the crowds, the police escort, the colour of it all. But the wait once into the dressing room was interminable; it seemed to take ages. I made a mental note that if I was ever in the same situation again, I would arrange some pre-match entertainment in the dressing room just to break the nervous anxiety, even monotony, for the players. Unfortunately I am still waiting for the next opportunity. The players did have a walk out to soak up the atmosphere but when, at long last, the time came to walk down the tunnel that was an even stranger experience for me. I was at the head of the QPR team and as I looked across at the amber-shirted Oxford lads, Malcolm Shotton, John Aldridge, David Langan, Kevin Brock and the rest, I couldn't help thinking I was in the wrong place. Maurice had let Ken Fish lead them out because he said that it was not his but Jim Smith's team and it certainly felt that way. I finished up talking to them more than my lot.

The *déjà vu* sensation carried over into the game because we played poorly and Oxford took us to the cleaners. The writing was on the wall after Trevor Hebberd scored the first goal. We just could not get into the game and Ray Houghton and Jeremy Charles scored one each to complete a 3–0 victory. So much for superstition because I had an expensive Crombie overcoat which I had worn for every round and kept on for Wembley. It was a warm spring afternoon and I was sweating buckets. When we lost I took it off, laid it down somewhere and that was the last I saw of it. It was a total nightmare for us – the fans gave the players plenty of abuse and it was a long walk back down the tunnel to the dressing room. I was as sick as they were but as I trudged off feeling pretty down in the mouth, the fans at the Oxford end began to chorus 'There's only one Jimmy Smith', which gave me a tremendous lift. Then Aldo popped his head round the dressing room and shouted, 'Get in here, boss – we've got the champagne out. This is your team.'

Of course I had to put up with Maxwell gloating like the cat who had fallen into a vat of double cream. 'I knew you were going to lose today, Jimmy,' he sniggered. I asked how he did know and he replied: 'Because when I shook your players' hands before the match, they were all sweaty.' It was typical Maxwell but he may have had a point because in the games against teams like Forest, Chelsea and Liverpool we had been the underdogs but we were favourites to win the final and I think that affected the attitude of the players. We managed to drown our sorrows in style back at the Royal Lancaster. But Gregory was peeved enough to throw out two or three members of the *EastEnders* cast, including Nick Berry and Gillian Taylforth, who had been invited by Eric Hall but did not have tickets. Jim did not stand on ceremony and so-called celebrities meant nothing to him unless of course they were in his inner sanctum.

It goes without saying that my £25,000 bonus went out of the window and Gregory seemed to take great delight in telling myself and Frank Sibley, who did not get anything either, that he had paid the secretary a grand for doing well with the tickets and various members of staff were also given bonuses for their good work in helping with the administration. It was his way of letting us know that, although he felt they had done their jobs well, he was not happy with us. I could not help wishing I had taken his advice and put a few quid on Oxford. Gregory's disappointment at losing in the final, and so badly at that, cut deep and I think it sparked another demonstration of childish pettiness at the start of the following season when he suddenly decreed that back-room staff would no longer be allowed in the boardroom after matches, delegating me to pass the message on to those it concerned. It was particularly difficult for me to tell our physio Dave Butler who had been at the club for ten years and had always been invited upstairs after matches with his wife. I mentioned it to another director Tony Chandler, who was a pal of Dave's, and together they came to an arrangement whereby Dave went into his suite instead although he was obviously very unhappy about it.

Some time after the final we played Aston Villa at home and I went into the boardroom afterwards to find a Villa player, Simon Stainrod, who had been at QPR, enjoying the chairman's hospitality. After Simon left I had a right go at Gregory. I told him he was right out of order banning the staff but putting the welcome mat out for opposing players and that, if the boardroom was not good enough for them, it was not good enough for me, and stormed out. The following Monday I got a message from the club secretary telling me I had been suspended for a fortnight for being abusive to the chairman. Gregory also said, through the secretary, that he would not be saying anything to the press but he could not help it if they picked it up. As it happened they never did. It was a farcical situation because that evening I was supposed to be spearheading the launch of a new bingo ticket at Hammersmith Palais. Dennis Signy pleaded with me to go ahead with the launch, so I did and I must say I did a great job. Dennis and a few others rang Gregory afterwards to tell him how well the evening had gone and it was largely down to my spiel.

Two days later we were due to go to Newcastle United

and I wanted to be there, so I decided a little friendly diplomacy was the order of the day. I rang Gregory and told him, 'Look, things have been said that should not have been but I have to go to Newcastle with the team.' We had won two games in succession against Watford and Villa, I had just signed Sammy Lee from Liverpool and I felt I had to be there. Under sufferance he agreed and I am sure he was waiting with his gang of hangers-on to pour on the vitriol if things had gone wrong – but they didn't. We won 2–0 and that was the last I heard about the suspension.

CHAPTER NINE

GETTING IT SORTED

It troubled me that in the first few months at QPR I did not have a great rapport with the players. At Oxford we were all in it together. The London lot were somewhat flashier, a bit spivvy, the sort who would go straight from training to an upmarket restaurant and have a lunch complete with wine and all the trimmings. There seemed to be something on the go all the time, people popping in all the time trying to do deals over anything from a suit length to a sports car. I'd had my card marked about a few of them by Frank Sibley, who had been acting as caretaker manager following the sacking of Alan Mullery but had made it clear he did not want the job permanently, and I knew the ones to watch out for. The feeling was that a few of them had let down Mullery after he had taken over from Terry Venables and had only lasted a few months. Venables was undoubtedly a tough act to follow. In his four years he had taken the team into the top division, qualified for Europe and reached the final of the FA Cup. Most of the team had been at the club under him and I sensed a resentment at any attempt to do something in a different manner to what he would have done.

I encountered another major problem which concerned me deeply. Whenever a player, such as Terry Fenwick, Steve Wicks or John Gregory, had a problem they did not come to me – they went to the chairman instead and he encouraged that. I also detected quite early that Gregory's judgement of a manager inevitably meant a comparison with Venables whom he loved like a son. It all made for the kind of oppressive atmosphere that I felt would ultimately do me down unless I did something about it. I resolved to sever the Venables–Jim Gregory connection as quickly as possible and one of the first players to go was John Gregory who was sold to Derby County for £100,000. It was a move that suited everybody as John was a good player who did even better when he went to the Baseball Ground.

I valued Fenwick as a player. He might have been one of Jim Gregory's men and a ducker and diver off the field but I could never complain about his outlook when he went on it. He was my skipper and a terrific influence. He combined skill with a fierce, determined attitude that served the team well on more than one occasion. He played a pivotal role in the sweeper system which we subsequently employed successfully. However, I still got the impression that, whatever my instructions, if it suited him to do something else he would. A clear example of that was when we went to Carlisle United, a struggling Second Division side, to play in the third round of the FA Cup.

The game had been postponed twice because of the conditions and it was eventually played one freezing Monday night when the ground was swept by gale-force winds. I instructed Fenwick to take the wind in the first half if he won the toss – I have always believed it's best to do that because you can gain a valuable advantage and there is always the possibility it could change direction later in the game. Clearly Fenwick did not agree because he called correctly but opted to kick against the wind. Carlisle scored before half-time and although we only turned round one goal down the match developed into one of those terribly frustrating occasions when we did everything but hit the net and lost 1–0. I asked Fenwick later why he had gone against my instruction and his explanation was that he felt, because they were a poor side, we could hold them against the wind and then make our superiority count afterwards. In fairness he was never afraid to take responsibility as skipper but my point was, whether he thought I was right or wrong, he should not have gone against his manager.

He had a problem over a new contract which he was continuously sounding off about to the press. There were rumours about a move to Tottenham and speculation that his former boss Venables wanted to take him to Barcelona, but neither club were in touch and I was pleased when he did eventually sign a new deal when the club made him the highest-paid player in their history at over £1,000 a week. It seems ludicrously low when you think that was barely thirteen years ago and players like Roy Keane are now earning more in a week than he would have made in a year. Fenwick had my total respect as a player but I have to say I never knew which camp he was in – I was not sure whether it was mine – and our paths would cross again, of which more later.

I have been given credit for giving Les Ferdinand his big chance in professional football but in truth the man who did more to get his career off the ground was Gordon Milne, my old adversary from our days in non-league football at Boston and Wigan. I got to know about Les through Frank Sibley, whose mate was the manager of Hayes Athletic and had pestered the life out of Frank about this powerful young striker they had at the club. Frank went to see him and came back to tell me he was worth another look. I made a personal check one Tuesday night when it was pouring down with rain and the pitch was like a mudflat. It was hardly the sort of conditions in which anybody could really shine and Les did not do a lot apart from once when he beat about four men and hit a shot that nearly snapped the bar in two. That was enough and I decided there and then to get him. The trouble was I was not the only manager who fancied him and I had to move quickly. I spoke to the Hayes manager and did the deal that evening for £15,000. I rang Gregory and told him what I had done and he did not say too much at the time but he always maintained later that he was responsible for getting Les to QPR. I suppose if he had turned out to be a real duffer he would have kept quiet and let me take the blame.

Les certainly did not pull up any trees when he first arrived. He was a big, powerful twenty-year-old whose job had been delivering paint before he joined us in March 1987 but he seemed completely under-awed by life as a professional footballer. In fact he was so laid back and easy-going I began to worry about just what was going to motivate him. He had a couple of first-team games towards the end of his first season but he played mostly in the reserves, all over the place – even at the back – as I tried to put some fire in his belly. The following pre-season he came with us on tour to Holland when one of our opponents was a Greek team. I took him to one side before the match and warned him about some of the antics the Greeks were likely to get up to, such as shirt-tugging, spitting and obscene gestures. The last thing I wanted was for him to break the habit of a lifetime and lose his rag in a match that did not matter too much. Sadly my words fell on deaf ears – one of the Greeks did spit at him and he promptly laid the guy out! There was another occasion on that same tour when Les exhibited a rare tendency towards violence when the players had a problem with a gang of the locals in a club. They got Dave Seaman on the floor and were giving him a real going-over when Les went in and sorted four or five of them out.

But demonstrations of temperament were all too infrequent and it was reflected in his performances. I could not for the life of me stick him in the side because I was worried that if the crowd got at him it could do irreparable damage. He could not handle the rollickings I gave him. To be fair, I used to hand out some real verbal volleys and I know he has said he thought I went over the top at times, which I probably did, but I was trying to get more from him. Finally Gordon, who was coaching Besiktas in Turkey, rang me, asking whether I knew of a big, typically English type of centre-forward that he could take on loan. I told him I had just the player. I called Les in and gave him a lot of guff about how he could get valuable experience playing in Europe and he agreed to go. I always believed he had the potential to go right to the top but I could never have imagined the difference going to Turkey would make to him. He went out there, took to the white-hot atmosphere of some of the games like a duck to water, became a star and the rest . . . as they say. According to Gordon, Les quickly became accustomed to the environment and the people, the locals loved him and his confidence grew visibly day by day. Gordon used to regale me with stories about how he used to destroy defences and I know he and his president at Besiktas would have loved Les to stay on a permanent basis, but by then we had become aware of how well he was doing and stuck to the loan arrangement. He stayed out there for a year and I had gone by the time he came back but he continued to develop as a player, especially under Gerry Francis, and was eventually sold for £6 million to Newcastle United where he won the PFA Player of the Year award, before moving on to Tottenham Hotspur for a similar sum. Les's later career has been bedevilled by injury, which has been a great shame, but at his best there were not many better and I am proud of the part I played in getting him started.

David Seaman was a different proposition because he already had a reputation as an up-and-coming goalkeeper when I took him from Birmingham City to Loftus Road for £250,000 just before the 1986–87 season. I had seen him perform well in a game against Coventry City and targeted him as a replacement for Paul Barron who was coming to the end of his career. We were playing in a tournament in Sweden when I rang the chairman and told him I wanted to buy David. Gregory went through the normal routine of asking, 'Now, are you sure you want this lad?' But in fairness he did the deal without any more fuss. David had a similar character to Ferdinand when he came – a lovely disposition but casual in the extreme. I realized he needed some extra tuition so I decided to bring in Bob Wilson to give him some specialist coaching. Bob had been doing bits here and there as well as his television work and he did a great job on David. In my opinion Bob Wilson made David the 'keeper he is today. He made him realize how good he could be and worked him because if I hadn't brought in a goalkeeping coach, he would not have done anything off his own bat. He would have spent his time fishing, which he has always loved.

David's first league game for us turned out to be a nightmare because he had to pick the ball out of the net five times at Southampton on the opening day of the 1986–87 season, but I can clearly remember the day I knew I had bought a real 'keeper. It was a fortnight later when we went to Everton and got a goalless draw which was a complete contrast to our game at Goodison Park the previous season. We had led 2–0 but they scored from a penalty just before half-time and made it 2–2 early in the second half. We scored again but they started bombing high balls into our area for the likes of Graeme Sharp, and Paul Barron could not quite handle it and we ended up losing 4–3. Everton tried the same tactics when we went back but this time David was in goal and he came out and caught everything. I knew then I had the best 'keeper in the country – and it did not take long for others to get the same message. I like to think I was one of the fore-runners in organizing personal coaching for goalkeepers. Most top clubs have them now but in those days they were a rare breed, which is difficult to comprehend when you consider the importance of having a 'keeper who knows what he is doing. What with introducing fitness coaching at Boston United and then a goalkeeping coach, I suppose I can consider myself a bit of a football visionary.

I have also blazed a few football trails in my time in the game and one that I was particularly proud of was the day when I became the first manager to join the 92 club – whose exclusive membership is restricted to those who have managed or coached at every club ground in the league. The venue could hardly have been more appropriate because it was Hillsborough, the place where as a kid I watched more football than anywhere else. I suppose when you have been involved at every level from the basement upwards like I had been in the first fourteen years of my career, you deserve some recognition but I knew nothing about it until I was contacted by somebody from the 92 club. And when he said the picture would be completed when I took QPR to Sheffield Wednesday, I don't think he realized what that meant to me. The saddest thing about my playing career was that I never kicked a ball on the Hillsborough pitch. It was always my boyhood dream to play for Wednesday but they never came for me and I joined Sheffield United instead. There was one year when United were drawn away to Wednesday in the FA Youth Cup and the game was due to be played at Hillsborough. I thought my big moment had arrived but I was promoted to play in the reserves on the same night and the chance never came again.

We wasted our good start to the 1986–87 season by winning only two out of sixteen matches in the three months up to Christmas. The fans were not happy, and who could blame them? Some even organized a campaign to get me the sack, distributing leaflets before matches and generally making life difficult. I managed to ride out that crisis but the supporters' agitation then was nothing to the storm of unrest that erupted over the proposed merger between QPR and Fulham in February. I was never party to the negotiations that went on but Jim did tell me he would be selling his interest in the club to a property group called Marler Estates. They also owned Fulham and Stamford Bridge and the idea was to shut Fulham down at the end of the season and create a new club called Fulham Park Rangers which would be headed by the Fulham chairman David Bulstrode. I had been assured by Mr Bulstrode that I would manage the new club and Ray Lewington, who was in charge at Fulham, would be my assistant. I think I could have been forgiven for thinking 'here we go again' because the whole business smacked of Robert Maxwell's attempt three years earlier to merge Oxford United and Reading and call it Thames Valley Royals.

The similarity did not end there because when news broke of the proposal the supporters of both clubs decided on the same kind of protest action that I had been through before. They organized a sit-down demonstration before a home match against Manchester City. The kick-off was delayed for about twenty minutes and the game only got under way after I went out on to the pitch and assured them that their club was not going to disappear. The Fulham fans were equally angry to the extent that the lives of Bulstrode and another director, Robert Noonan, were threatened if they went ahead with the scheme. Whether that had any effect or not the following day came an announcement that the merger was off. It was blocked at an emergency meeting of the Football League Management Committee but by then Bulstrode had decided to pull out anyway. The irony was that Fulham were eventually saved when a consortium headed by my old friend Jimmy Hill bought out the players' contracts, clearing the way for Bulstrode to take over from Jim Gregory as my new chairman. In a way I was not sorry to see Jim go because, although we had been through a lot together, I think if he had stayed I might have been looking for another job that summer. QPR had been his life for twenty-three years but he obviously felt the £6 million offer was one he could not refuse. Even after he left he used to telephone me from his yacht to ask about the score. But I was in no position to dwell too much on the wheeling and dealing in the corridors of power, I was still more concerned for my own welfare. We had finished the season in a blaze of mediocrity losing our last three games – one of them a 7–1 defeat at Sheffield Wednesday – and I was wondering whether this new brush intended to sweep the manager's office clean.

As it happened David and I enjoyed a terrific relationship and the short time I spent working with him until his untimely, premature death was one of my happiest in football. He was a committed football follower who knew plenty about the game but was always willing to listen to learn more. He was a fair man who left me to get on with the job the way I wanted to do it. His first love was Aldershot where he had once been a bank manager and whenever his QPR commitments allowed he would dash off and catch an Aldershot match. That gave us a great affinity because we often used to chat about each other's experiences with the club – me as a player and him as a supporter. The first big decision he made at Rangers was to get rid of the plastic pitch, which had my full backing. There were also a couple of transfer deals which I had to get involved in as a result of his previous links with Fulham. They were broke and he told me I had to buy two players from them to give them a much-needed cash injection. After giving the matter careful thought I chose Paul Parker, whom I rated as a defender, and their centre-forward Dean Coney and I think we gave them something in the region of a million pounds for the pair.

I also bought John O'Neill, a big centre-half from Leicester City, for £65,000 and paid Southampton £30,000 to renew my association with Mark Dennis, a deal that many people believed qualified me for a stint at the funny farm because in the time that had elapsed since our days at Birmingham he had developed a reputation as a bit of a nutter who was always causing problems both on and off the field. But I felt I knew him as well as anybody. I liked his devilment and I thought I could control it And the bottom line for me was he had a sweet left foot and he could play. I know the lad tried to turn over a new leaf. When he signed for me he told one reporter, 'I am more mature now and I feel I can control myself. I know players are going to wind me up and try to get me sent off but that is pressure – that is football.' That was certainly true but unfortunately his best intentions always seemed to get overtaken by his quick temper. As it happened he did not play that many times because he was unlucky with injuries but when he did, not only did he land himself in trouble, he dropped me in it as well. He came back after an absence of thirteen games, while he recovered from injuries he sustained in a car crash, for a game against Tottenham Hotspur. The pre-match publicity was all about Ossie Ardiles making his 300th appearance in English football. Well, that might have been the story at the start but it certainly wasn't by the end. Dennis, never one for being out of the limelight, helped Ardiles to celebrate by allowing him to feel the weight of his elbow and was sent off – for the eleventh time in his career. From the touchline I thought Ardiles had made a meal of going down and I did myself no favours by suggesting at the time that he had contributed to Dennis's dismissal.

There was more fuss over that than the incident itself and it kept the papers going for days. Ardiles threatened legal action unless I withdrew my remarks and accused me of trying to switch the responsibility from Dennis and myself on to him, saying, 'Smith has questions to answer about the handling of the player. Something must be wrong. Are we to suppose there were ten previous con men before me?' He had a point and I quickly realized there was no other way out for me but to apologize. I was also getting grief from the Professional Footballers' Association and Gordon Taylor acted as a mediator to get the thing sorted out. I issued a public statement admitting I was wrong and explaining that what I said was in the heat of the moment. I also rang Ardiles privately and said I was sorry and that was almost the end of the matter . . . almost, because the following summer he and Dennis became team-mates after I took Ossie to Loftus

Road. He had been released by Spurs and did not have a club and Peter Shreeves, who had worked with him at White Hart Lane, said he would do a good job for us. And he certainly did. We signed him just before the season started and he had not done a great deal of training and was not fully wound up when I picked him to play at Manchester United as a sweeper. We drew 0–0 and he gave one of the best displays I have ever seen from a player in that position.

I had resolved to play with a sweeper the previous year because I felt we had the quality of players to make it work. I had seen foreign teams employ that formation and there had been occasions at Oxford when we were losing when I turned to it, pushing the full-backs on, and invariably we salvaged something from the game. I was conscious of a certain scepticism among the staff, who went along with the idea because they felt that, in time, I would get that system out of my system. I had changed the coaches around, switching Peter Shreeves from the reserves to the first team and moving Frank Sibley in the other direction. It was a difficult decision that Frank was not happy about but it was no reflection on his ability. I just wanted a change of voice, a different face and method, and Peter, who was out of work when I brought him to replace Bobby Campbell, who had left to become Chelsea manager, had done a terrific job with the stiffs. I discussed my 'sweeper' theory with Peter, who smiled and said, 'Fair enough, you're the boss; let's give it a try.' I am not sure the players were convinced it would work either but events proved me right and the doubters wrong.

I used a pre-season tour of Norway to test my options. We were one of three foreign clubs over there, the others being Dundee United and Nuremberg, and we all played the same three Norwegian teams. Parker played as a right wing-back, Alan McDonald in the centre of defence and Fenwick as sweeper. It worked well enough because we won two games and drew the other without conceding a goal. I could not wait for the opening league match at West Ham but my eagerness was tempered with a couple of serious doubts. Parker was quick and a good defender but he could not pass wind and you need to be able to distribute the ball well in that position. I was also worried that McDonald's lack of mobility could be exposed by Tony Cottee and Frank McAvennie, the two very nippy West Ham strikers. I moved Parker to right-side centre-back to go man-to-man on Cottee and he never gave the lad a kick. It worked a real treat. We won 3–0 and I was convinced I had hit upon a magic formula with Parker the marker, McDonald the stopper and Fenwick the sweeper. We let in only one goal in our first six matches; won eight of our first ten, drawing one and losing only to my bogey team Oxford, and topped the First Division table until well into October.

Then came my not so happy forty-seventh birthday – beautifully timed to coincide with our visit to Liverpool who were then in second place. I decided on a special build-up for the game and we travelled up to Merseyside on the Thursday afternoon, having arranged with Howard Kendall to train at Bellefield the following day. That night we were in our beds in the hotel when the fire alarm went in the early hours and we all had to get up, grab whatever clothes we could and assemble outside. We had a head count to make sure every one of our bleary-eyed players had come down and just as I was thinking it was the worst kind of preparation for the game I bumped into the Liverpool manager Kenny Dalglish standing on the pavement alongside his players, who were also staying at the hotel. It was some consolation but not much when Saturday came around. We played really well and should have been three goals up before Craig Johnston scored for them just before half-time. It was the worst kind of time to go behind and it opened the floodgates. They took us apart in the second half with John Aldridge converting a penalty and John Barnes adding two more.

Liverpool leapfrogged over us to the top of the table and stayed there for the rest of the season. We finished in a respectable fifth – my highest-ever finish as a manager. Ironically I did one other piece of what turned out to be significant transfer business just before the transfer deadline when I took Trevor Francis from Glasgow Rangers. We had not got a lot of money and I had always regarded Trevor as one of the top players England had produced and he was available for £25,000. By then he was thirty-four but I knew he was a very fit guy who always looked after himself, so I rang the Rangers manager Graeme Souness and we did the deal. Trevor had been all over the world but he quickly showed he retained his appetite for the game and he did a tremendous job for me.

We finished fifth in the league in 1987–88 which, but for the continuing European ban following the Heysel tragedy, would have meant us qualifying for a place in the UEFA Cup. As it was, it meant we competed in the league's centenary tournament at the start of the following season. We entertained Arsenal at the end of August and lost 2–0 in a thrilling game that we deserved to get something from. I was in my office afterwards with the chairman and we enjoyed a glass of wine together and he was in a terrific mood in spite of the result. 'I really enjoyed the game, Jim – I know we lost but I think we are going to have another good season,' he said with a huge grin on his face. Then he took his leave with an assurance that he would see me the following day. Sadly it was an appointment he never kept. He died as a result of a massive heart attack at seven o'clock the following morning. And, if the truth be known, my feelings for QPR died with him.

I am sure David Bulstrode and I could have gone on to great things together. I had committed myself long-term to the club a year earlier when I signed a contract that should have kept me there until 1992 because I was so optimistic about the future under David. Those who did not know had him tagged as just a property dealer but he was very much a football man at heart. It was never the same afterwards. His successor Richard Thompson was a nice enough chap but it was a strange situation because he was in his early twenties and when we got together I felt like a father talking to his son. I remember one particular lunch together at a restaurant of his choice. 'You'll enjoy this place,' he told me. 'They do a fantastic knickerbocker glory.' I felt like saying, 'Sod the knickerbocker glory – do they do a decent wine?' We drank nothing more potent than water, which I would welcome in the desert – if I was ever unfortunate to be stranded in one. I was not convinced Richard was that interested in his role as chairman. Under the circumstances Mr Noonan, who had come from Fulham with David, became a bigger influence in the day-to-day running of the club and he was not my cup of tea. While Mr Bulstrode was alive he stayed in the background somewhat but I became acutely aware of his increasing profile after Thompson assumed control. I think he felt he could manipulate the new chairman and I was uncomfortable with some of the decisions that were taken. I don't think Mr Noonan liked it when he voiced his opinion about a certain football matter and I called him an amateur.

I began to get the feeling that it was not going to work mainly because I felt then, as I do now and have always done, that the relationship between chairman and manager is more important than anything in a football club. Around that time the papers were full of speculation that Sheffield Wednesday wanted me to take over from Howard Wilkinson, who had gone to Leeds United. I would have been tempted because it was always a job that appealed to me because of my background. There had been similar talk about me going to Hillsborough even before Howard was appointed five years earlier. In fact he rang me up one morning to find out whether I knew anything about it and I told him I didn't. That afternoon I was driving to a game when I heard on the car radio that he was the new Wednesday manager, so I think he was just checking whether I was involved.

The managerial merry-go-round was spinning furiously because in addition to Wednesday there was also a vacancy at Newcastle United after Willie McFaul had been sacked. Arthur Cox, who was at Derby County, had been tipped to return to St James's Park, supposedly leaving the way open for me to become reunited with Robert Maxwell who was now at the Baseball Ground, but that did not happen either and just when I thought I was going to be stuck with having to make the most of what was becoming an increasingly frustrating working atmosphere at QPR, Newcastle came to the rescue. We had a scout called Joe Vine who had been with me at Colchester and Oxford but also had connections with United through his friendship with their former manager Joe Harvey. I had mentioned my disquiet to Vine who rang me up out of the blue and asked if I fancied Newcastle. Ironically, a couple of days before, Willie had telephoned me requesting tickets for our home match against Coventry City because he and a pal and their wives were coming to London for the weekend and he thought he would take in the game. We had a drink afterwards and chatted about what had happened at Newcastle but at the time it was of no more than passing interest.

It was the very next day that I received the first tug from Vine. Out of courtesy I phoned Willie and told him: 'You'll never guess what's happened – I have a chance of the Newcastle job.' For some reason he did not sound too pleased and I don't think we've ever spoken since but my conscience is perfectly clear. The interest could not have come at a better time but there was definitely no prior contact. There are too many examples in football of managers getting tapped for jobs while others are still in employment. I am certain I have been the victim of such circumstances but I would never hasten the departure of any manager by going behind his back. Newcastle did not have a manager when I was approached and I felt it would be a good move. I arranged to meet the United chairman Gordon McKeag at his daughter's house in London and we quickly agreed a three-year contract at £100,000 a year – again more than I had ever earned and about £25,000 more than I was getting at Rangers. I knew Newcastle were a big club with a big reputation and I was looking forward to getting out of QPR and going up there. What I did not know was the depth of all the hassle that was going on in the take-over battle being spearheaded by property developer John Hall's Magpie group.

When I informed Thompson and Noonan of my decision to leave, they hardly raised any obstacles. Thompson came out with the usual quotes saying he did not want me to go and he wanted the maximum compensation possible but he was just paying lip service. I could sense that Noonan in particular was delighted that I was getting out of his hair. I recommended Peter Shreeves for my job but within a fortnight they had given it to Trevor Francis. That figured because Thompson was a young chairman and it suited him to have a young manager.

CHAPTER TEN

THE IMPOSSIBLE DREAM

I was Newcastle United's thirteenth post-war manager – was that number ever more unlucky? It had seemed like manna from heaven to get the opportunity to manage a club with such tremendous support and fine traditions especially after the way the QPR situation had turned sour. In fact it appeared such a perfect opportunity that I went headlong into the job without doing any homework on the playing staff or the boardroom situation. Somebody had mentioned there was unrest at the top with a group led by John Hall trying to take over the club but I never realized how deep the bitterness was and I had every confidence in my ability to calm any storm by getting things right on the field even though Newcastle, at the time, were two points adrift at the bottom of the First Division table. I quickly realized that it was not going to be that easy. The day after the announcement about my appointment, the *Daily Mirror* carried a story quoting Hall saying that his first priority after taking over the club would be to sack Jim Smith. It was an astonishing statement, especially as it came from somebody I had never met or spoken to and it made me very angry. It also made me even more determined to stuff his premature judgement down his throat.

I relished the challenge at Newcastle and, as challenges go, they could not have come any tougher. I appointed Bobby Saxton as my assistant – I had known Bobby for a long time and knew he was a good coach and motivator. He arrived at the hotel we were staying in on the evening after I had taken my first training session. He looked and sounded a bit apprehensive so I just told him, 'Relax, Bobby. This is the worst set of players I have ever come across. You'll have your work cut out to coach this lot.' And I don't think the supporters felt too optimistic either – while Bobby and I were sitting together having dinner one of the locals came up to me, shook my hand and said, 'Best of luck, Jim, you're gonna need it.' And there were plenty of others who questioned the state of my mental health. They joked and had a laugh but behind the humour was a serious yearning to have a team they could be proud of and I was determined to give it to them.

I introduced a rigorous training routine which involved double sessions on most days. We spent a great deal of time on basics, working on skills, set-pieces and all-round fitness. My aim as always was to win matches playing entertaining football but I knew I had to act fast to improve the squad. In hindsight I probably made too many changes too quickly but the situation called for desperate measures. I had been warned by McKeag that any buying would have to be self-financing as there was not a penny in the kitty. There was an offer of £750,000 from Hearts for John Robertson on the table almost immediately and, under the circumstances, I thought it was too good to refuse although I respected John as a player and he did really well after he left. I used some of the money to bring in Kevin Brock, a player I knew I could rely on from our days together at Oxford United and QPR.

We could not have had a better start. Before I took over the team had gone six games without even scoring a goal, equalling a fifty-year-old club record, but we beat Wimbledon 2–1 in my first game in charge. The supporters gave me a tremendous welcome which flew in the face of all the adverse comments coming from Hall and company and I felt they, at least, could bring stability to the club. The following week we drew against Southampton and then we went to Sheffield Wednesday and won 2–1 to lift us two places off the bottom. Sadly the run did not continue and I have always maintained we suffered physically and mentally from our third-round FA Cup marathon against Watford, which went into its fourth game in eleven days before it was decided by an extra-time own goal from our skipper Glenn Roeder. We won only three matches from the end of December, picked up a measly two points from our last nine games and were relegated in bottom position.

Of course the players and I were fair game for the critics and John Hall was prominent among them. While McKeag offered assurances that my job was not in danger, Hall was singing a different tune, calling for the chairman to quit and urging the supporters to boycott our final home game against Millwall. They didn't, but those who turned up created such an atmosphere of tension and hatred that when half-time came and we were losing 1–0, I went into the dressing room shaking with rage. I had nothing but sympathy for the players and I told them so. 'I just don't know how you are managing to play out there,' I said and urged them to just try and stay calm, retain their dignity when all around were losing theirs, and hopefully salvage a result. John Anderson scored a superb equalizer and we drew 1–1. The truth was although the final relegation card was not played until we lost at home to West Ham three days earlier, I believed we had done really well to survive until then. When I looked at what we had when I arrived, I thought we would be down by Easter.

We had a mishmash of players, the most celebrated of whom was Brazilian international Mirandinha who was a favourite with the supporters. However, despite press reports about his love for the club and his desire to stay, I knew he wanted a transfer. He could play when he turned his mind to it and that was certainly the case when two successive victories in March against Everton and at Norwich City gave us a glimmer of hope about getting out of relegation trouble. Mirandinha scored in both games and I felt if he could turn it on again in a crucial bottom-of-the-table match against Sheffield Wednesday at St James's on Easter Monday it could give us a real platform to beat the drop. He scored from a penalty but missed other good chances and we lost 3–1. Clearly his form was slipping. I think we both knew the time had come for both of us to go our separate ways. To me Mirandinha was never the kind of player you could hang your hat on. He was often on the treatment table for one usually minor ailment or another, which he built up into something akin to career-threatening. I was relieved when we eventually did ship him back to Brazil.

There was a lot of coming and going during that summer. I fancied us to go straight back up and I believed experience would be the key factor in the Second Division. I wanted to revamp the attack completely and during the summer I brought in Mark McGhee from Celtic for £200,000 and signed Mickey Quinn from Portsmouth for a figure the transfer tribunal fixed at £650,000. Mickey was a character who became an instant hit. I always knew he would score goals because he had a great record but neither of us could have dreamed he would have the start he did, four goals in his first league match for us, a 5–2 hammering of Leeds United, and nine in his first five matches. He may have had more of the look of a Sumo wrestler than an athlete, but he trained hard enough and just lived for scoring goals. He liked his pop, was great in the dressing room and was ultra-reliable, missing only one league game in that first season and scoring thirty-two goals. Mickey is now trying his hand as a race-horse trainer and doing very well at it. That figures because he loved a bet as well. It used to mystify me when he came in at half-time punching the air and claiming he had backed another good winner. Then I found out how he knew. His dad, who was in the crowd with a radio, would whistle either once or twice depending on whether the horse had won or not. Mickey knew where he was sitting and he would wait for the whistle as he came off the pitch.

McGhee was an altogether more quiet and serious character but his appearance record was even more exemplary, a magnificent 100 per cent in fifty-eight league and cup matches, scoring nineteen goals. They were a fearsome striking partnership but sadly neither could come up with a goal in the two games we needed them most – the end of season play-offs against our deadly rivals Sunderland. It had been a topsy-turvy season with a disastrous December when we picked up only one point in five games, culminating in a 4–1 New Year's Day home defeat by Wolves after which a supporter braved the cold to whip off his shirt and throw it at me in the dug-out. That compared with a marvellous April when we won six successive matches and went up to second place. Somewhere in between was the key match at Sheffield United when we conceded a late goal and drew 1–1. As it turned out that point put the Blades up and condemned us to the play-offs. By then I had splashed out £500,000 to bring experienced Scottish international Roy Aitken from Celtic. Billy McNeil, the Celtic manager, got a bee in his bonnet about the way the deal was done, with broad hints that we had made it known illegally that we wanted him. There had been some stuff in the papers but it had nothing to do with us and anyway our interest had been sparked by a Celtic circular indicating that Aitken was available. Maybe in the end McNeil had second thoughts about letting him go and I could understand that because Roy became a wonderful skipper for Newcastle.

Losing to Sunderland at any time was bad but in a match where the stakes were so high it was regarded as nothing less than a disaster. We had finished third in the table, six points ahead of the three other play-off teams Swindon Town, Blackburn Rovers and Sunderland. We played the first game at Roker Park and did well to get a goalless draw, especially as John Burridge saved a penalty. That made us favourites to win the return leg at St James's but it was a quagmire of a pitch, nothing went right for us and we lost 2–0. Eric Gates scored the first goal and when Marco Gabbiadini scored the second the place erupted with a pitch invasion that held up the game for over twenty minutes. I don't think I have ever felt as low as I did on that afternoon. The players were spat at and the crowd called for me to be sacked. I am told somebody at one of the local hospitals stuck up a Newcastle team picture, blacked out the faces, and wrote underneath it, 'These are the people who let Newcastle down.'

I have never been a believer in the play-off system. It is a money-generating exercise that contradicts the age-old football saying that you get what you deserve over a season. But that year it counted against us twice. It was the year that Sunderland went on to play Swindon Town in the final and lost 1–0 and should have been beaten by a lot more. But because of the betting scandal involving Swindon we had been tipped off that, whatever the result in the final, they would not be promoted to the First Division. It was also touch and go whether we would go up as the highest-placed club or Sunderland because they reached the final. We understood the voting to be 2–2 but the deciding vote went to the Football League president – my old Blackburn friend Bill Fox – who cast it in favour of Sunderland. Bill, one of the instigators of the play-off system, was hardly going to vote any other way.

I would not hide behind the boardroom turmoil but, if it was not the biggest contributory factor to our performances, it certainly did not make life any easier. It was an intolerable situation with a continuation of demonstrations against the board and the team, whipped up by the publicity-seeking Magpie group. My problem was I inherited a dressing room that was not good enough to handle reasonable situations, let alone what was happening at Newcastle. I knew after a couple of months that I had jumped out of the frying pan into a blazing inferno of emotion and irrational behaviour. I knew it was the hardest job I had had or was ever likely to have. It got so bad it was difficult at times to persuade players to pull on a black-and-white shirt, especially in home games, because the stick was flying about almost from the pre-match kick-in. Even a top player like Kenny Sansom, with a wealth of experience playing in front of fiercely hostile crowds, could not handle it. I signed him from Arsenal just after I arrived but once the fur started flying Kenny could not wait to get away from the place.

The battle to buy shares owned by the chairman and his supporters intensified to such a stage that they were changing hands for up to 12,000 times their original 50p value. I felt sorry for Gordon McKeag, who acted with dignity in the face of some horrendous criticism, but he was always fighting a losing battle to hang on to control as his support gradually began to dwindle. It might have been better all round if he had chosen to come to some accommodation with Hall which would have allowed both to have been involved in the running of the club. Inevitably in time the thousands of pounds spent on buying shares paid off and the Halls – John and his son Douglas – forced their way on to the board and from that moment I knew my days as Newcastle manager were numbered.

I did not, in fact, meet John Hall until 1 September 1990 after our first away game of the following season at Blackburn Rovers. We won 1–0 without playing particularly well – as a matter of fact I roasted the players afterwards because I thought we were that bad. As I was going into the boardroom, he was walking out with his wife Mae. His only words were, 'That wasn't very good, Jim.' I replied: 'It wasn't as good as that,' and those were the only words we spoke. I felt I needed to clear the air; to establish where I stood with the Halls. I wanted to be able to manage the club to the best of my ability and I could not do that in the kind of oppressive atmosphere that seemed to hang over the place like a black cloud. I called for a special board meeting at which one of the directors, Bob Young, introduced me to Douglas, who was attending his first such get-together. I had made up my mind to get a few things off my chest and Douglas was the first target. There had been all sorts of newspaper speculation about people being lined up to take over as manager. In the circumstances I did not think Douglas and his father were doing a lot to prevent it and I was very uptight about it. I just blew my top at that meeting, calling both Douglas and his father a few choice names. I tried to make my position clear in the light of all the rumours. I pointed out that nobody was more upset than me about the results but I told them the present playing staff was neither big enough nor strong enough to sustain the kind of injuries we had suffered and I needed money to spend on players to ease what I felt was a growing crisis. The tirade went on for about twenty minutes, during which time I also gave them both an ultimatum to back me or sack me before I sat down.

Young, who had been instrumental in trying to break down the barriers between the old and new factions, told me I should apologize to them and I did because I may have spoken out of turn and then I left the meeting and went downstairs where Bobby was waiting in my office. I told him what had happened and he said I had done the right thing and we got out a bottle of Scotch. I had apologized for the language I had used but I still felt justified in saying my piece and I needed a drink to calm down. And it turned out I was not the only one because while we were sitting there having a chat and wondering where we were going next, all the directors, apart from the Halls, came into the office, shook my hand and said they wished they had had the courage to say what I had. A few days later another director, George Forbes, came to me and asked if I could work with the Halls. I responded that I could and that I hoped what had been said at the meeting could be left in the past to rot.

Forbes then told me about a financial proposal that John Hall had come up with – a £500,000 interest-free loan; £1 million to spend on players and a £50,000 bonus for me if I took the team back up. I also had to agree that if I did not win promotion I would resign. I thought that was very fair and went along with the deal. Not long after that John Hall left the board at the same time that McKeag resigned as chairman and handed the role to Forbes, a nice man who had been involved with the club for some time. Unfortunately, as far as I was concerned, the financial package never materialized.

The Halls had this bright idea of floating a new share issue with the intention of raising £8 million in capital. It was made clear at the outset that anything that came to me to spend on players would be carefully monitored. 'Jim Smith will not be allowed to squander the money,' was one of John Hall's comments. As it turned out the timing of the issue, only a few weeks before Christmas, was all wrong and it was subsequently aborted. I think I carried the can for a lot of that because the team were not doing very well at the time and the people behind the share issue claimed there was a lack of confidence in my management. That was a constant undercurrent, stoked up by the odd comment from either John or Douglas.

We had a lot of problems with injuries halfway through the season, especially losing McGhee for weeks on end, and were never better than being on the fringe of the play-offs. We did have a bit of a run in February and March and I thought we could still get into the top six if we managed to keep it up but then something happened which made me realize I was only flogging a dead horse. It was after a game at Portsmouth which we won 1–0 that I agreed to do an interview with a Tyneside-based local radio reporter. His first question nearly knocked me sideways – 'Can you comment on a statement from John Hall that he would not put the £500,000 in while you are still manager?' I managed to gather myself together enough to say that it was his money and he could obviously do with it what he thought fit but I was truly staggered by what I had been told.

It was on the team bus on the six-hour journey back from Portsmouth that I thought long and hard about the situation and by the time the coach pulled into St James's Park I had made up my mind to quit. I could not see the point of banging my head against a brick wall when we were all not pulling together. As I got off I turned round to Bobby and said to him, 'That's it, old son – I'm out of here.' Bobby urged caution, telling me not to be too hasty, but there was no turning back. I rang George Forbes and arranged a meeting and I told him I wanted to resign and I wanted my contract paid up. He said he understood and it was sorted out without any fuss. I later spoke to the players, who I believe were genuinely sorry to see me go. They believed they still had a chance of making the play-offs and maybe under different circumstances we might have done. But I know if we hadn't I would have been out anyway.

Forbes got Bobby in and asked if he would organize the team for the match at Swindon Town the following weekend and gave him reason to believe he had as good a chance as any for the job if things went well. Bobby was quite excited about it – but it seemed we had both been made fools of which was rather appropriate two days before 1 April. There had been speculation that Ossie Ardiles was being lined up for my job even before I left but he was certainly appointed with indecent haste after I left. Ardiles had started the week in charge at Swindon but by the end of it he was the new manager of Newcastle. It must have been a strange game for him to watch that weekend and you had to wonder where his loyalties lay. But I did not envy his task at Newcastle. The politics were the worst I had ever come across. I just wondered whether he would get a better chance to manage than I had. Having said that, I also felt he owed it to me to tell me the smoke signals that had been coming out of St James's Park were giving the wrong message. I had taken him on at QPR when he did not have a club and we had a good relationship until I left. I would have thought that counted for something.

After saying my goodbyes to the players I went back to my flat in Tynemouth to collect Yvonne and prepared to head back to our home in Woodstock. I closed the door, not only behind me, but also on what I thought was the most gut-wrenching twenty-seven months of my life. Emotionally I felt stripped bare but I also felt relieved. Finally I had had to ask myself – 'What am I doing here?' As I said at the time my former QPR chairman Jim Gregory was an expert on heart attacks, having survived four, and he had warned me the way I was going I was heading for one myself. I was fifty years old and just did not need all the hassle. What I did want was another job – anywhere I felt I could get an even break – and when I closed that door in Tynemouth I never believed for a minute the opportunity to work again would keep me in the North-East – wrong again!

As I was driving south I took a call on my mobile from Colin Todd who had been managing Middlesbrough for a year. 'Can you come and see me? I want you to join me at Middlesbrough,' he said. I glanced at Yvonne and she threw me a 'here we go again' look. But I decided to meet Colin at his house in Chester-le-Street, dropping the missus off at the nearby home of my old pal Gordon Hughes. Toddy wanted me as assistant for the last few weeks of the season because Boro still had a chance of promotion. I agreed in principle and the details were sorted out after I met his chairman Colin Henderson. The club called a press conference and there were a few surprised faces when I walked in to answer questions from the same journalists I had talked to about why I left Newcastle a couple of days earlier. Boro did well enough while I was there – even reaching the dreaded play-offs where I again had the misfortune to finish on the losing side, this time to Notts County. Colin wanted me to stay on to the extent of suggesting I took over as manager and made him my number two but I did not think that was right and I was ready to move on by then.

It will always be the biggest regret of my managerial career that I did not get it right at Newcastle. Notwithstanding the fact there were factions working against me from the word go, I was still daft enough to believe I could do it. Now I realize it was an impossible dream. I made mistakes and I'll take my share of the blame for them but mine were minuscule compared to the incessant wrangling that ripped the club apart. The North-East as a whole is different to anywhere else and I've managed all over the country. It will not change – you would not want it to but the key is to strike the right balance between passion and patience. My good friend Peter Reid has done a tremendous job at Sunderland, lifting them to their highest league finish for nearly fifty years by buying players such as Kevin Phillips, Niall Quinn, Thomas Sorensen and others for bargain prices. And yet he has been constantly criticized because he did not go out and spend even more money. How many other sets of supporters would have settled for finishing one place behind Sunderland? Certainly those who follow Watford and Bradford City, the two clubs who were promoted with them from the First Division at the end of the 1998–99 season.

When I took over Newcastle's record of recent success was a pretty thin volume. Maybe I and others who immediately preceded and followed me picked up the tab for all that frustration. Indeed I believed the club had suffered in the past because previous managers had been too eager to satisfy supporters' demands to sign star names. All I ever heard were stories about Malcolm Macdonald, Kevin Keegan, Paul Gascoigne, Peter Beardsley and the rest. The supporters worshipped personalities but personalities had never won the club anything. What I hoped to do was give them a team that would win regularly playing decent football – a team that starred as a collective unit. I wanted the place to be so full of good players, the fans could not just talk about one or two. At times I despaired of ever getting it right because the demands were so great, far greater than at any other club with which I had been associated. In the past supporters at places like Manchester United, Liverpool and Arsenal have always expected success but the clubs had the wherewithal to provide it – it was expected at Newcastle too but it rarely arrived.

There can be no short cuts – Newcastle have tried that route too. What has happened since I left at the end of March 1991 was what the club desperately needed – somebody who realized its awesome potential and attacked that with unlimited finance. It needed somebody like John Hall to come in and bring it kicking and screaming, if you like, into the twenty-first century. The family dynasties who had controlled Newcastle United for years had had their day and change was essential. I just wish it had been done differently. I just wish I had not been the manager who was caught in the maelstrom. We did not gel as employer and employee but he has gone his way and I have gone mine and when we meet now in Spain, where he lives most of the year and I have a place, we sit down and enjoy a bottle of wine together.

And the supporters are still searching for that Holy Grail. In the wake of the Hall family gaining total control, they may have become established as one of the biggest clubs in the country with an annual turnover second only to Manchester United, but a succession of managers starting with Keegan and followed by Kenny Dalglish and Ruud Gullit have spent over £100 million and the trophy cabinet has remained empty. My situation was similar to my time at Blackburn Rovers before the gold rush – nobody gave me any open chequebook. In my search for the right formula I probably did too much wheeling and dealing. I bought twenty-three players and sold twenty-four – some I would have liked to have kept but I needed the money to reinvest and offers for players like John Hendrie, £500,000 to Leeds United, and

Dave Beasant, £750,000 to Chelsea, were too good to turn down. But I left them with a better squad than I took over and players like Gavin Peacock and Andy Hunt have both gone on to have good careers in the game.

Manchester United's success may be due to brilliant management but Sir Alex Ferguson would be the first to admit it has been based on the development of home-grown talent such as David Beckham, the Neville brothers, Ryan Giggs, Paul Scholes and Nicky Butt, coupled with shrewd buying of players like Roy Keane, Jaap Stam, Andy Cole and Dwight Yorke. Now that's the kind of formula for success that I and most managers are looking for – simple, isn't it?

CHAPTER ELEVEN

POMPEY AND CIRCUMSTANCE

Things happen in football that make it either the greatest game to be involved in or the most frustrating and miserable. There's a song lyric that sums it all up: 'Nothing's impossible I have found/But when my chin is on the ground/I pick myself up, dust myself off and start all over again.' Colin Todd was kind enough to give me the opportunity to do that and maybe more at Middlesbrough but by then I had lined myself up for another football adventure with none other than my former QPR chairman Jim Gregory, whose self-imposed exile from the game after he left Loftus Road ended when he took over Portsmouth in 1988. I didn't need a lot of persuasion to link up with Jim again. Unlike when I dived into the unexpected at Newcastle, he was the devil I knew who illustrated his addiction to football by moving in at Portsmouth barely a year after he sold out at QPR. He would be hard work but I knew that too and I was happy to sign a two-year contract. Portsmouth was a big club and I was anxious to put it back on the map and I felt that this time I would be given the support I needed to try and do that. I was a little older and, as I thought, a lot wiser than when we worked together three years earlier but wisdom comes at a price and, as it turned out, apparently I was yet to pay my full dues. By the time I left Portsmouth four years later that account was settled in full. I was a victim of circumstance and I consider that I was not the beneficiary of a relationship between the Gregory family and Terry Venables.

Gregory had sacked Alan Ball and made Tony Barton care-taker-manager. I appointed Barton as chief scout when I took over but quickly realized I owed a debt of gratitude to the people whose responsibility it had been to stock the youth team with budding talent. I was lucky enough to inherit a clutch of good young players whom I had not known about – lads like Darren Anderton, Andy Awford, Kit Symons and Darryl Powell. There was a wealth of skilful experience too in players such as our goalkeeper Alan Knight, full-back John Beresford, midfield players Warren Neill (whom I had at QPR) and Martin Kuhl and a couple of good strikers in Guy Whittingham and Colin Clarke. It did not take me long to realize the potential of the younger players, especially Anderton. He was a Southampton boy who had come to the club straight from school. Off the field he was very quiet and unassuming but on it you could not come across somebody with more confidence. His strength and stamina belied his frail-looking appearance – in training he would win the sprints as well as the cross-countries. In matches he could play anywhere down the right side – even right wing-back where he excelled and went on to perform in that role for England.

Anderton in particular gained maximum exposure in the team's tremendous FA Cup run which took us to the very brink of Wembley in 1992. The following summer Jim Gregory sold him to Venables, who was then in charge at Tottenham Hotspur, for £2 million plus Paul Walsh. By then most of the top clubs had been banging on the door – Liverpool were probably first in before we played them in the semi-final but Darren turned them down. I remember him telling me at the time he was happy to stay at Portsmouth and his big ambition was to help us get into the First

Seats in the sun with Bobby Robson (left) and Jim McLean (centre) in the south of France.

Should have stuck to football – great style but the middle stump has gone.
So much for cricket.

Paulo Wanchope – a shooting star I
had to bring down to earth.
©Action Images

A happy Sir Alex Ferguson after United's win
against Palmeiras… his Brazilian trip paid
handsome dividends. ©Shaun Botterill/Allsport

Thank heaven for little girls... we had six in the family before one of
the boys came along. This is Yvonne and me with our daughters Suzanne, Fiona and
Alison and granddaughters, twins Sophie and Phoebe, Olivia and Poppy. Later there was
Matilda and Daisy and at last little Alfie! ©News Group Newspapers

Division. We might have fulfilled that ambition too but the chairman and Venables came up with a package between them that was attractive enough for him to move on to Spurs. Jim obviously regarded it as a good deal especially because he always fancied Walsh as a player having tried to sign him from Liverpool a year earlier, but I thought at the time Venables was getting him cheaply and events have proved me right. Anderton has been a somewhat unlucky player in recent years, sustaining a number of injuries which have earned him the rather caustic nickname of 'sick-note'. But, fully fit and on his day, there are not many better or more honest players around and he deserves a trouble-free few years to give him the chance to silence the cynics.

We had a little taster of cup glory when we went to Manchester United in the Rumbelows, which was what the League Cup was known as in those days, and played well although we were beaten 3–1. The FA Cup was much, much better. It started very low key with a 2–1 third-round win at Exeter City but rapidly gained momentum after that. Anderton scored both goals when we knocked out Leyton Orient in the next round and helped himself to another couple in round five when we won a replay at Middlesbrough, after they had held us to a 1–1 draw at our place. That took us into the quarter-finals and a home match against Nottingham Forest. The Forest team was packed with talent and experience with players like Archie Gemmill, Stuart Pearce, Nigel Clough, Teddy Sheringham, Des Walker and a young but highly competitive Roy Keane. Four of our players were twenty-one or under but I still believed we could bridge the gap between the Premiership and First Division if we played to our potential. Forest had been the best cup side in England for ten years but the pressure was all on them because nobody expected us to win. I told my players the only thing they had to worry about was putting on a performance for our supporters but, in spite of the high standard of the opposition, they were oozing with confidence.

There have been some great football occasions at Fratton Park. They once packed in over 51,000 for a Cup quarter-final against Derby County in 1949. There was barely half that number at the Forest match, although the receipts were a record £208,000, but they certainly got their money's worth. I doubt whether the atmosphere could have been more emotional on that previous occasion because there was many a missed heartbeat and chewed fingernail on this one. We provided the crowd with plenty to cheer about when we scored early on – Mark Crossley dropped a ball and Alan McLoughlin, whom I had paid Southampton £400,000 for a couple of weeks earlier, was presented with an easy chance which he accepted gratefully. From then on it was the Alamo revisited as Forest piled forward and we defended brilliantly. I could not have picked a star man but it was a great education for the likes of Awford and Symons who stood up to the barrage really well. I had been on television the previous evening talking about the game and was asked about Brian Clough's great ambition to win the FA Cup. 'That's all very well,' I said. 'But I'd like to win it too.' Cloughie must have seen the programme because he came to me after the match, shook my hand and said: 'Quite right too, young man. And I hope you bloody well do.'

That meant a semi-final – the first of my career – at Highbury against the mighty Liverpool. The younger players had not only proved they could handle the big occasion, they positively revelled in it and I had no worries about their temperament or ability. Some people had suggested that, by their own gigantic standards, this was not the best Liverpool side of all time but I had seen them previously in a UEFA Cup game against Italian side Genoa and they played some great stuff. I remember thinking at the time that if this is mediocre God help us if they decide to turn it on. With those thoughts of Divine Providence on my mind, I decided to leave nothing to chance in our preparation for the game – even to the extent of taking in a local Sunday church service on the morning of the match. But just to be on the safe side we also attended to the more earthly matter of devising a game plan that I felt could expose Liverpool at the back where I believed they tended to play very square.

It was all about getting the ball back from our front men and playing it over the top for a midfield runner. Anderton's pace made him an ideal candidate and when the chance came it worked a treat, but not before our defence had again played out of their skins to keep the game goalless after ninety minutes. Then we played our ace card – a knock-back from Colin Clarke, Wally Neill lifted one over the top and Anderton ran on to stick the ball in the back of the net. We managed to hold on to the lead until the last few minutes of extra-time when Liverpool won a free-kick; John Barnes bent it in against a post and Ronnie Whelan tucked it away. It was a well-worked set-piece – a typical example of how skill can be a great saviour – but I was still steaming about the goal because Whelan should not have been on the pitch to score it. Not long before that he had put Mark Chamberlain out of the game with a particularly bad tackle. Chamberlain had come back from a long injury lay-off and had been running Liverpool ragged, and if he had stayed on I am convinced we would have won. Whelan's challenge not only finished him for that match but he never kicked a ball for us again that season.

The replay was eight days later at Villa Park and, because the FA ruled there would be no room in the calendar to slot in a second replay, it was decided that, for the first time in the 111-year history of the competition, if the game was level after extra-time, there would have to be a penalty shoot-out to decide who went on to Wembley. I did not believe it was pos-sible to feel any prouder about my players than I did after the first match but I was wrong. They were even better the second time – and not just defensively. We took the game to Liverpool and there were times when we really had them rocking. And we had a glorious chance to win it at a time when they would have found it difficult to come back. Three minutes from the end of normal time John Beresford went racing down the left wing. Liverpool thought he was offside and, to be fair, he looked it, but there was no flag and no whistle. He got to the line and pulled the ball back for McLoughlin, running with the goal at his mercy. I thought, 'That's it – Wembley here we come.' But from barely eight yards out he crashed the ball against the bar. I would have bet you could have heard the groans back in Portsmouth. Dean Holdsworth missed a great chance against Aston Villa to put Bolton Wanderers in the 2000 final but this one was just as good if not better. Liverpool knew they had had a real let-off and you could sense their relief. The game stayed goalless throughout extra-time, taking us through to the dreaded penalties. I was still reasonably optimistic about the outcome. We had some excellent spot-kick specialists and it was a case of trying to get them to stay as calm as possible in a situation which demanded cool heads and clear thinking. Whether or not the occasion finally got to us I don't know but our penalties were poor and Liverpool won it 3–1.

Our name clearly was not on the Cup. That certainly became evident when I heard later that Graeme Souness, the Liverpool manager, who had been rushed into hospital for a heart by-pass operation after the first game, was sitting up in bed in hospital watching the second match and, in extra-time, he kept shouting at the screen, 'Get Barnesy off – he's knackered, he can't run.' And he couldn't. But the wily old Ronnie Moran, who was in charge of the team that day, had other ideas – he wanted Barnes on the field if and when it came to penalties. He was right – Barnes scored and we missed our first efforts and that set them on their way. They say that the semi-final is the worst round of the Cup to lose in but surely there cannot have been unluckier losers than Portsmouth that year.

The dressing room was like a morgue afterwards with players, some with tears in their eyes, staring at the floor in silence. What could I say except that I could not have felt more proud if they had hit Liverpool for six? Ray Houghton asked permission to come in and went round shaking everybody by the hand, telling them how unlucky they were and how relieved Liverpool were. Another couple of Liverpool players followed him in; then all our lads went into the home dressing room and everybody ended up swapping shirts. That gave the lads a huge lift and by the time we got on the team coach, they were telling each other that if they came that close to beating a side like Liverpool over two matches, they could not be far behind the best in England. The sad thing was that Sunderland, a Second Division side like ourselves, stole some of the Portsmouth thunder by reaching the final where they were well beaten by Liverpool. The width of the bar prevented us getting to Wembley and I am sure we would have beaten Sunderland.

But the FA Cup and I have never been great friends. Later that year I was hauled over the coals by the FA after a ticket for the final that had been issued to me ended up being sold on the black market. I had nothing at all to do with that. It was a matter of being badly let down by somebody I thought I could trust. I was sent six tickets for the Liverpool–Sunderland match and passed them on to people in the North. The ironical thing was I did not even charge for them myself. I certainly did not give them to touts or anything like that. I understand that the authorities have to take strong action to try and prevent tickets being sold illegally but I did not enjoy the publicity that surrounded the affair – especially when I was banned for five years for receiving final tickets. It was a nasty stain on my character that I did not deserve and it taught me a salutary lesson that you do not really know who you can trust.

If I could alter the lyrics of Frank Sinatra's 'My Way' very slightly they would read 'I've had my fill . . . more than my bloody share of losing'. And being a three-time loser in the end of season play-offs is no fun, I can tell you. As if the FA

Cup did not bring enough heartache to everybody connected with Portsmouth Football Club, there was more to come the following year when we missed out on promotion to the Premiership by one goal and were then beaten by Leicester City in the play-offs. It was all the more galling because, just before the transfer deadline, I went to Jim Gregory and told him, 'Chairman – we need a centre-forward.' I wanted to buy the Cambridge United striker John Taylor, a big powerful lad who is now back at the club. By that time Jim's health had declined and he was not performing his normal hands-on role at the club. He consulted with his finance director Brian Henson and together they decided we could not do it. The reason they gave was twofold – the fee of around £300,000 was too much, and the lad wanted too much wages. I accepted neither objection and I was unhappy about being knocked back. 'Do you realize,' I explained, 'if we get into the Premier League we will receive something like £3 million in television money – this deal is chicken feed compared to that.' But they would not budge; we missed out on promotion by that one goal but if I had been allowed to sign Taylor I am certain we would have gone up.

But there were another three key turning-points in that season: an uncanny trio of events and personal decisions which came back to haunt me. When I was at QPR I had a 'keeper in the juniors, a Worksop-born lad called Ian Bennett whom I thought of highly enough to take up to Newcastle. He spent two years on Tyneside without breaking into the first team and to try and help his career I let him go to Peterborough for nothing. In that season at Portsmouth we missed a penalty in each of the two games against Peterborough and Ian Bennett saved both of them! Paul Walsh, who had come to us from Spurs as part of the Anderton deal and did really well, was the unfortunate first victim in a 1–1 draw at London Road. The second was indirectly down to another of my gracious acts of kindness. In the return game at Fratton Park we were 3–0 up and coasting when we were awarded the all-important spot-kick. As Whittingham had scored two goals and was going for a club scoring record, I called for him to have a go instead of Warren Aspinall, who was our regular penalty-taker. Bennett saved the kick from Whittingham, who later underlined the futility of my generosity by completing his hat-trick anyway. If I had not done Bennett a favour back at Newcastle . . . if he had been made to pick either one of those penalties out of the net . . . if I had made Whittingham wait for his hat-trick and let Aspinall take the kick . . . destiny decided it just wasn't to be.

But the 'ifs' were not confined to the two games against Peterborough. At the beginning of November I was back on familiar territory at Oxford United and by half-time Portsmouth had cruised to a 4–2 lead. With less than fifteen minutes to go it was 5–2 and it could have been ten, so I did not panic too much when they pulled one more goal back. As the game went into injury time we were still two goals to the good – and then the ceiling fell in! Oxford were awarded a penalty and Jim Magilton made it 5–4. The referee said to one of our lads, 'Kick off and I'll blow the final whistle.' And he had the thing to his lips when we restarted the game but he hung on for a vital few seconds. The ball got to Gavin Maguire, who punted it right down the slope straight into the hands of the Oxford 'keeper Paul Reece, who promptly booted it back up the field again where it took a couple of bounces, hit a couple of heads before landing at the feet of a young lad called Chris Allen, who scored the tenth goal of an incredible match. I have to say I went raving mad in the dressing room afterwards and I remember telling the players, 'This result will come back and give us sleepless nights' – and it did.

In the final analysis there were a number of factors that I was not happy about, including our own charity, that cost us a top-two place. Our incredible generosity continued right until the penultimate match of the season at Sunderland. If we had won it would have committed them to Third Division football but again it all went

went wrong. They scored with two penalties, our full-back Ray Daniel missed two chances from eight yards, Paul Walsh got sent off and we ended up losing 4–1. The results that Saturday meant Swindon were guaranteed a place in the play-offs without having to kick a ball – their game the following day at home to West Ham was important in as much as the Hammers were our chief rivals for the runners-up spot in the league, which by then had been won by Newcastle. I was at the game working for television and Swindon lost 3–1. In my opinion Swindon's performance was not what it had been throughout the season. Maybe they considered Portsmouth to be easier opponents should we meet in the play-offs, I don't know. But the timing of the games raised inevitable possibilities of opportunism, so much so that from then on the League have made sure that all important end-of-season matches kick-off at the same time.

As it turned out Swindon were promoted without having to play Portsmouth in the play-offs. Like Quinn and McGhee at Newcastle, Whittingham, who scored goals for fun that season, becoming the first player to score over forty league goals since Ted McDougall twenty years earlier and smashing a club record which had stood since 1927, could not manage one in either of the two-legged semi-final matches against Leicester City. I had a bad feeling about the game; a terrible sense of *déjà vu* – my mind kept going back to what happened when I was at Newcastle and I hoped against hope I would not have to go through it all again. Filbert Street, City's home ground, was out of commission because they were constructing a new stand so we played the first match at Nottingham Forest's City Ground. If anything I thought we just edged it so I was not very happy when Julian Joachim scored the only goal of the game four minutes from the end. I was even less happy in the return at our place when we shared four goals and City's second was as clear a case of offside as you can get. I had a go at the referee Roger Milford afterwards but he said he was sticking by his decision. He changed his mind the following season when he came with us to Bari where we were playing in the Anglo-Italian Cup. I buttonholed him again about the decision and he admitted he had made a mistake. 'But that's the way it goes, Jim, it's only a game,' he laughed. But I was not in the mood to share the joke. 'It's more than that, Roger,' I told him. 'That decision cost this club £3 million.'

I have to admit to a certain volatility which has caused me to have a few brushes with authority from time to time. The memory of Milford's mistake was still fresh in the mind when we started the following season with a game at Oxford. It was tough to get everybody in the right frame of mind for the new season. Naturally there was a feeling in the dressing room that we should have been in the Premiership and instead of the exciting prospect of taking on the best teams in the country, we were facing the also-rans again. I had to make sure the players had put the disappointment behind them and were in the mood to prove that, at least, we were the best team in the First Division. It did not help much when Oxford went two goals up but we fought back to level and I thought we had a great chance of winning the game when the referee Steve Dunne, who is now one of the Premiership officials, gave a penalty for handball against Mark Chamberlain. It was a disgraceful decision because it was clear even from where I was watching in the dug-out that there had been no contact between hand and ball. I was so angry I ran on to the pitch to protest but it did me no good. Oxford scored and we lost 3–2 and I am afraid my protests did not end there. I went into the referee's room after the game and I saw red, tearing into Mr Dunne, calling him many things and doubting his parentage. Of course he then reported me to the FA and I was charged with bringing the game into disrepute. I asked for a personal hearing and took a video of the incident as evidence. I'm certain those on the commission agreed there should have been no penalty but I still got done for insulting the match official. I was fined but

I felt so incensed at the decision of the commission that I did consider not paying the fine and accepting the consequences. But I was persuaded that would have been an act of folly.

Overall, although we just missed out on the Premiership, I was pleased with the way the team, particularly the young lads, had stuck at it throughout the season. We played some terrific stuff, apart from the odd form dip, and I looked forward to the future with some optimism. What a pity it turned out to be misplaced. As far as I am concerned, the problems I began to have at Portsmouth coincided with the serious deterioration in Jim Gregory's health. Heart attacks led to circulation problems which eventually resulted in him losing one and then both legs. He still retained his humour, even to the point, when he had one false leg, of turning it back to front so his feet pointed in different directions. His antics used to bring the place down. But gradually Jim's grip on the club lessened. He suffered a major setback when the council refused permission for the club to build a new stadium. We thought we would get it – in fact the chairman was counting on it and it seemed to knock him back further when it was turned down. That decision, coupled with failing health, virtually killed Jim's interest in Portsmouth. His son Martin Gregory came on the board but he was never the driving force his father was and the club lost its impetus.

All in all it was a poor third season for me – neither the team nor the board seemed to know which direction they were heading in and I became very disillusioned. Martin was desperate to sell the club. In fact, he and another director were due to fly to Belgrade to meet Milan Mandaric, the Yugoslav businessman who has since bought it, but they changed their minds because they did not know enough about the chap. Obviously I was concerned enough to ask to be kept in the picture and Gregory mentioned to me that he was going to have lunch with Venables instead because he knew people who wanted to buy into football clubs. I remember remarking that it was a good idea because I felt that a change of ownership might give the place a lift and we could pick up from where we had left off the previous season. The fact is I could not wait for Gregory junior to do any sort of a deal and clear off and let experienced football people get on with the job of running the club. I did not suspect for a second that when the change came it would be me who would be on my way. The next morning I got a call from Gregory, 'Jim, I'd like to have a chat . . . can you come and see me.' My immediate impression was that he was going to tell me about a deal he had struck as a result of his chat with Venables. I certainly never saw the chop coming.

He sat me down in his office and suddenly blurted out, 'I think you should have a sabbatical.' I looked at him in amazement – 'I'm not having any sabbatical,' I retorted. 'Look, Martin – I've been connected with your family long enough for us to put our cards on the table.' I told him if he wanted me out he had better get in the finance director Brian Henson to sort out a deal. As it happened I had another ace up my sleeve but I was a bit reluctant to play it. It has always been common in football for managers to chat to each other on a regular basis and I had mentioned to Howard Wilkinson that I was getting more and more disenchanted every day with what was going on at Portsmouth. Howard was chairman of the League Managers' Association, an organization geared to protect the security and livelihood of team bosses which he had been instrumental in forming, and he had already let me know there was a job for me as chief executive if I wanted it. We had a chat one night, ironically outside the Baseball Ground at Derby, after he asked to go and watch Leeds Reserves play Derby Reserves. We sat on the Leeds coach and Howard spelled out what the chief executive's job was all about. I listened and thought about it but I still regarded myself as a hands-on manager and I had no urge to pack in just yet. It appeared, however, that the decision was being made for me.

I told Gregory to stuff his sabbatical and my concern was

to get the best deal possible for myself. But I did say that if he wanted any guidance in choosing a new manager I would be only too pleased to help. He did not respond to that and no wonder. I turned on the sports news when I was driving back home to hear that, not only had I been sacked, but that Terry Fenwick had been appointed as my successor. Clearly, my destiny had already been decided by others and I cursed my stupidity at not being able to read the tell-tale signs. The plain facts were that the day after Gregory and Venables had their lunch, I was being moved out and Fenwick was moving in and Venables was allowed to come in as chairman after allegedly buying the club for a pound. I may have been putting one and one together and coming up with the wrong answer but I am normally pretty good at maths. I made my feelings known in an interview for Sky television. I felt I had been done no favours by the man who was the current England coach and said so. I added that I thought it was a bad football decision and subsequent events at Portsmouth have not proved me wrong. They had their most successful time for years when I was in charge and I do not believe I was to blame when things began to go wrong. I was forced to sell our best players and the uncertainty over whether the club was going to change hands, a situation created by the board, meant there was an atmosphere in which it was difficult to do the job properly.

I had something of the last laugh, though, when the Pompey wheel turned a full circle. Mandaric and Bob McNab, the former Arsenal and England full-back, who had worked for him in America, came to see me early in 1999 looking for advice on whether the Yugoslav should take over the club which by then had so much debt it was in danger of being wound up. Mandaric, McNab and David Deacon were part of a consortium that was attempting to take control. Venables by this time was long since gone, and Gregory was back as chairman. I told them I thought the club would benefit from a change at the top and a couple of months later the creditors accepted the consortium's ten cents on the dollar compromise. Gregory made a last-ditch attempt to stop the take-over but was beaten, which to me was poetic justice. Portsmouth are a club with a marvellous history and I would love to see the new regime go some way to recapturing former glories. We came pretty close to that but the responsibility for what has gone wrong since should be weighing pretty heavily on certain shoulders.

CHAPTER TWELVE

GOODBYE AND HELLO

I was sickened by the way I had been treated at Portsmouth. So much so that I looked at my situation seriously and thought, 'I am in my fifty-fifth year – do I need this any more?' In the circumstances the League Managers' Association seemed to present an ideal opportunity to head down another and altogether revolutionary football direction. The LMA was an infant organization, a carefully conceived attempt to unify managers in a common purpose, which was to improve the conditions of employment and ensure the financial security of its members. But such a purpose calls for trust and co-operation in an industry where people jump into chairs that have barely yielded up the shape of the previous incumbent's backside. Although I thought what had happened to me at Portsmouth made a nonsense of getting a strong managers' union together when the people involved did not even act with common courtesy to one another, I felt strongly that some constructive attempt should be made to change the circumstances in which managers are hired and fired. I believed, and still do, that if managers are to have any standing in the game we have to behave professionally within our own ranks.

With some doubts about whether I could exorcise the daily

routine of mixing with players, organizing the training, listening to and trying to sort out their problems, vetting opposition, choosing line-ups, deciding on tactics, sweating through matches, enjoying victories and hating defeats, I agreed to become the LMA's chief executive in March 1995. As I feared, it did not take long for the doubts to be realized. To me management is like a drug and four months of cold turkey was more than enough. At the outset I really believed my days as a manager were over without knowing exactly what the LMA job entailed. I replaced Steve Coppell, who had returned to club life, and worked closely with an appointed committee whose members included such football luminaries as Howard Wilkinson, Alex Ferguson, Frank Clark, Dave Bassett and Brian Little. Nowadays the association is on a much more professional footing with its own offices and a bigger staff but I worked from home, dealing with various football matters. I would attend FA and other meetings such as disciplinary commissions and referees' discussions about new rules but I was only there as an observer and rarely allowed to offer an opinion – when I did it was never minuted. The LMA had no clout as such and they could only advise on matters.

Most of my calls were from sacked managers wondering how they were going to get their money paid up. A typical example that illustrated my daily routine of telephone calls was after Russell Osman had been ousted at Bristol City. His compensation had still not been settled when he came on to me, even though a few months had gone by, and I soon found out why. Osman was determined to squeeze every penny he could out of his former employers, including bonuses for the remainder of his contract which included the following season. Although Joe Jordan had taken over at City, who were struggling near the bottom of the First Division table and were eventually relegated, Osman's case rested on his belief they would go straight back up and he felt he was entitled, under the terms of his deal at City, to any attaching bonus. My immediate impression was that he did not have a prayer. I listened to what he had to say and suggested he might have to settle for something less. I told him if I could get him two-thirds of his contract up front he should accept it. I travelled to London to meet up with the City chairman and after some discussion he finally agreed to do that, but Osman still would not have it. I thought it was a fair offer and I warned him it was unlikely he would do any better but he was adamant. And it was still dragging on when I left the LMA, so I am not sure whether he did any better or not.

I don't blame Osman for trying to get as much as possible – after all I had been in his position myself and it's natural to want to screw the people who have got rid of you. But it pays to be reasonable and there were times when I found myself banging my head against a brick wall because of the unreasonable demands of the managers. Having said that, I have not come across many chairmen who have paid up without a quibble. One of the finest achievements of the LMA has been the Managers' Arbitration Tribunal, the charter drawn up with the full agreement of the Premier League that stipulates that any sacked manager must have his compensation agreed within twenty-eight days or it is referred to the MAT for a ruling over which there is no appeal. By the same token managers are required to honour their contracts and can only move between clubs if the respective chairmen are in full agreement. It is a sound arrangement which has done much to bring job stability at the highest level. I know John Barnwell, who is doing a great job as the current chief executive, is working hard to get a similar process ratified by the Football League instead of the current watered down agreement. It is far from a perfect world yet but we are getting there.

Life at the LMA was interesting at times but also very frustrating and by the end of that season I realized it was not for me. I suppose I was in the safest job of all. I could have been there until I was seventy – well, I would not have expected the sack from my fellow managers – or would I? I stayed active by jogging daily on the sea-front and that was when my brain started ticking over again. The four months I had away from management gave me the chance to sit back and take stock of my situation. The longest period I had out of the game before that was the three-week gap between leaving Oxford and taking over at Birmingham. It was the time of the annual managerial merry-go-round again and jobs were becoming available thick and fast – at one period there were about eight vacancies. But only two appealed – Sheffield Wednesday and Derby County. My brother-in-law had contacts at Wednesday and it was made known to the chairman Dave Richards that I would be interested. Apparently he wasn't. Then Ray Harford was confident enough about getting the job to invite me to go to Hillsborough as his assistant, but that did not materialize either and anyway, in spite of my close relationship with Ray, I did not think I was suited to that kind of role.

The situation appeared to resolve itself when Graham Smith, who has always been something of a lucky contact for me especially as he has the ear of several chairmen and club officials in the Midlands area, telephoned to say I could be in the frame at Derby and suggested I ring one of the directors, Stuart Webb. Stuart arranged for me to see the chairman Lionel Pickering, who had bought control of Derby after the death of its previous owner Robert Maxwell, and we met at his house, Ednaston Manor. I had been first introduced to Mr Pickering during my second season at Portsmouth when we went to Derby and won 4–2. We had a chat and a laugh – he complimented me on the way the team played which was how he liked to see the game played. I hoped I had made a lasting impact . . . after all, you never know in this game. My own impression of him was confirmed when we got together at his home to talk about Derby County. For all his wealth and business acumen, he is a down-to-earth chap who would be comfortable in any company and the bottom line is his love for football in general and Derby in particular. A journalist in his younger days, he discovered free newspapers on a trip to Australia and saw the possibilities of them being popular over here. He came back, built up a network of local free-sheets and then sold the business on for a lot of money.

I looked forward to our meeting. My spell out of management had whetted my appetite and I was ready to come back in spite of all the hard luck stories I had been listening to at the LMA. I had done my homework on Derby. Without being the kind of fairy godfather that Jack Walker had been at Blackburn Rovers, Mr Pickering had still invested a lot of his personal wealth into getting a successful team, at least one that could get into the Premiership, and it had not happened. It was more of an informal chat than the normal full interview in front of a board of directors. It was a glorious spring day and we sat outside in his garden talking football. It was an opportunity for us to weigh each other up; to hear what the other had to offer. Mr Pickering painted a picture of what he thought had been underachievement but made it clear there was no more cash swilling around and that any spending money would have to be self-generated. I had become used to missing the gravy train and my enthusiasm for the job drowned any minor problems like having to wheel and deal again.

I came away from the meeting buoyant and optimistic. I felt encouraged by what he had to say and I thought he would be a terrific guy to work for. All in all I was pretty confident about Derby giving me the opportunity to return to football management. So it was with the heaviest of thuds that I was brought back down to earth when I read the papers the next day. It was painfully apparent I was not the only one in with a chance of the job. One headline screamed that Barry Fry was all but appointed; another claimed Steve Bruce would be going as player-manager . . . and over the next three weeks there were a few other names mentioned like Ossie Ardiles, Steve Coppell, Martin O'Neill, Mike

Walker and Neil Warnock – and, about me, not so much as a peep. Enough time went by for me to start believing the worst and I had almost given up completely when Stuart telephoned to put me in the picture. He told me there was one other serious contender who at that stage was slightly favoured to get the job. 'If he doesn't take it, it's yours,' he said. The plot thickened when my rival identified himself as Brian Horton. 'Nobby' rang me and asked if it was true that I was involved as well. I told him I was but made a genuine offer to withdraw and leave the way open for him. I wanted it all right but I still had my job with the LMA and Brian was out of work at the time. To be fair to 'Nobby', he told me to hang fire because he was talking to another club as well.

That was how I would have left it – feeling that I had just missed out and suitably depressed about the whole business. I was pretty elated when a day or two later Stuart called to say, 'Congratulations . . . you are the new manager of Derby County.' It all happened that quickly and I did not know whether I was on my head or my heels. But when the dust settled I had to wonder how everything had worked out to my advantage. In fact when the question was put to me in a television interview I remember saying I was delighted to get the job but that I was not too sure whether I had been the chairman's choice. Those doubts were cleared up by Mr Pickering himself some time later. Early in the season I was driving him to a reserve-team match at Stoke City when he suddenly asked me why I had said what I had and I told him that I had heard it was Stuart Webb who had persuaded him to appoint me. 'That's not true,' he retorted and then proceeded to lay the facts out before me. Apparently on the day that Brian Horton was coming to get the job he had been asked to wait outside the chairman's house while the board tied up one or two loose ends inside. Then one of the directors said he was uncomfortable about giving 'Nobby' the job because there were bad vibes from the supporters and the media and he thought the club should go for somebody like Trevor Francis or another top name. But Mr Pickering cut the discussion short by declaring, 'Gentlemen – if we aren't having Brian Horton, we're having Jim Smith and nobody else.' And then he took it upon himself to go out and give 'Nobby' the bad news before telling Stuart to call me and tell me the job was mine.

I am not too sure I was flavour of the month with every Derby supporter. I would say it was about fifty-fifty with half being all right about me taking over and the other half disappointed it was not somebody like Kenny Dalglish or Graeme Souness. I know that Steve Bruce was favoured by some directors but he was unable to get his release from Manchester United. But I could not let that bother me. As far as I was concerned their loss was my gain. Of course I then had to inform the LMA that I was leaving, so I rang the executive chairman John Camkin to tell him what had happened and at the same time recommended Gordon Milne to take over from me. I thought he would be great for the job and Camkin agreed. They had shared a Coventry City connection – Gordon was manager and John used to be on the board. So the three of us arranged to meet for lunch at the Bear Hotel in Woodstock to discuss the matter. I had known Gordon from our non-league days – what I did not know was what a magnificent negotiator he was because by the time the lunch was over, he had been appointed at twice the salary I had been getting! It was also a profitable lunch for a certain member of the media. Seated a couple of tables away was Gary Newbon, the ITV sports commentator. He came across and greeted us with a mixture of delight and suspicion, saying 'Hello, fellas – what are you doing here?' Then the penny dropped – 'It's Derby, isn't it, Jim? You've got the Derby job.' The cat was out of the bag and I saw no point in denying it. Gary got very excited and asked permission to bring over a camera crew because he wanted to break the story on Central Television that evening. And that's how the story came out – Newbon was in the right place at the right time and got himself a double scoop . . . me going to Derby and Gordon taking over at the LMA. As it turned out Gordon only lasted a year before he went back to coach in Turkey. Thankfully the LMA has a more stable person than either of us in charge now and I believe the association will go from strength to strength under John.

My brief at Derby was simple – I had to reduce the wage bill and sell those players who had it in their contracts that they could move on if the team did not win promotion. 'I make no bones about it,' said Mr Pickering. 'Your job will be a difficult one and if we finish mid-table you will have done well.' But he was my kind of bloke – straight and down to earth. If I wanted to have a chat the place he preferred to meet was his local pub – the one he enjoyed so much he bought it. I found it incredible that players should have been allowed to dictate their own release terms even to the extent of the transfer fee but I was bound by the consequences. In Craig Short's case it was £2.7 million and Mark Pembridge could go for £1 million. This was the situation that greeted me in my first week behind the manager's desk. I was determined to get it right from the start. I viewed Derby as my last throw of the dice as far as top-class management was concerned and I was going to make the most of it. I realized quickly there was a lot to be done and worked from eight in the morning until eight at night and sometimes later sorting out players' contracts, organizing pre-season games and structuring the coaching staff. One of my first decisions was to bring in Steve McLaren as my first-team coach – but more of him later.

But my list of priorities was pre-empted by the parade of players who wanted out. Short was the first to knock on the door and announce, 'I'm leaving . . . I'm going to Everton.' I told him he was going nowhere unless they came up with the money. He was really aggressive because he was desperate to join Everton and deep down I was as anxious to get rid of him as he was to go because I needed the money to bring in a few new recruits. In the end I took Gary Rowett in part-exchange from Everton in order to push the deal through. The next player to present himself was Paul Williams, who was equally belligerent, declaring, 'I didn't care who came in as a manager – whether it was Alf Ramsey or Joe Bloggs. I'm on my way.' I asked him if he had a release clause in his contract and he said he hadn't but he was going anyway. I told him the same as I had said to Short – 'If the deal is right for Derby you can go but not before.' He came back a couple of days later and demanded to know if I had done anything about his move. I replied that I had more important things on my plate. 'If your move comes it comes and if it doesn't, it doesn't,' I told him. He did not seem too happy about that or the way I told him to clear off because I was busy.

He remained awkward even when it came to pre-season and I was ready to talk business when Ron Atkinson, who was now at Coventry City, came on and asked if I would take Sean Flynn in a player-plus cash deal for Williams. We agreed £1 million plus Flynn but Williams's agent Kevin Mason contacted me and said he did not want to go to Coventry. In fact he rang me on the morning the deal was due to go through and said he had heard Aston Villa and Nottingham Forest had been in touch because Williams would prefer either one of those clubs to Coventry. I told him nobody had been on and asked him if he was trying to botch the deal. We had a few words but the transfer finally went through. As it turned out Williams has enjoyed a good career at Highfield Road but, take it from me, he was hoping somebody else would come in for him right up to the time he signed on the dotted line. I also sold Pembridge to Sheffield Wednesday where he rejoined his former Luton Town manager David Pleat, which meant I had received £4.7 million for three players who did not want to play for the club and had brought in two others who might be useful assets. It turned out to be particularly good business in the case of Rowett, who had three good years at Derby before moving on to Birmingham City for £1 million.

But my recruiting did not stop there. In successive days I went back to Portsmouth to sign Darryl Powell, who has been with me ever since and has been worth his weight in gold, for £750,000, and then took Dutch striker Ronnie Willems from Grasshoppers of Zurich for £300,000. I had been tipped off about Ronnie by a good contact who advised me he had been one of the top young goalscorers in Holland but had been unlucky with injuries. I liked what I saw when I watched a video of him and he impressed me when he came over to train with us. He had played in the side that won the Swiss title but had been disappointed by the apathy of the fans and felt he would enjoy the passion of English football. Unfortunately he picked up an Achilles tendon injury after just two matches which kept him out for a couple of months but he came back to become a key player for us.

I felt, at a time when domestic transfer fees were going through the roof, there was a lot of value on the Continent, particularly Holland, and for that reason I also signed Robin Van der Laan, another Dutchman, from Port Vale for £475,000 and made him skipper. He was a tremendously competitive midfielder whom I had tried to buy when I was at Portsmouth but could not get. He had been at Port Vale for four years and had already adopted a Potteries accent which was highly amusing. He combined Dutch technique with an English midfield approach – tough and uncompromising – and I did not feel there was any risk at all in signing him. And so it proved – he was tremendous in the first season, hardly missing a game, and it was entirely appropriate that he should score the goal at Crystal Palace that ensured promotion to the Premiership.

I was convinced by the time the pre-season games came around that I had struck a nice team balance and nothing happened in those matches to change my mind. Everybody was really up for the opening match at home to Port Vale – nobody more than me. There is nothing like the eager anticipation of the opening day of the season – the buzz of expectancy from the crowd; the smiles on the faces of the directors; the heart-thumping excitement of bringing the players to a pitch of mental and physical effort. This is what I had missed during the last four months of the previous season – this is what I was all about . . . not perched behind a desk answering a telephone and listening to everybody else's troubles. Sod that for a game of soldiers! Vale were no great shakes and I fancied us strongly to get off to a good start . . . but you would think by now I would have learned my lesson – ninety minutes later I was beginning to wonder if I should have stayed behind that desk. And the feeling had not gone away by the end of that August during which we picked up only two points from our first four matches. The Vale match ended in a goalless draw, we went to Reading and lost, drew at home to Grimsby Town and then got well stuffed at Wolves.

So it was not without some relief that we broke our duck with a win at Luton Town at the beginning of September. Dean Sturridge had started the first two games on the bench but he came on and scored against Reading. I thought he deserved his chance and he took it brilliantly, scoring four in his first five starts including the two that beat Luton and the only goal in our first home win, against Southend United. Sturridge had been on loan at Torquay United in the season before I arrived and was available to them for about £75,000. He would have gone but fortunately for us they could not raise the cash. He had been playing on the wing but came to me and said, 'Boss, I'm a striker not a winger, please give me a chance down the middle.' So we did, trying him out first in training and then in the first team, and he proved as good as his word, scoring twenty league goals in that season. When I think he could have been lost to us, and remembering the goals he has scored since, I have to consider myself lucky that Torquay were skint.

But we were still stuttering in the first weeks of that season, taking two steps forward and one back – there was something missing in the side and I could not quite put my finger on it. The supporters were remarkably patient but that changed slightly when we lost at Barnsley at the end of the month when one guy, albeit fired up with drink, started calling me all the useless old sods in the world. He was shouting that I should be sacked and somebody younger should come in. It got very nasty but I felt the best thing to do was let it pass without reacting. Things might have got out of hand if the team's fortunes hadn't changed – gradually at first but then with a fantastic run of results that carried us from one end of the table to the other. I believe there were two catalysts for our success – the first was a 2–0 victory at Sheffield United when I made a controversial decision to change our goalkeeper at half-time. I replaced Steve Sutton with Russell Hoult because I felt Hoult would be better equipped to deal with the aerial stuff United were throwing into the box. The chairman came to me later and admitted that he thought I'd had a rush of blood but paid me the compliment of saying it was the bravest change he had ever come across.

The second important factor was the arrival of Croatian international skipper Igor Stimac, who is definitely one of the best signings I have ever made. Stimac was a defender who was highly regarded in Europe and quite frankly I thought I had no chance of getting him when I heard he might be available. I could not believe a player of such high quality would want to come to a club which at that time was below halfway in a minor English league. We were approached by an agent who informed us that his club Hadjuk Split were prepared to let him go because they were in considerable financial difficulties. We then spoke to his manager, who flew over to England and established that he would indeed come to us if we could come up with the £1.5 million. I decided to put it to the chairman. 'We've got to have him because he will take us up,' I urged. Mr Pickering got the board together and they came up with the money that allowed us to go ahead with the deal. I had helped to rewrite the transfer record books years earlier with Trevor Francis but it had taken me a long time to join the million-pound club myself. By that time, however, the transfer fees were beginning to spiral out of control and I was still a long way behind the really big spenders. My aim was to get value for money and I knew I had that with Stimac. We met, convinced him about the club's ambitions, agreed his wages, which were the highest the club had ever paid, and the signing went through without a hitch. The hitches did not materialize until later – first when he crashed his car on his second day in England driving on the wrong side of the road and then after we gave him his debut at the centre of defence at Tranmere Rovers. We were 3–0 down at half-time and lost 5–1 and the only consolation I had was that Stimac scored our goal.

But it was the failings of other players and to a great extent the pattern we played that proved our undoing and I decided to change things around and make Stimac the main man in a new system. I went to three at the back with him as a sweeper and brought in Ronnie Willems behind the front two of Sturridge and Marco Gabbiadini. We worked all week on a 3–4–3 formation and the whole thing just took off. We beat West Brom 3–0 and Charlton Athletic 2–0 in successive home games and then had a massive 4–1 victory at Birmingham City. That was the game that told me how good we could really be but by then I had also fully realized just what a gem we had in the Croatian. I should have guessed what kind of man he was when I asked him, 'Do you prefer to play on the right or the left.' He just threw me a look which seemed to say, 'Look, you daft bugger – I can play anywhere you want.' Stimac was simply magnificent – a charismatic character who played with poise and great assurance. He took the team to a new level of class, composure and confidence on the field. And off it he threw himself into the dressing-room mixture and quickly became popular with his teammates. His English was passable but it was not very long before it improved enough for him to join in the mickey-taking, giving as good as he got. He spent only three days in a hotel before he moved into an apartment; within less than a month he had brought his family over and installed them in a house. And it was normal practice when he got on the bus after an away match for him to write down all the results and then work out the league table.

That did not take much doing when we got to around Christmas time because we displaced Sunderland at the top with a 3–1 win at the Baseball Ground on 23 December. Even I had to catch my breath at the way we had rocketed up the table. I remember early in November, when we were in the bottom half, Yvonne and I had dinner with Trevor Francis and his wife at Howard Wilkinson's house in Sheffield. I told them then that we would go up. I felt so confident that everything was coming together – but I never guessed how dramatic the change would be. We jumped from seventeenth to number one in forty-three days on the back of a golden December during which we won every one of our five matches. The turkey had never tasted better. The phone was hot with calls from friends and fellow managers offering their congratulations but there was one in particular I valued more than others – and I was not in to take it. I heard a familiar voice when I caught up with my messages: 'Eh – Mr Smith, this is old big 'ead Brian Clough here. I just thought I'd ring to say thanks for putting the smile back on the faces of Derby supporters – ta-ra!' Coming from THE man – at a time when football seemed to have forgotten his magnificent achievements – that meant everything.

I passed yet another milestone in March when I reached 1,000 league games as a manager. Fittingly the game in question was at Norwich City – not that far away from where I began my league career at Colchester United. I would have enjoyed the occasion even more had we won but the Canaries spoiled the day when Jeremy Goss scored the only goal midway through the second half. Later my friends in the

LMA marked the achievement by presenting me with a memento – the only trouble was the engraver had missed a nought off the inscription and it has stayed at a hundred ever since. It must have been done by an Irishman.

It was always between Sunderland and ourselves for the top spot until Peter Reid's team turned the tables on us in March when they won 3–0 at Roker Park to go back to the top of the table. It was our first defeat in the twenty games that Stimac had played for us since that traumatic debut defeat at Tranmere Rovers and it underlined just how much Sunderland had kept pace with us. But then another major promotion rival emerged towards the end of the season in the shape of Crystal Palace. Harry Bassett had taken over at Selhurst Park in February and worked a minor miracle. Palace were in sixteenth place in the table when Bassett arrived but they took forty points from their next eighteen games, shot up to third in the table and came to the Baseball Ground for the penultimate match of the season threatening a victory that might have doomed me to another dreaded play-off disappointment. But there was extra spice in the fixture because Harry and I had become something of promotion kings throughout our careers. He had managed six promoted teams, two more than me and I was definitely keen to pull one back.

We needed to win the match to clinch promotion behind Sunderland, who were already up, and the pressure was all on us. Palace had won their last three matches and we were going into this game on the back of two successive draws. I decided to get the players away for a few days to try and relieve the tension and we prepared for the game at a hotel in Yorkshire. Howard had arranged for us to use the Leeds United training facilities at Wetherby and we lined up a few social activities to keep the mood as buoyant as possible. But you could have cut the atmosphere with a knife on the day of the match. I was desperate for us to get off to a good start and we could not have had a better one because Sturridge scored after only three minutes. But we hardly had time to settle down before Kenny Brown, a full-back who had spent most of the season loaned out by West Ham to a variety of clubs, smashed in an equalizer three minutes later. It was anybody's game after that until Van der Laan scored with a great header in the second half and we held the lead until the end. It was hugs and kisses all round at the final whistle and Harry was first to congratulate me but that's typical of him. 'You deserve it Jim, that's one in the eye for the young brigade,' he said.

So I cut Harry's lead. I wish he could have come up with us but, although Palace won their play-off semi-final against Charlton Athletic, they got done at Wembley by Leicester City in the last minute of extra-time. He deserved better than that but you cannot keep a bloke like Bassett down – he still managed to go further ahead again by getting Nottingham Forest up two years later and I hope he stays ahead – my days of fighting promotion battles are over. They say the first time is the best and the Colchester success certainly gave me the confidence to go on and prove myself as a manager but this promotion was something very special as well because it proved I could still do it. It also proved a lot of people wrong; people who had written me off either because they thought I was too old and past it or, in a couple of particular cases, because I was never up to it in the first place. Getting to the Premiership was everything but I would not be human if I said I did not take any pleasure in sticking two fingers up at the likes of John Hall and his son Douglas; at Martin Gregory, who had dispensed with my services at Portsmouth a year earlier – the same Portsmouth who, under my replacement Terry Fenwick, had avoided relegation to the Second Division on goal difference; and at the doubters at Sheffield Wednesday who clearly did not believe I was up to the job. The chairman had indicated I would have done well to get us in the top half – I had always felt we could do better – but we exceeded his expectations and fulfilled the ambitions he had when he bought the club. I was pleased for him because he had seen his faith in me justified. He may be the type who likes to know everything that is going on, which is only natural, but, unlike one or two others I have worked for, he keeps his distance and lets people get on with the job. And he was generous in his moment of triumph. I picked up a nice bonus for winning promotion and my contract was extended by two years with a substantial salary increase into the bargain. My only disappointment was we did not win the championship because I thought we were good enough and should have done.

CHAPTER THIRTEEN

McGRATH AND WANCHOPE

When I first walked into my office at Derby there were already extensive plans for a £10 million redevelopment of the Baseball Ground, a stadium that had housed generations of Rams supporters since the reign of Queen Victoria. The plans entailed knocking the main stand down in the first year and replacing it with a much bigger one going right across the road, and then over a period of time replacing the other main structures and bringing the whole stadium in line with other top Premiership grounds. I was going to have to put up with inconveniences like temporary dressing rooms, which I did not fancy too much because I did not believe they would be conducive to us winning matches, but that was the price we were going to have to pay. But the council were also regenerating a site which had housed the gasworks and some railway sidings and had become a bit of an eyesore. This was the Pride Park scheme and they hoped its centrepiece would be the Millennium Dome. Building it in Derby might have made it accessible to more people but, as usual, those responsible for making the decision could not see past London and it went to Greenwich instead. Fortunately the loss of the Dome was Derby County's gain. The club vice-chairman, Peter Gadsby, had his ear to the ground in his capacity as one of the area's largest property developers and he and the council got together and it was decided to build a new £16 million stadium on the Pride Park complex and make that the focal point of the development. The deal was done very quickly and instead of having to make do and mend over a period of years, which is what would have happened at the Baseball Ground, the new stadium was up and running within eighteen months.

It was important that we paved the way for our departure to pastures new by saying farewell to the Baseball Ground in style. After all, its dressing rooms – home and away – had echoed to the voices of footballing legends such as Raich Carter, Sammy Crooks, Peter Doherty, Hughie Gallacher, Dixie Dean, Tommy Lawton and Frank Swift, to mention but a few. In its heyday in the 1970s under Brian Clough and then Dave Mackay and with players such as Colin Todd, Roy McFarland, Kevin Hector, Archie Gemmill and the rest, the old ground had resounded to the sound of 'champions'. We might not be able to achieve that lofty pedestal but we had to make sure that we did not allow these memories to be disturbed by failure in this particular season.

That was my job and to do it properly I knew we needed to strengthen the squad with quality players. Promotion had come pretty cheaply – well, that is if you call around £500,000 cheap. My sales had amounted to around £6 million and the million pounds I spent bringing Ashley Ward from Norwich City just before the transfer deadline had pushed my buying just beyond the £6 million mark. Ward has been something of a late developer who looked to be going nowhere as a player until his career blossomed, as many do, under Dario Gradi at Crewe Alexandra. He had done reasonably well at Norwich and I felt he could get us a few vital goals in the promotion run-in and then do a job in the Premiership if we got there. But there were a couple of early surprises which I had not expected.

The first was in his debut game against his old club at Carrow Road when he missed an open goal. Sitting in the directors' box I heard one of the City fans behind me remark, 'Good old Ashley – he hasn't changed. That's another open goal he's missed.' I thought, 'Now he tells me . . . after I've just paid a million quid for the bloke.' The miss probably cost us the match because we lost 1–0 at a time when we were desperate for points to maintain our promotion challenge. Then I found out he was not as fit as he should have been – he had to have a hernia operation which made him miss the first two months of the following season. He struggled to win over the crowd when he came back but nobody could fault his effort and application and I was more pleased for him than myself or the team when he hit something of a purple patch towards the end of the season and grabbed some vital goals. But all in all, although he worked his socks off, I never felt he did himself enough justice in front of goal and that's why I eventually sold him to Barnsley. To be fair, he did much better there for Danny Wilson, certainly well enough to persuade Brian Kidd to pay £4.25 million to take him to Ewood Park just after he was appointed.

My priority during the summer was to bring in players who I believed would help us bridge the massive gap between the First Division and the Premiership. The first one was another Croatian, Aljosa Asanovic, who had been a team-mate of Stimac's at Hadjuk Split. He was followed by Jacob Laursen, a Danish international defender from Silkeborg, and then I bought Christian Dailly from Dundee United, who at £1 million was the most expensive of the three. Stimac was instrumental in the move that reunited him with his countryman. He let us know Asanovic was available and I was immediately interested. I had seen him play for Croatia in Euro 96 and did not have to be convinced of his quality. I thought at just under £1 million he was a real bargain and I was not wrong. He slotted in on the left side of midfield and, like Stimac, gave us a new dimension. He was absolutely magnificent for six months and his class was a key factor in us finishing in a respectable twelfth position at the end of the season. Unfortunately, he picked up an injury during the following pre-season, by which time I had signed two Italians, Francesco 'Ciccio' Baiano and Stefano Eranio, and he struggled to get in the team and when he did he found it difficult to pick up the pace of the game again. The other thing about him was, and this is typical of many foreigners, he was not prepared to roll up his sleeves and say, 'I'll show you.' He got moody and started making noises about wanting to leave, so I decided the best thing to do was accommodate him. He moved to Napoli for £350,000 in December but still did well enough to make the Croatian team which lost to France in the semi-final of the 1998 World Cup.

We had a useful tip-off about Dailly and I and others watched him and liked what we saw. I had a good relationship with the Dundee United chairman Jim McLean which went back to the managers' trip to Marseilles during the European Championship all those years earlier in 1982. The snag was that I had read in the papers that Manchester City were keen on Dailly but when I rang Jim he told me there was no way the player was going to Maine Road. He believed they had let it out they wanted him and anyway they were messing McLean about because they could not come up with the £1 million United wanted. I told him we would pay the asking price and we were given permission to talk to the lad. The next day I got the strangest of phone calls from Jimmy Frizzell at City. 'Is it true you are in for Dailly,' he asked. When I admitted I was he said, 'I'll tell you what. Let's put the same bid in at £400,000 and let him choose who he wants to come to.' I honestly thought it was a wind-up but quickly realized he was serious. 'Oh yes, we'll certainly do that,' I replied. 'By the way we've just bid £1 million.'

So Dailly came to us and did a terrific job as Jim McLean said he would. Jim also gave me a piece of advice which also turned out to be invaluable. 'He is coming as a midfield player but take it from me his best position will be at the centre of defence,' he said. I remembered these words some time later when Stimac got injured before a cup-tie against Aston Villa and I switched Dailly to centre-back. He was outstanding and established such a reputation in that position that he became a regular in the Scotland side. It was his qualities as a defender which must have appealed to Roy Hodgson, then at Blackburn Rovers, who asked me about him after he had been with us for two seasons. I told him straight away that Dailly was not going anywhere but the next thing I knew they had made an offer of £4 million and I could tell the board were feeling edgy about it. But I still recommended we did not sell and I told the chairman, 'If it gets to £5 million, I accept we'll have to take it.' I sat in the room while our chief executive Keith Loring dealt with his opposite number at Rovers, John Williams. It did indeed get to £5 million but I thought we could squeeze more out of them. 'Ask for £5.5million,' I urged Keith – and he did, at which point Williams balked. 'I can't go to that,' he said. 'I'll have to speak to Jack Walker,' and then put the phone down. Keith's face was a picture. 'Bloody hell, Keith, it looks like you've knackered the deal for £500,000,' I told him. Fortunately they came back with an extra £300,000 and the deal went through.

In that first Premiership season I took a chance with Paul McGrath who came from Aston Villa after a couple of months. McGrath was nearly thirty-seven and his best days were definitely behind him but I was looking at a short-term situation and I thought his experience would be an asset in keeping us tighter at the back. I made a few inquiries about him and was told quite categorically that there was no way he could do anything approaching normal training because his knees were shot. But people like Big Ron and others whose opinions I valued told me I would be getting a great player and he was only going to cost me £100,000, so I thought, why not? His first game was against Newcastle United at home and although he had done nothing on the training ground during the week before the match I wanted him involved on the Friday when we do all our set plays practice. I told him he would be marking Alan Shearer and nominated one of the young lads to stand in for the Newcastle striker while we practised corners and free-kicks. I have to say that the stand-in won every ball in the air against McGrath and I was beginning to wonder what I had done. He must have known I was a bit worried as well because he came to me after training and said, 'Boss, you don't think I can jump for the ball, do you?' I had to admit that I didn't, going on what I had seen during practice. He just smiled and told me, 'I never head the ball on Fridays – but don't fret, I'll head them all tomorrow.' And he was as good as his word – even if Shearer did have the last laugh by scoring the only goal of the game.

And that was him. During the week he would do no more than a casual jog but you would never guess it when he went out on match-days. He was good value for what we spent and what he earned. Football came easy for him – too easy at times. Two matches summed up how he could be exasperatingly good and frustratingly nonchalant. We played Wimbledon at Selhurst Park and he gave an unbelievably bad square ball straight to Marcus Gayle who set off for goal like a shot. I still don't know how McGrath managed it but he flew after Gayle and got in a brilliant tackle just as he was preparing to shoot. I congratulated him on the challenge later and he replied: 'I had to get there, boss – it was my mistake and I had to put it right.'

Then there was the day we went to Middlesbrough for a league match three days before they were due at our place in the quarter-final of the FA Cup. Juninho, Middlesbrough's Brazilian forward, was flying at the time and I knew he would be a big danger to us if we allowed him to run the game, so I told Laursen to go man for man on him. It worked well and I thought we were unlucky to be a goal down at half-time – but that's when my best-laid plan went sadly wrong. Laursen picked up a calf injury and had to come off and I replaced him with McGrath who was on the bench because his knees could not really stand up to two full games in a week. I passed on the instruction for him to go into the middle at the back and tell Dailly to assume the man-marking role on Juninho. Unfortunately nothing like that happened. We ended up with four centre-backs and Juninho running the show with the complete freedom of the park and me bawling and shouting to try and get somebody to pick him up. Middlesbrough walloped six goals past us with Ravanelli scoring a hat-trick and all we managed was a Paul Simpson consolation in the last minute.

I asked McGrath after the match why he had not done what I wanted and he just shrugged his shoulders and said, 'Sorry, boss, I forgot.' Not only did it not improve our chances of survival but that defeat handed Middlesbrough a decisive psychological lift before the FA Cup match. Bryan Robson stifled the threat of Asanovic by marking him tight and we never got going at all and lost 2–0. That was a big chance for us that we threw away and even though we stayed up I regretted another missed opportunity to realize my greatest ambition, which is still to get to the final of the FA Cup. McGrath was supposed to have a drink problem but I saw little evidence of it. He certainly did not go missing or anything like that. The reason I let him go after a year was simply because he did not train. It gets harder and harder in the Premier League and it was always difficult for the coaches to work with the team without the man who filled one of the key positions. Not many players could get away with what he did but he was well thought of in the dressing room because to them he was something of a legend and they loved him. He went to Sheffield United after he left us and broke down badly after only a couple of months, which was a great shame, but the miracle was he managed to go on for as long as he did.

We managed to bury the memory of the Middlesbrough nightmare with a good home win against Tottenham Hotspur but in the meantime I made three signings just before the transfer deadline. I paid £500,000 for my former Portsmouth 'keeper Mart Poom and then a day later splashed out £600,000 for each of two Costa Ricans called Paulo Wanchope and Mauricio Solis.

Poom's story is an interesting one. I had originally signed the young Estonian for Portsmouth for £200,000 after he came over on a month's trial. Unfortunately, his face did not fit with Terry Fenwick and he was not able to muster enough first-team appearances to keep his work permit. Although he returned to Estonia I never lost track of the lad because I thought he had qualities that could take him a long way in the game. He re-emerged in the national team which played Scotland in a replayed World Cup qualifier in Monaco and I asked the Scottish national goalkeeping coach Alan Hodgkinson to run a check on him. The problem was Poom had such a blinder in the goalless draw against the Scots that a few other teams sat up and began to take notice. Hodgkinson was unequivocal in his verdict, coming back with just two words, 'Sign him', and I jumped in ahead of the queue and had the deal done before anybody else could step in. As any manager will tell you, and for proof you only have to look at what's happened at Manchester United since Peter Schmeichel left, the goalkeeping position is one of the most vital in any club. I believe that Poom is one of the best in the Premiership – I would certainly rate him in the top three.

Around the same time I took a call from Bob McNab, the former Arsenal and England right-back who was involved with football in America. He said he was sending me a video of a game involving Wanchope, a tall, gangly-looking striker, and Solis, who played in midfield. The pair had been on trial at Queens Park Rangers, who had declined an option to take the matter any further, and the video was of a reserve team game in which they had taken part while at Rangers. It was not the best picture in the world but I saw enough to want to take the matter further. I arranged for them to come to Derby for a week to have a look and they played in a private practice match against Manchester City. I could not go to the game but my assistant Billy McEwan came back with glowing reports of both of them. 'Boss, I think we have something here,' he said. We then played them in the reserves at Preston North End and this time Steve and I both decided to have a look. Wanchope missed a couple of open goals but still showed enough and, at only twenty, he was certainly worth a chance. If anything Solis, who was four years older, looked even more useful. What also impressed me was they had been at Rangers in the middle of winter when the weather was not the best without having apparently made it and they still wanted to come back to England.

We did the deal with their club CS Heridiano and ten days later the three of them, Poom and Wanchope making their debuts, and Solis on the bench, were introduced to Premiership football at Manchester United of all places. We had gone up a couple of days early and prepared for the game at Mottram Hall. While I was there I bumped into the BBC's television commentator John Motson who was also staying at the hotel. That was significant only inasmuch as he later got the blame from Sir Alex for divulging United's team secrets to me – which he did not and I was rather insulted about because the game plan was entirely down to me. I decided to change the formation and played with a straight back four; Laursen was given the job of marking Eric Cantona and we played with two wide men – Sturridge and Wanchope – and Ward through the middle. The nostalgic return of McGrath took a lot of the pressure away from the trio and he certainly played his part in what was a great afternoon for everybody concerned with Derby County. But there was only one name on everybody's lips afterwards and that was Paulo Wanchope. We were already one up with a good strike from Ward when Wanchope picked the ball up about twenty yards inside our half. He set off on his run and beat about three or four opponents before crashing in a magnificent goal. It should have been awarded the goal of the season but the *Match of the Day* man Alan Hansen, who has never had a high opinion of Wanchope, put it down to luck and gave it to somebody else.

Wanchope did well for Derby. He is hardly the most orthodox of strikers, giving the impression of being awkward and leggy, but he developed his skills well and was always a handful for opposing defences. The problem was as he got better the more I felt his attitude declined. Steve McLaren had numerous run-ins with him over his refusal to release the ball at the right time. He would say something like 'Every coach keeps telling me that', more or less telling Steve to stuff his opinions because he was going to do what he wanted to do. I was also concerned about his apparent lack of effort in matches and I had three major bust-ups with him about it. We lost 1–0 at Barnsley and he was having a stinker so I took him off and he did not like it, flouncing off like a big kid. I'd had enough of his tantrums and tore into him in the dressing room after the match, telling him to start behaving like a grown-up and cut out all the prima donna histrionics. I told him in no uncertain terms he was not only letting himself down but his team-mates and the supporters. I'll admit I pushed him hard – obviously past his breaking point because he leapt to his feet and jabbed his finger in my direction, accusing me of having no respect for him. For a minute or so it got really tasty – I moved towards him maybe a shade too aggressively and he stood his ground. Fortunately, maybe for me as it happens, Steve McLaren and a couple of the lads got between us and eventually things cooled down.

But at times Wanchope continued to behave exasperatingly like he could not give a toss. At half-time in a match against Arsenal I completely lost it with him. 'Get changed and get in that bath,' I bawled at him. But the other players persuaded me to keep him on. 'All right,' I told him. 'If I was in their shoes I'd be giving you a smack, not supporting you.' He must have got the message because he did all right after that. There was yet another time when we played Coventry

City in our last home game and it was goalless when right on full-time he missed the biggest sitter I have ever seen missed in my life. When he walked in I lambasted him. 'I'm glad you missed that because that's all you deserved for your lack of effort.' This time he just sat there and said nothing. The following Sunday we went to Chelsea for the last game of the season. After the game I was disappointed that Wanchope was the only one missing when the staff and players all went out to dinner at a restaurant partly owned by Mikkel Beck, the Danish striker we had signed from Middlesbrough. He preferred his own company and had flown home to Costa Rica for the summer. As far as myself and everybody else was concerned it was a case of good riddance. We had been having discussions with his agent Dennis Roach and Harry Redknapp about a move to West Ham but nothing had happened by the time he returned for pre-season training. He seemed all right when we had a chat about what he wanted to do. I asked him if he was going to West Ham and he smiled and said, 'No, I don't think so', so I left it at that.

We had arranged a series of pre-season games in America and at that stage I regarded him as part of my team plans and let him know he would be part of the trip. He looked non-plussed about that. 'Do you mean you are taking me to the States?' he asked in total amazement. I told him that last season was forgotten – whatever problems we had were forgotten. He was still a Derby player and it was time to start again. He accepted that to the point of being kitted out for the trip but the next morning he came to me and announced he was signing for West Ham after all. I believe that a big factor in his decision was that he felt, after all the speculation which had come to nothing, he would lose face by staying at Derby. He was supposed to be wanted by a string of top clubs ... Juventus, Inter Milan, Barcelona, Real Madrid – even Arsenal ... but I never heard a peep from any of them apart from struggling Italian outfit Reggiana. For him it was West Ham or nobody and he went there because he could not face the fact that he would lose face by sticking with us.

Having said all that, I do regret that he left and I desperately wanted him to stay at the club. He has now joined Manchester City and I am sure he will be a tremendous success with Joe Royle at Maine Road. We offered him a massive contract when he had a year left but he hesitated because he said he wanted to see how the season went, but the impression I got was he did not think Derby was big enough for him. I also believe he had his mind swayed by agents supposedly tapping him on behalf of the top Italian clubs. Juventus even invited me over there, I thought on the pretext of watching a match but maybe to discuss Wanchope, but all they wanted was to talk about a possible link-up between our two clubs which in the end did not amount to anything, and his name was never mentioned at all. I did get a call from a guy who said he was connected with Reggiana whose story was fanciful at the very least. He said he would like Wanchope but they did not really have any money and I advised the lad to avoid them like the plague.

You could say that Wanchope had the last laugh on me when he returned to Pride Park at the end of the 1998–99 season and scored both goals for West Ham in a 2–0 defeat that hardly did our hopes of survival much good. I always knew he was a handful and he certainly proved it that afternoon. His first goal was a superb header and then he took advantage of some poor defensive play on our part to score again. We got at them after that and he was very quiet but the damage had been done. I had no problems with Solis, who was a really nice lad, but unfortunately he did not exactly cut it in Premiership football. Eventually we had to let him go back to Costa Rica because he did not make enough appearances to qualify for a renewal of his work permit.

There was always a brisk turnover of players and I have never made any apology for shopping in foreign markets. I felt there were better bargains on other continents, especially with some of the prices being asked for players in this country. I thought I was paying over the odds when I tried to take Tommy Johnson back to Derby in March 1997. Johnson had spent a couple of years at Aston Villa after Brian Little had bought him for around £1.5 million and he had done all right. I thought with his pace he would do a good job for us but I had to go to £2.5 million before Villa agreed to let him go. But when we got down to talking about his wages it seemed clear that Johnson did not want to come back to Derby and I did not push it too hard because I thought we were better off without players whose hearts would not be in the club. In the event he probably did us a favour because he went to Celtic soon afterwards for £2.4 million and has not pulled up any trees in Scotland. I then turned my attention to a young striker who was struggling to keep his place in a First Division side. I thought he had potential and might benefit by being allowed to develop at a higher level. When I asked about him I was quoted a staggering £1.8 million and it absolutely blew my mind. I think my reaction, somewhere between a yell and a loud guffaw, underlined what I thought and I did not even haggle. When you are asked to pay that kind of money for somebody so young and relatively inexperienced it forces a club like ours to look overseas for a better deal.

And that's what I did, and quite successfully even though I do say it myself. In the summer of 1997 we recruited two Italians who have done a magnificent job in helping Derby survive their longest spell in the top flight of football for over twenty years. Eranio came on a Bosman free transfer from AC Milan and a month later I paid £1.5 million for Baiano from Fiorentina. I knew about Eranio from his days in the Italian team and I also spoke to Trevor Francis who knew a lot about the Italian scene. Although he was coming up for thirty-one when he arrived I was still confident he would be useful to us playing either as a right wing-back or in midfield. I am happy to say he is still with us because technically he is one of the best I have ever managed in the whole of my career. He is also willing to do a specific marking job when required, as he did last season when we went to White Hart Lane to play Spurs. I was conscious of the threat posed by David Ginola so I asked Eranio if he would look after him. His expression – a little smile and a wink – told me everything. The Frenchman did not get a smell until Justin Edinburgh gave Eranio a thump on the back of the head and he was carried off suffering from concussion.

But you win and lose in the buying business and, for me, one of the biggest fish ever to slip out of my grasp was the great Roberto Baggio. Again I had been tipped off that his club AC Milan would let him go but immediately dismissed the possibility of him coming to Derby because either the fee and his wages would be too high or he would rather sign for one of the so-called more glamorous outfits. I was contacted by his manager who informed me that to get him we would have to come up with a package that would cost us £6 million over three years – half for Milan and the other half for the man who had been one of the greatest post-war stars in Italian football and who had once changed hands for what was, at the time, a world record £8 million when he moved from Fiorentina to Juventus in 1990. I laid the deal on the line for Mr Pickering: 'Look, chairman, we can sign Baggio, somebody who would fill the new stadium, and wouldn't it be fantastic to begin our new era at Pride Park with one of the biggest names in the game wearing a Derby County shirt?' He was as excited as me about it all and gave me the green light to do the deal. I flew to Milan with a Birmingham-based Italian called Johnny Palladini, who was going to advise and translate, to meet Baggio and his representatives. Our plane was delayed for some hours and it was 10 p.m. when we arrived at our hotel.

It had been a long day and the plan then was to grab some dinner, have a chat with Baggio's people and get some sleep before meeting the player the following day. That went out of the window when his agent insisted we saw his manager that same night – 'You must see him straight away – that is important and he is waiting,' he insisted. So we were driven to another part of Milan, through some massive gates into a huge courtyard in front of a block of flats, and taken into this sumptuous apartment. I was ushered into a separate room and that's when I realized why the agent had been so insistent . . . I went in to find, not only the manager waiting, but Baggio himself. He certainly looked the part. He may have turned thirty but he was still in great shape, lean and in excellent physical condition. We shook hands and had a chat about Italian football and Derby and what I believed he could do for us while, at the same time, Palladini talked to Baggio's people. We had walked out on a terrace overlooking the city when Palladini came out and informed me the goalposts had been changed – 'The deal is now £3 million for the club, £3 million in wages, plus an additional £3 million signing-on fee to be paid offshore.' My immediate reaction was to tell them to stick it but I hesitated because I did not want them to think we were cheapskates and I said: 'Tell them to give me some time to think about it.' It was while I was wondering what the hell I was doing there and what a wasted journey it had all been, that a young lady added to the growing farce by asking me if I would like some ice cream. I replied, 'Ice cream, dear? What I would rather have is a large glass of red wine after what I have just heard.'

I did get the wine and as a matter of fact I had a few more when we got back to the hotel, where I wondered if there was any way we could come up with this ridiculous amount of money. We even kicked it around the following day, hoping to find some leeway that could broker the deal, but in the end I had to give it up. I went back home and told the chairman what had happened and he and the rest of the board were genuinely disappointed Baggio would not be signing for Derby, but I think everybody realized, under the circumstances, it was out of the question. I had to smile when I read later that he had signed for Bologna where he did very well before eventually returning to Inter Milan.

Still, even that dark cloud had a silver lining. I had already signed Eranio and I regaled him with the whole Baggio story. 'Don't worry, boss,' he smiled. 'Instead you go buy Baiano from Fiorentina – he will be better for Derby than Baggio.' So I took him at his word, but not until after I made a few inquiries from people who knew and received all the right responses. The pair did magnificently for us in helping us to a top-ten finish in their first season, linking up together to give the midfield strength and style. There was not much of Baiano but he more than punched his weight and he was not bad in front of goal either. Only Wanchope scored more in that first season. But some foreigners find the competitiveness and sheer fatigue of our football season difficult to handle and he was one of them. He struggled to maintain his form the following season and I felt we had seen the best of him. It suited both him and the club to go back to Italy and he signed for a Serie 'B' club for a small amount.

CHAPTER FOURTEEN

COACHES COME . . . AND GO

I am reliably informed that Derby County lost their first-ever league match at the Baseball Ground to Sunderland. I know for a fact that we lost the last one 3–1 against Arsenal over a hundred years later, which put the dampener on what had otherwise been a successful return to top-flight football. If somebody had offered us twelfth position in the Premiership table at the start of the season I am fairly sure we would have grabbed it with both hands. And in deference to Francis Ley, a local industrialist whose introduction of baseball into this country gave our old stadium its name, it was appropriate that we should win the first completed league match at Pride Park. The word 'completed' is significant. In the game against Wimbledon which marked the debut of our Premiership stage we were playing well and leading 2–1 (with Ashley Ward claiming the distinction of scoring the first league goal, and Stefano Eranio adding a second) when suddenly a power failure plunged the ground into darkness. Uriah Rennie, who was refereeing his first Premiership match, took the players off the pitch and we got the lads back in the dressing room and tried to keep their muscles warm while outside the lights flickered and failed at regular intervals.

Derby's record against Wimbledon was a poor one and it

was sod's law that just when we looked like beating them for the first time in years something should go wrong. The Wimbledon manager Joe Kinnear was anxious to get it called off for obvious reasons but I was determined to buy as much time as possible. I even instructed Jim Fearn, our press and communications manager, to talk to the referee and tell him we were doing everything possible to restore the lighting. Unfortunately I was told later their conversation was over-heard by Kinnear and good old Vinnie Jones who followed Fearn on to the pitch and shouted to Rennie not to take any notice of him. To be fair to him the match official gave it as long as he could and when there was still no sign of the lights coming back on after a good half-hour he abandoned the game. Ironically, as the announcement came the lights did come on again, which got the crowd at it a bit, but the decision stood which was fortunate because a few minutes later they went out for good. An investigation later revealed that the power failure was caused by an incorrect setting on the circuit breaker. There were rumours that the lights had been sabotaged by a betting syndicate. They were taken seriously enough by the police for them to interrogate the Stadium project manager Arthur Burns before he convinced them there was no sinister reason behind the blackout. It was a costly lesson because Wimbledon came back to Pride Park a few weeks later and went away with a point.

So Ward was robbed of a place in posterity – and he was not the only one. There may have been no floodlight failure to save Barnsley, who were our next visitors, but the game still provided plenty of talking points – not the least of which was the scorer of the first official goal to be scored at Pride Park. The game was goalless when we were awarded a penalty. Ciccio Baiano was handed the opportunity to mark his debut by taking it but his shot was pushed away by Barnsley's German 'keeper Lars Leese and Stefano Eranio followed up to score the rebound. But the referee ordered the kick to be retaken after ruling that Leese had moved too early. This time Eranio himself, who must have fancied his chances more than his Italian team-mate, grabbed the ball and cracked it into the net cool as you like. That was the only goal of the game but there was no sense of anti-climax even though we had to wait for that first win. We were poor and were lucky to get the three points but beating Barnsley was the proud culmination of maximum effort by all the different factions of the football club: the directors and those responsible for constructing the magnificent new stadium and the players and coaching staff, including myself, who had helped to get the show on the road.

The dressing room by now had a distinctly cosmopolitan look with around ten foreign players from countries such as Estonia, Italy, Denmark, Croatia, Holland, Jamaica and Costa Rica and a smattering from the home countries. In fact it was a situation which drew comment from no less a person than the Duke of Edinburgh himself – and rather a wry one at that. The occasion was the official opening of Pride Park on Friday 18 July 1997 by Her Majesty The Queen, who was accompanied by the Duke. It was a proud day for everybody connected with the club and an especially memorable one for me and my family. Yvonne and my daughters were there and four of my grandchildren presented posies to Her Majesty. Usually a manager has to get his team to an FA Cup final to enjoy a brush with royalty but since that pleasure has escaped me thus far I would more than settle for doing the honours on a occasion like this.

The players, staff and myself were lined up on the pitch when she walked into the stadium and the noise was unbelievable. I made a mental promise to myself to make sure we enjoyed a similar atmosphere on match-days. I was introduced by the chairman and then in turn I introduced the Queen and the Duke to the players. Her Majesty did not say a lot but her husband was very chatty. 'You have a lot of foreign players here,' he remarked. 'You obviously like them a lot.' I agreed and we talked about one or two he had heard of. Then later the Queen, Duke, chairman and myself boarded an open car for a tour of the ground. Mr Pickering conversed with Her Majesty while I continued to point people out to the Duke, among them a group of our young apprentices. 'Over there, sir, those lads in the tracksuits are all our apprentices,' I ventured. Quick as a flash he retorted, 'Well, they haven't got much hope here with all those foreigners, have they?'

I don't know if he meant to express what has become a general opinion in the game. Certainly I have done my share of shopping abroad. We have scouts covering a great number of games in Europe because I believe, and in my case it has been proved, that's where the bargains are. I do not subscribe to the view that the more mature foreigners in English football are stunting the progress of home-produced players or that they are damaging our international prospects. The Michael Owens will always be there – the cream will always come to the top and the current crop of young players are as good as they have been for a long time. Rather than have a detrimental effect I believe they have learned from playing with or against or just simply watching the continentals. The fact that the livelihoods of domestic players could be affected if the influx continues to grow means that there may be a case for restricting their numbers but I fail to see, under current regulations regarding freedom of movement within the European community, how this can be applied.

But there is one concern I have about foreign imports and it is a major one. There is a growing tendency in the Premiership for clubs to recruit young players from foreign countries, and by that I mean teenagers who then become part of the youth development scheme. I believe it is creating a dangerous precedent which could certainly have a long-term effect on the number of home players coming into the game. I would certainly like to see some import restrictions on the ages of players to prevent what could become a mass invasion.

But my foreign players helped me to enjoy another red-letter day in my career when I celebrated twenty-five years as a manager in June 1997. I was pleased to welcome Arsenal to Pride Park for the occasion, hopefully to get our revenge for the Gunners spoiling our final league match at the Baseball and also to renew my acquaintance with their extremely talented manager Arsène Wenger. It has always been my custom to invite the opposing manager into my office after a match for a drink and a laugh – win or lose – and I had done that on his previous visit to Derby. Then, as now, it had been something of a gala occasion and he came in, had a glass of champagne and we had a chat. He was just as friendly the second time around – even though this time his team, then in second place and later to be crowned league champions, were beaten 3–0 with Paulo Wanchope scoring twice and Dean Sturridge getting the other. That victory took us to sixth in the table – it was our highest placing that season, which ended with us in a very respectable ninth.

I was quite surprised later when I was told by the Arsenal press representative Clare Tomlinson that it was the first time any manager had shown Wenger the same after-match courtesy. I believe he is a charming man, honest and forthright, and although he was a little reserved on the first meeting, he has opened up since, particularly some time later when we met in Milan when we both attended a Juventus–Bologna match. We were in a group who went out to dinner and had a good discussion about the merits of French, English, Italian and even Japanese football. He also talked with some incredulity about the money, around £20 million, Juventus were prepared to pay for Nicolas Anelka, who later moved to Real Madrid instead. What he did not mention was his interest in Thierry Henry, which I suspect was the real purpose of his visit, and I had to smile when he subsequently did the deal. Did he regard me as a potential rival for Henry? Somehow I think not.

The postscript to the twenty-five-year celebrations was I

won the Carling No. 1 award and the chairman presented me with a set of golf clubs and a trolley. I wondered whether he was trying to tell me something! But maybe not . . . because although the season again ended without any trophies I was convinced we were making slow but sure progress. The last-day victory over Liverpool was a result of some significance because it was Derby's first win over the Merseysiders for twenty-two years and ended a sequence of defeats that had stretched back over ten years. Sadly, that was Roy Evans's last game in sole charge at Anfield – some time later it was announced that he and Gérard Houllier would share the managerial duties. I never believed that would work and I was sorry for Roy when he eventually left the club he had served at all levels since leaving school. He was under a lot of criticism when they played us, which I thought was unfair and made no allowances either for his loyalty or the excellent job he had done for the club. Liverpool still finished third in the table, which under the current qualification system would have earned them a place in the UEFA Champions' League – their disappointment the previous season under-lined just how well Roy had done under difficult circum-stances. I am amazed that somebody with his experience at the highest level still continues to be ignored when good jobs became available.

My great vision for Derby still is to put some silverware in the trophy cabinet – and I mean something worthwhile. Being realistic, the title will always be on a distant horizon but I believe we are capable of winning one of the cup compe-titions or even finishing high enough in the league to qualify for a place in the UEFA Cup. I did have another aim which has been side-tracked somewhat – that was to stay on as manager for as long as I am wanted and then pass the job on to the young man I was grooming to be my successor, Steve McLaren. Unfortunately, the lure of becoming Sir Alex Ferguson's number two at Manchester United was too great for Steve and he left us in February 1999. I had made him my first-team coach during my first hectic week in charge. I had resolved as I pounded those miles on the seafront at Portsmouth that, if I was ever lucky enough to get back into management, I would not go for the older, established number two-cum-coach, I would appoint a younger man with a modern approach and outlook.

Steve had first come to my attention on my regular trips to Oxford United to watch matches when the likes of Maurice Evans, and later Brian Horton and Denis Smith, were in charge. Latterly I had been impressed with this bright, young character who would come into the office after the game, enjoy a beer and talk sensibly about football. I liked his manner and attitude and, when I asked around, I also liked what I heard about how he had performed with the reserves and the kids. I spoke to Maurice about Steve and he had no hesitation in recommending him. 'He has everything to go a long way in the game as a coach,' he said. So I contacted Denis and asked for permission to talk to Steve, who jumped at the chance to come to Derby. Not only was he moving up from reserve- to first-team coaching but he was also returning to the club he had been with as a player. Oxford wanted a nominal compensation figure of around £30,000 which we were happy to pay.

Steve made an immediate impact with a wonderful, fresh approach that went down well with the players and the rest of the staff. He introduced innovations such as regular stretching exercises; massages; diets; technical data and fitness routines in conjunction with the specialist coach. We always discussed everything with the staff but it was a whole new training and match preparation routine which put the accent on the athleticism as well as the skill of the players. We also did a lot of work studying videos and it was not just reviewing matches. We had separate cameras strategically placed to be able to provide not only evidence of where we might have gone wrong in defending or attacking set-pieces but also a detailed analysis of any player's performance.

Steve's arrival was perfectly timed to coincide with my strategy of widening the club's horizon. The trickle of foreigners had become a flood. They were accustomed to the kind of day-to-day care and attention that few clubs in England had the facilities to provide. It might have been a far cry from the twice-weekly sessions with the part-timers at Boston and a lot different to anything I had done at my previous clubs, but the face of football was changing fast and Derby County were certainly not going to be left straggling behind the rest. I viewed Steve's role as essential in that progression and he turned out to be everything I expected and a lot more. The players who came from Italy and Holland viewed with some incredulity the fact that we had no full-time masseur. At their previous clubs there would be up to half a dozen on hand to provide daily massages. We made it a priority to appoint one although a few eyebrows were raised when we gave the job to a woman, Helen Bretnal, who had been with Derbyshire County Cricket Club before she came to us. Helen was terrific at her job but unfortunately I had to let her go when she and one of my players, Rory Delap, became an item. I did not feel it was appropriate to have that sort of close relationship within the club, especially with the kind of publicity it might attract from the more lurid sections of the media. They understood my point of view and accepted the situation without any problem. But we were fortunate to bring in another top masseur, a mad Scouser called John McEwan who is well respected by the players for his ability and a near-lavatory humour which ensures there is never a dull dressing-room moment. We also use a top biomechanics expert called Alan Watson who deals with the players' movement and rhythm, and I don't think there is a better medical back-up team in the country than our physio Peter Melville and his assistant Neil Sillett.

It was Steve who instigated the appointment of Bill Beswick as the team's sports psychologist. He had been on coaching courses when Beswick had been lecturing and felt he would be useful in enhancing the performances of the players. And he has been a terrific asset to the club in making sure the players' mental preparation is equally as important as their physical preparation. There have been many Beswick success stories but one in particular was Chris Powell, who was struggling with his confidence so much after he joined us from Southend United that I feared the £750,000 I spent on him would be wasted because he did not look as though he would handle Premiership football. But Beswick's influence was so great that Chris turned out to be one of our most consistent players and actually won the player of the year award.

I suppose there were players at every club who did not respond to or like the coach as much as others but I felt that everybody respected Steve for his knowledge and coaching talent. We had a great relationship, both professionally and socially. I was godfather to his youngest son Josh and his family and mine were and still are very close. As the partnership developed he assumed a lot of the responsibility for training and coaching. I still determined the team, tactics and buying and selling and got involved with the set plays in the countdown to match-days but generally speaking he was in charge on the training pitch. It all seemed to be going well until I heard that Fergie had been asking questions about Steve with a view to him being a possible successor to Brian Kidd, who had left United to take over at Blackburn Rovers. I kept quiet and hoped it would go away but my worst fears were realized when we went to Old Trafford early in February to play a league game which, ironically, we had agreed to bring forward from Easter Monday to help out United's European Champions' League schedule. We lost 1–0 but that was far from my only disappointment of the evening.

Fergie took me into his inner sanctum after the match and said, 'Jim, I want Steve McLaren as my number two and I would like your permission to speak to him.' I half-expected the approach and was ready with my reply. I said: 'All right,

Alex, you can have him but it is going to cost you £500,000. He is a top man and that sort of figure would be chicken feed if you were paying it out for players.' He said he thought I must be joking and then mentioned how much he was prepared to pay Steve, which made me think the deal had already gone somewhere down the road. Anyway the discussion was left in the air and I got on the team coach with Steve and the players for the trip back. I never mentioned what had happened and neither did he until we arrived in Derby much later when I pulled Steve to one side and told him I wanted to see him in the office that morning. 'I am sure you know why,' I told him. 'Is it Manchester United?' he asked and I nodded and asked him outright, 'What do you want to do?' I was half-expecting the reply – 'I want to go.' I just said: 'Fair enough – I don't want to stand in your way so if we can come to the right arrangement with United, it's on.' And that was it. Steve went without any haggling, argument or bad feeling.

I viewed his departure with mixed emotions – sadness that the line of succession had been broken and that we would not have his input during the week but satisfaction and, to a certain extent, flattery that somebody whose talents I had spotted when he was just an obscure reserve-team coach with a Division Two club should become coach to what became the most successful club in Europe. The compensation figure was only token – in the end we settled for £250,000. Life goes on. People and personalities are just pieces in a jigsaw that is rarely completed at a football club. Losing Steve was a disappointment but far from a tragedy as we actually finished one place higher at the end of that 1998–99 season than we had the previous one. I brought my old friend Ray Harford in straight away to steady things and preserve continuity. I had known him a long time and valued his friendship but the reason why he came was purely professional. Ray is a top coach and his arrival took away the sting of Steve going. He had a totally different approach which, it must be said, was better suited to some of the players, especially those who had not got on that well with Steve. Some of his training sessions were excellent and drew a terrific response. But when it came down a more permanent arrangement he was undecided about what he wanted to do. The bottom line was he preferred to live in London and I needed him above the shop, so to speak. To be my chief coach he had to live in the Derby area and he would not move. If you ask him now he would probably say he regrets that decision but things have now moved on.

Ultimately that was also one of the reasons why things did not work out with Malcolm Crosby, who was appointed first-team coach before the start of the 1998–99 season. I knew Malcolm from my days at Newcastle when he was part of Denis Smith's back-room staff at Sunderland. There was a link inasmuch as he played at Aldershot after me and had stayed in the same digs as I had. It was important I chose the right man, especially after the strong influence Steve had wielded in the dressing room and then the successful three months Ray had spent at the club. And therein lay Malcolm's problem. It was always going to be a difficult job for the lad filling their shoes and things did not work in his favour when we started badly, taking only one point from our first four matches.

At the end of the day I have to say I made the wrong decision. I had taken on somebody whose CV was a contradiction of the type of coach I had promised myself I would get when I appointed Steve – young, eager to learn and someone who would develop his talents with the team. I tried to explain my reasons for letting him go – that it was not the gel I was after, it was not the system I wanted – and I had to change it. I also looked for the same commitment about moving to Derby that Malcolm had promised he would give when he took the job but, for one reason or another, had been unable to fulfil. I did not believe the ninety-minute to two-hour drive from his home in Oxford was the ideal preparation for training sessions and I should know because I have done it myself. At Derby, in order to keep our heads above water, everybody has to be 110 per cent in tune with the job because we cannot afford to splash big money in the transfer market. We have to squeeze every last drop out of the players we have by being ultra-professional on the training pitch and I just felt that it was not happening. It had been on my mind to effect the change for some time but when the crunch came it was really done on the spur of the moment. Malcolm understood my position and accepted it and we struck a deal that he was happy with. He has now joined Colin Todd as part of the new managerial team at Swindon Town and I hope they are both very successful.

I have to confess that my mind was swayed by the fact that I had been impressed by the knowledge, attitude and application of my reserve-team coach Stevie Round, whom I have since promoted to take over first-team duties. Stevie's playing career at the club ended when he was only twenty-two because of injury, which is always a great shame, but he decided to do what he believed was the next best thing. When I arrived he and another young lad, Steve Taylor, whose career also ended prematurely, were helping Gerry Summers run the youth scheme. Taylor is now doing well as the Under–19 coach at the youth academy but at the start of 1998–99 season I put Roundy in charge of the reserves and moved up Billy McEwan to assistant manager to help with organizational matters. Later when Crosby left I switched Billy and Stevie's duties, with Billy going back to looking after the reserves while retaining his status as assistant manager.

On reflection I did not handle the changeover as diplomatically as I might have done. In the first place I hate getting rid of anybody and I did not enjoy doing it to Crosby. In the second place I acted without consulting Billy, which I should have done, especially with regard to him reverting to reserve-team duties. Billy got a bit of a shock when it was presented to him as a *fait accompli,* which was understandable and I apologized to him. My excuse was that it was a sudden decision, premeditated in its perception but not in its execution. I believe the changes have suited everybody, Billy is happier with clearly defined and vital responsibilities and Stevie has adapted well to his new role and I believe has the potential to be a top-class coach. He was a disciple of Steve McLaren's and has a similar modern if not futuristic approach to the job. Naturally people will compare them and they have a lot in common but I believe Stevie has everything it takes to be just as good if not better.

What with one thing and another I don't believe we performed as well as we were capable of last season although our results in the second half made up for our mediocre start. I was quoted in the papers at the start of the season saying I believed I had the strongest squad I had ever had in my time at Derby and I still maintain that. But there were problems which have since been resolved and should not stand in the way of our progress this season. I was sorry to lose Wanchope during the summer and equally sad when Stimac followed him to West Ham. But I felt we'd had the best out of Igor. He had been instrumental in Croatia reaching the semi-finals of the World Cup in 1998, playing in every game in spite of having a back injury before the tournament, but he only made a limited number of appearances for us when he came back and in my opinion was no longer giving us value for money.

On reflection we may have made a mistake in breaking away from our normal pre-season preparation in La Manga to go to America where we played matches in Chicago and Denver. The training facilities were not as good and it was a little like going on holiday rather than working in a training camp. The trip also had significant repercussions for the club in the saga of Esteban Fuertes. He was an Argentinian striker who had been recommended by Steve Wicks, who played for me at Queens Park Rangers. We had him watched and the reports came back that he was definitely worth pursuing. I had him brought over to Derby where we discussed contracts with his representatives and he finally agreed to join us. We were led to believe that Fuertes did not need any work permit because, although he did not fulfil the international requirement, he had an Italian passport courtesy of his grandparents.

I can say now that I was never one hundred per cent committed to the deal; there was a feeling of unease, the reason for which I could not put my finger on. His passport situation took about five weeks into the season to sort out but I kept being reassured by his agents telling me everything would be all right. Normally I would have said, 'Look, forget it. I'm not happy about the way it is dragging on', which I wasn't. But he was on the training pitch with us and, although he had a major fitness problem when he arrived in the middle of July, it was just like having him on trial – we were not losing anything and besides he kept knocking loads of goals in. He certainly had something – good skills and a tremendous shot. He looked a good player but it took us until the end of August when he made his debut against Sheffield Wednesday to get him into match condition. But he was certainly worth waiting for. We were desperate for a break after taking only one point from our first four matches and Fuertes helped to provide it. We beat Wednesday and then he scored the only goal in the next game against Everton.

Unfortunately he also had a fiery Latin temperament which did not go down too well with match officials. He was booked in three successive matches and then got himself sent off when we lost at home to Bradford City. The referee had already red-carded one of the City players and we were in control of the game when somebody pushed Fuertes and he retaliated. Things got worse after that, especially when we gifted them the points with an own goal. So our hot-blooded Argentinian picked up a three-match ban, but little did I know then that, compared with what was around the corner, this was chicken feed. Neither did I suspect anything was wrong when I brought him back at the first opportunity and he played really well in a good 3–1 victory over Chelsea. It was November and getting chilly, so I decided to take advantage of a two-week fixture gap by taking the players and their wives or girlfriends for a short break in Portugal. When it was over I stayed over at my place in Spain and missed the drama that transpired when the party arrived back at Heathrow. Apparently the immigration officials chose to scrutinize every detail of every passport, even down to using infra-red, almost as if they were looking for something in particular. If they were they certainly found it when they came to Fuertes and discovered that his Italian passport was a fake.

They immediately slapped a no-entry ban and he was led away. After some hectic bargaining and consultations it was agreed that he could spend one night in a hotel while a return flight to Argentina was arranged, and out he went the following day. It seemed clear to us that somebody knew about the fake passport and had tipped off the authorities. When I got a call about it, it confirmed my worst suspicions. I should have realized I was in murky waters when we were trying to sort out the complications of his contract and where we were supposed to pay the transfer money. Fuertes had been owned by one Argentinian club who could not afford to pay him and they loaned him to Sante Fé. They were not much better off, so a management company bought a slice of him. It meant that three different groups had a piece of the action,which caused a problem when it came down to making the initial £1.3 million instalment of the £2.8 million transfer fee. In the end we handed it over to the Argentinian FA to let them sort it out.

As the situation developed, our concern was how were we going to get our money back but that problem became more acute when it became apparent that, not only would that not be forthcoming, we might also be liable to cough up the rest of the fee. It was a right mess and it dragged on for months until it was finally sorted out in the summer when Fuertes signed for French First Division club Lens. In the meantime we had to lend him back to Santa Fé and the frustrating thing was he notched twelve goals in eleven games for them and ended up one of the country's top marksmen. It was altogether a highly unsavoury episode which has certainly made us wary of getting involved in similar situations again. As a result of what happened, the FA and Premiership have changed their system when it comes to giving the green light to foreign players. Whereas in the past it was enough to send a photostat of a passport, clubs must now send the passport itself to be checked before a player's transfer can be approved.

The whole Fuertes affair cast a cloud over the club and created an atmosphere of instability that certainly did not help results. We needed to strengthen the side; we desperately needed somebody up front and there did not appear to be the money available to do it. That was when the chairman and the other directors pushed the boat out to allow me to bring in Craig Burley from Celtic, take Giorgi Kinkladze on loan from Ajax and sign Branko Strupar, a former Belgian Footballer of the Year, from Gent, and I think all three made a big difference to our season. Burley was a major acquisition with his drive and leadership; Kinky did well and became an immediate hit with the supporters because they like big-occasion players. I have since made the deal a permanent one and I know we will not see the best of him until into this season. He is a player I rated when he was with Manchester City. I once saw him give a brilliant individual display for City against Oxford United when I was commentating for television. He did not have the best of times in Holland but when the opportunity came for me to get him, I jumped at it. Strupar was also an instant success when he scored twice in his first full game against Watford.

They all contributed to us staying out of relegation trouble at the end of the season but it was tight in the end, mainly because Bradford City put pressure on all of the teams near the bottom of the table. We did ourselves no favours when we missed penalties at Watford and Bradford that would have given us four more points and lifted us comfortably clear but I was heartened by our results from the turn of the year which, stretched over a season, would have given us a mid-table finish. But that is not good enough. I may be a little long in the tooth but I remember the comment my teachers used to write on my school reports: 'Must do better.' It is as applicable now as it was then.

CHAPTER FIFTEEN

A MANAGER'S LOT

If posterity remembers me for anything, it might be as the man who arrived at the bank, plastic at the ready, only to find somebody had already emptied the cash machine. I am proud of my record as a wheeler and dealer. My deficit at Derby, turning them from a mid-table First Division team into one which is looking forward to its fifth successive season in the Premiership, is only £6 million which is minute when compared to the finance which has been generated by the club being in the top flight. There was a twenty-year time span between me breaking the British transfer record by becoming the first manager to sell a player for £1 million and being able to buy one for seven figures. During those two decades there has been so much money swilling around in transfer dealings it is almost obscene. I wish I could have had a slice of the action. Bobby Saxton, who was my coach at Newcastle, has always maintained that if we had had the money that John Hall subsequently threw at the club we would have won everything. I would not disagree with that or even dismiss the suggestion that I could also have done it at Blackburn had Jack Walker's millions been available to me while I was at Ewood Park.

If you are being absolutely honest, to win the top prizes or even do consistently well in the highest league, you have to be able to buy the best and they come at a price which is well in excess of the £3 million or so that has roughly been the average for those who have come to Derby over the past year or so. It costs nothing to be ambitious in football . . . even the lowliest can dream about having their day. It is only when you try to fulfil your ambition that you have to start paying the bills and the trick is not to overstretch yourself by aiming higher than your budget allows. We had a disappointing season at Derby last time but before that we finished twelfth, ninth and eighth in the Premiership and that is the kind of standard we have to set ourselves. At the start of any season you set yourself what you consider realistic targets and for us a top-ten finish and a good run in both cup competitions is the aim.

So what do you do when you cannot join the élite band of bosses who can spend up to £18 million on a player? The answer is of course you try and beat them on the field and, if you cannot manage that, you do your best to out-bargain them – and you get a hell of a kick when you do. Like when you buy Les Ferdinand for £15,000 and he is sold for £6 million. Like when you buy David Seaman for £225,000 and he goes on to be the best in England. Like at Newcastle where I gave debuts to home-grown players such as Steve Howey, who I believe would certainly have established himself in the England side but for a succession of injuries. Like when you nurture a kid like Darren Anderton, give him his first big chance and then watch his progress to international stardom. Like when you make a £4.3 million profit on Christian Dailly in just two years. Like when you unearth a gem like Malcolm Christie who came from Nuneaton Borough last year for £30,000, which could and almost certainly will go up to £100,000 depending on appearances. He has not only become a Premiership regular but also made it into the England Under-21 squad. Spotting and developing your own stars certainly compensates you and gives you as much pleasure as buying your way to success.

Of course, the almost unbeatable combination which has helped Manchester United to harvest the game's top prizes over the past seven years is when a club can have the best of both worlds – a conveyor belt of home-produced internationals and a budget which allows the manager to pick off top players from anywhere in the world. But even that takes good judgement. A bad judge can prove that money is not everything but even the most successful make mistakes. I pride myself on the fact that most of my buys have been reasonably successful for what they are and what they cost. Alex has had his turkeys like everybody else but they have been few and far between and they diminish when put alongside successes like Roy Keane, Jaap Stam, Dwight Yorke, Andy Cole, Ole Gunnar Solskjaer and Teddy Sheringham. You could say he was lucky to get players like David Beckham, Paul Scholes, the Neville brothers, Nicky Butt and Ryan Giggs through the youth scheme but he had the foresight to first blood and then nurse them along at the right pace.

Alex was also cute enough to manipulate what was a political situation and exploit it quite blatantly for the good of his team. They ran away with their sixth title in eight years but there is no question their championship and European Cup ambitions were aided by them having a midwinter break in Brazil and being allowed to opt out of the FA Cup. Having said that, nobody could say it was worth the whole of the eighteen-point difference between United and Arsenal – it would be unfair to describe it as a 'tainted title' which is a view that has been expressed in some circles. United were the best and would have won it under any circumstances although maybe not as comfortably. And they are certainly no penalty-kick this season. I can see the likes of Arsenal, Liverpool, Leeds United and Chelsea pushing them all the way and, from a purely selfish as well as professional point of view, it will be for the good of football if they do. From Derby's standpoint it is better they are under some pressure and not able to approach a game totally relaxed and brimming with confidence because it makes it just that little bit harder for them to be at their best.

Although it could be said that it is happening already I would not like to see one team dominating the English scene in the way that Rangers dominate in Scotland. In spite of United's recent record, the competition is tougher than the one set of rivals Rangers have to worry about. It would be quite understandable if both Glasgow clubs wanted to remain big fishes in a small pool but I believe it would be better for their long-term standing in the game if they were able to compete against Premiership teams in a British League. That's as far as I would want to go. UEFA have already stretched the definition of 'champions' by allowing third-placed teams to compete in the Champions' League. I do not believe a European League would have enough appeal for English supporters – their pleasure is to sustain the rivalry between English clubs which has been established over decades. Derby v Dortmund will never pack them in as much as Derby v Newcastle. Matches against teams like Real Madrid and Barcelona may be mouth-watering prospects but the average fan isn't going to go to Barcelona, Madrid and then Munich week after week because they just could not afford it. It will all become dependent on television. Once they start making the travelling distances so great, they will be making the game purely for TV. I can see why the TV people are all for it but they will be creating a different type of football fan.

You have to worry for the future of domestic football as we know it now. It seems inevitable that some time in the future there will be two divisions of the Premiership with the other leagues perhaps becoming part-time and regionalized. It may be the only economic solution but we lose the lower leagues at our peril. Not only them but also non-league football as well still provide a valuable source of good players. I may have bought a lot of Europeans but I have also made it my business whenever possible to buy young British players from the lower leagues, as I have proved with several who have become regular members of the first-team squad at Derby, players like Rory Delap, Seth Johnson, Lee Morris, Malcolm Christie, Andy Oakes and Richard Jackson.

Delap came from Carlisle United after their chairman Michael Knighton, he of Manchester United fame, rang me to say he had a couple of good youngsters who he thought we should have a look at. He was not wrong either – Delap and a young team-mate, Matt Jansen, had a week's trial and both were very impressive. Delap, a tall right-sided defender, was more what I wanted and I signed him for £500,000. On the face of it, I might have made a mistake in turning down Jansen, who later went to Crystal Palace for £1 million and then on to Blackburn Rovers for an astonishing £4.1 million. But I was not looking for his type of player – someone who played just off the front men – and I have no regrets about that. I later went back to Carlisle and signed another young left-sided defender, Paul Boertien, for £250,000. These players are the future of Derby and the signs could not be better. The young lads who were already at the club as part of the Academy system are very promising and Derby won the southern section of the Premier reserve-team league.

It is a sad thing that whatever changes come about in the game – and there seem to be some every year – they will be dictated by the revenue football is getting from television and not by the paying public. There may be more money in the game than ever but everything is relative – transfer fees are rocketing and so are wages. Even at Derby we have players who are taking home close on a million pounds a year and their number can only increase. It is this subject of players' earnings which to me represents one of football's major future problems. Even the average Premiership player has only to compete in the top flight for six to eight years to achieve riches beyond his wildest dreams, and the big question is will wealth and security take the edge off their professionalism? Will they still hunger to win enough matches to lay down a challenge to Manchester United? As the cash avalanche continues and gets even stronger with the new television deal, the focus will be on good management more than ever before and anybody who wants to topple United will first of all have to equal and even better the managerial qualities of Ferguson. He seems to have discovered the secret of how to retain his millionaires' appetite for success.

You don't have to look further than a player like Beckham for evidence of that. The lad has his faults – sometimes his temper gets the better of him and he can be a bit petulant – but when you recognize the amount of work he gets through on a football pitch in every game, you can only admire him. Forget his football profile, which is high enough – if he never earned another penny and lived to be a hundred he would die a rich man . . . and he has a wife who earns more than he does! But Beckham is the perfect example of the wealthy player who is still not satisfied. He wants to be a winner, he wants to be the best and I have a lot of admiration for him. To me he is the sort of player any manager would love to have in his dressing room because he motivates himself and it rubs off on others.

To my mind, being able to get the best out of your players is an essential part of the job. And there are different ways to handle different players. You can't afford to be too hard on somebody with a weak temperament and too soft on an individual who might take advantage of what he perceives as your weakness. It used to be common sense – now it's called sports psychology. But it has its place in the modern game and often during the week I will invite Bill Beswick to get his message across. You have to be especially careful with particular foreign players – you cannot go steaming into them like you would a Rotherham welder because you have to remember they are in a strange environment a long way from home. I suppose you could say that, earning as much as they do, players, whether they come from China or Chelmsford, should not need any outside help. The majority don't but that extra gee-up can produce that extra effort which might get you those extra points.

I would not hesitate to put Arsenè Wenger, whose teams also always want to win, in the same category as Alex Ferguson. The pair have built up an atmosphere of intense rivalry over the past few years, perhaps because they recognize the quality in each other. The response the Arsenal manager gets from his players will always make the Gunners a threat and he has been very shrewd in drawing on his knowledge of the French scene by acquiring players such as Patrick Vieira, Manny Petit, Thierry Henry and before them Nicolas Anelka. By the same token you wonder why Chelsea do not do better with the class and quality there is at Stamford Bridge. They have proved on their day they are a match for the strongest and yet they often struggle against the weakest. Theirs and supporters in general are entitled to demand value for money. Barring few exceptions, their wages have not mushroomed in anything like the proportions now being enjoyed by top players but the fans, even when they can ill afford it, are paying ever-increasing prices whether it be corporate or season-ticket charges. More than ever before managers are responsible for signing or producing footballers who have the character and professionalism to earn their huge salaries. At the end of the day it is all about players – they are the only ones who win you matches – but this is certainly a golden age for those in the top bracket. They are not only calling the tune, they are also being paid by the piper. If they want a long contract they get it; if they want a Bosman-style short cut to a big money deal they get that too. The danger is the balance of wealth is tipping too much in their direction. Howard Wilkinson once did a study on the Bosman situation and the conclusion he came to was it might be better to do away with transfer fees altogether. Give a player a contract, pay him what he is worth and let him move on when the agreed term is completed. Compensation would only be paid to clubs who want to sign players while they are still under contract.

It would need radical changes to the rules and I can see why directors would be wary of supporting them. They might not see the sense in developing a young player to the point where he might be worth millions under the present system, only to see another club come along and take him away for nothing. Certainly clubs like Derby exist by balancing their books . . . selling here, buying there. But doing away with transfer fees might loosen the control of the players and not allow them to dictate as much as they seem to be able to do at the moment.

It is a sad consequence of modern football trends that domestic competitions like the FA and League Cups have lost some of their glamour. They are certainly not being treated with the respect they deserve. Allowing Manchester United to opt out of their defence of the FA Cup last season was, in my opinion, an entirely wrong decision, notwithstanding the fact that United's non-participation gave others a chance they might not have had. As it turned out their fixture list could easily have accommodated cup ties that might have proved more attractive to their supporters than an armchair view of a contrived tournament on the other side of the world. And I do not think for a minute that our chances of staging the World Cup in 2006 depended on whether or not they went to Brazil. As the events of Euro 2000 proved, the hooliganism of a small but significant percentage who turned up in Holland and Belgium was always going to render diplomacy meaningless.

The League Cup, currently sponsored by Worthington, presents an even better opportunity to a club like ours to win a European place, mainly because the bigger outfits treat it like an unnecessary inconvenience. The reorganization of the European Champions' League makes that tournament a more attractive financial proposition than the more traditional cup competitions. It's a sad fact that, given the choice between finishing in the top three and winning the FA Cup, most clubs would choose the former because of the potential cash windfall involved. Not only that, the emphasis on European competition, coupled with the demands of television, has eroded the format of FA Cup ties. Gone are the days of second and third replays; now it's all about the heartbreak of penalty shoot-outs and instant dramas.

Sometimes I have to remind myself it really is only a game. In the context of what goes on elsewhere in the world you can be made to feel insignificant. Believe or not there are people out there who could not give a toss about who wins the championship or who gets promoted or relegated. But those of us whose lives are intrinsically linked with football would not swap places with anybody – even when good times go bad. Bill Shankly's famous quote – 'Some people think football is a matter of life and death – I can assure them it is much more serious than that' – came from the heart of someone who lived and breathed the game. And there is a lot of Bill in most of us. When I was younger I earned a reputation for throwing teacups around in the dressing room – it was a total exaggeration although I did smash one against a wall when I was player-manager at Boston. I later did it purely for effect in that first game as manager of Birmingham at Newcastle . . . and I knew they were plastic. Oh yes – and there was the occasion when I was in charge at Newcastle and we lost a game at Southampton that could have helped to keep us up. This time it was a plate of sandwiches that were too handy and I flung them against the wall and they landed on Bobby Saxton's head. But the sight of 'Sacko' sat on the bench, looking mournful and perplexed with egg and tomato trickling down his face, changed the mood completely and everybody creased with laughter.

To be fair, as you get older you have to change your tack. I'm not suggesting that cowardice sets in but some of these lads are just too big to grab by the hair like I did to John Bailey. I have had my moments of course, especially with Wanchope, but I only lost it with him because I felt he had his own agenda and was not giving enough to the team. There was a time when players handed out the bollockings to each other. I used to sit back and let them get on with it. People like 'Sacko' like to wind them up to make them even madder. I understand that Roy Keane does a bit of that at Manchester United but that is another thing which has generally gone out of the game. Players don't like not getting on with each other but as much as they rely on their team-mates, so does a manager's lot depend on how they perform.

Howard Wilkinson is one of only five managers who have carried off English football's top prize in the last decade. He won the league title with Leeds in 1992, having taken over at Elland Road when the side was struggling in the Second Division. Four years later he was out on his ear. I remember saying to him when he was getting stick from all directions, 'Why don't you take your money and get out.' Of course he did not do anything of the sort because like most in our profession, he is a born optimist; you always believe you can turn the corner. The reality of course is you cannot – that's why I resigned at Newcastle and why I accepted the situation at Portsmouth. When ultimatums like 'get us promotion or you're out' or 'keep us up or look for another job' are flying around, it is pointless hanging around. Whatever you do you will never win over the people in charge because their lack of respect for you is embedded in their minds and the day will come when they will grab any excuse to get rid of you. So why keep banging your head against a wall? At Newcastle the players pleaded with me not to throw in the towel. 'Stay and we'll get into the play-offs,' they urged. We might have done just that but I'll never be convinced that the Halls weren't just waiting for me to fail.

If there are exceptions they are few and far between. I have already mentioned how Howard Kendall turned the corner at Everton after they beat us in the cup when I was at Oxford. Even Alex Ferguson was supposed to be in trouble after he had been at Old Trafford for a couple of years. Allegedly his pivotal point was an FA Cup victory at Nottingham Forest in 1990. That may be true but in the normal course of events the only chance you get to prove people wrong is after you go to another club. It is my belief that if the signs are negative towards you, that negativity will never go away. Your time in the job is borrowed and yet, after either the axe has fallen or you jump before you are pushed, you cannot wait to give somebody else the opportunity to do the same. I have been fortunate enough in my job that I have not had the situation to consider too many times but there are others who have been in and out of jobs as regularly as clockwork. Like Tommy Docherty once said – they have had more clubs than Tony Jacklin. But what else can they do? Being a manager is their way of earning a living and many are not equipped to pay their mortgage any other way. When you have come into the game straight from school as an apprentice, then been a player, coach and finally manager, that's the only life you have ever known. Fine if you've been lucky enough to handle a top team – getting the sack can set you up for life – but for every glamour job there are a hundred that pay a pittance.

A manager will take a job at a struggling Third Division club in the hope that he can do well enough to persuade a chairman to give him a better one. I can only think of one person, Dario Gradi at Crewe Alexandra, who has remained in the same job for seventeen years, struggling to make ends meet in the Third and Fourth Divisions, when he could almost certainly have worked at a higher level. But his reward has been to take Crewe into the First Division and keep them there mostly with players he has developed himself. His has been a fantastic success story. Dario is a manager in the true sense of the word – profiting from the experience of having to operate on the breadline. It is an essential part of a manager's education missing in the CV of many.

CHAPTER SIXTEEN

JIM SMITH ON . . .

REFEREES

I have lost count of the number of times I have fallen foul of match officials. But in all cases I have to say that the men in the middle have been – well, not to put too fine a point on it – wrong! The plain and simple fact is whenever I have been in trouble, without exception it has been the result of unfair refereeing. My big fault is I keep using the word 'cheat' but I don't mean it when I say they have cheated. That's just an emotive word that shoots off my tongue in the heat of the moment. I have been done more times than not because of that word but unfortunately my vocabulary does not stretch to coming up with another less incriminating description which fits the mood of the time. Even my daughters have tried to get me to stop. They have pleaded with me to count to ten before blowing a fuse. 'Dad,' they said once. 'Instead of calling the referee a cheat, just look at him and say, "Referee, how do you sleep at night?" It will have the same effect and you won't get done for saying it.' I was determined to take their advice next time the occasion arose – and it did . . . very soon. I waited for him to come off the pitch after my team had been on the wrong end of another costly bad decision and I said, 'Referee, how do you sleep at night . . . you cheating bastard!'

But you never learn and you should learn. Even when video evidence has proved referees to be wrong, the disciplinary chaps will still fine you for questioning the official's integrity and/or parentage. My problem is I feel the decisions I go mad about are total injustices. We all make mistakes and I would prefer – win, lose or draw – to knock on the referee's door after a game, shake his hand and say congratulations on a good game, which I have done on many occasions. Quite recently I was talking to an assessor who smiled at me and said, 'Jim, I've seen your team four times this season and you have had the four worst refereeing performances I've seen.' During one of them at Liverpool Sami Hyypia went through Stefano Eranio and broke his leg and did not even get a yellow card from Uriah Rennie. Referees may have been given really low marks from assessors because they have been so poor, but they are still above criticism from managers. I will never condone players pushing or harassing officials but when the FA decide to clamp down on that sort of behaviour, as they often do, they never follow it up by saying they are going to look at the standard of refereeing. Except in rare cases, like Mr Harris's mix-up over the substitution at the end of the Tranmere Rovers–Sunderland FA Cup tie last season, a referee is never publicly accountable and I believe, with the game as it is at the moment, they should be made to attend press conferences after matches to explain their actions.

People talk about the probable advantage of professional referees but in terms of salary – their fees next season will be approaching a thousand pounds a match in the Premiership – and the time they have off work to handle matches both in this country and abroad, they are as near as you can get to being professional now. That has not and will not make them any better. What might is if we can all get round a table – referees, managers, coaches, players, anybody involved with the game – to talk openly and try and get a consensus of opinion. In the past I have attended meetings with FA and Premier League officials ostensibly to discuss rule changes like the tackle from behind or the new ten-yard regulation at free-kicks but when we get there it is not so much to debate the changes, more a case of being told they are coming into force. And then when in a match a player is tackled from behind, the referee applies the letter of the law and dishes out a yellow or red card. There seems to be no understanding of individual situations where a foul may have been committed but there was no intent and it might have been because the player in possession was just too quick for his opponent.

If I go back a few years to the days of Arthur Ellis, Jim Finney, Jack Taylor, Kevin Howley and Gordon Hill, they used common sense and talked to players. 'Any more of that, son, and you won't be in the book, you'll be in the bath', and that sort of thing. I'm not too sure whether they are allowed to do that any more. The good referees are those you never notice – they let the game flow. There was a brief spell last season when, because the authorities felt the whole thing was getting out of hand, referees were told to ease off and it was almost as if sanity prevailed. But it was back to normal before long. In our match at Tottenham Hotspur at the end of April, Neale Barry booked ten players including five of ours and sent off Stefan Schnoor, and there was only one bad tackle in the game. Where he and others go wrong is they dispense yellow cards like confetti early on for innocuous offences without allowing for the fact that something more serious might happen later on. They set their agenda too soon in a game. I believe things will only improve when referees are allowed to use their own judgement without having the worry of Big Brother, either in the shape of officialdom or a television camera, watching them. When rules are rigidly black and white you will always have a problem.

There are one or two who have seen the light. I remember when Graham Poll first came on the Premier League list he was a nightmare, but he has improved beyond all recognition because he has shown enough strength of character to impose his own personality on a game. I know I will not be too popular with several of my managerial colleagues when I say I am also a fan of David Elleray because I always think you get a fair deal with him. There are others, and in my experience Jeff Winter and Barry are tough disciplinarians who have reputations for being generous with yellow cards. When I see we have got them and people like them I urge the players to be extra careful not to give them any excuses to produce the cards – sadly at White Hart Lane it did not work. I am encouraged by the policy this season to mix and match referees between the Premier and Nationwide Leagues. The idea of an élitist group, responsible only for Premiership matches, did not work because some of them became too smart for their own good. Even so-called referees' assistants, the more politically correct term for what used to be linesmen, got into the act, brandishing their flags like semaphore fanatics, as if to say, 'Look at me, mum, I'm on telly today.' They just have to be noticed.

I accept that being a referee is a difficult job – but nobody forces them to do it. There are teams who have a reputation for giving them a hard time, for harassing and bullying, for using tactics that are nothing short of intimidation. We all remember the sight of Manchester United players crowding around Andy D'Urso during the game against Middlesbrough. It is not a sight that should be seen in football and the FA should be applauded for picking up on it. But it seems to work to such an extent that you sometimes wonder whether that sort of crime does pay. I would hate to think that my players forcibly challenge a referee's decision. They might protest in the heat of the moment – as I unfortunately do – but no action of theirs or mine is premeditated. And where force might not work, what price a little friendlier persuasion? I know of managers who blatantly court officials by ringing them up before a match to ask if they have any special requirements for when they arrive.

They will entertain them afterwards and perhaps leave a little token – a bottle of wine or of whatever the referee's favourite tipple might be – in his room. They would also never stoop to questioning a decision, maybe because the less they do the fewer decisions go against them . . . and a free-kick, penalty, yellow or red card could be the difference between winning and losing a match; between keeping and losing a job. Now why can't I be like that?

AGENTS

In an ideal world there would not be such a thing as agents but you have to recognize, with the millions of pounds involved in transfer deals, a player needs specialist advice. But the job description covers a multitude of different areas; contrasting situations and characters, some decent and others who are at best disreputable and at worst completely corrupt. There are manager-type agents who look after their players – his contracts, investments, mortgage, commercial activities, who look after them when they are in trouble, monitor their behaviour, and so on – like Mark McCormack's IMG Group for instance. And there are others whose only interest is making money from transfer deals. They employ a policy of disruption, encouraged by the success of approaching managers and saying things like 'I can get Joe Bloggs away and how much will you pay me if I do?' They will send you a list of their clients which is in fact nothing more than a shopping list – what they are saying is, if you fancy anybody in particular, give me a ring and we'll see what we can do about it. It is a phenomenon which has permeated into our game from other sports as players' earnings have matched and even topped those of top golfers, tennis stars and racing drivers. But the role of agents in football is different because of the power and influence they wield in transfer situations. They actually broker deals. I'm told in Italy a handful control every deal that goes down and it could happen here – already, where managers once dealt with one another when they wanted to sign a player, now they have to talk to his representative. As a result 'tapping' – the common parlance for an illegal approach – is more rife than ever.

As their impact and that of chairmen and chief executives has increased, so the involvement of managers in the nitty-gritty details of a transfer deal has been eroded. The problem is it used to be an essential part of the manager's professional remit and chief executives don't have the experience or know-how to make a judgement on a player's value – so they have brought in agents to do it for them, despite their interest in screwing as much as they can from all concerned. That certainly happens more with players who come from abroad but even with domestic deals, gone are the days when you could ring a manager up, settle on a fee, talk to the player and agree a contract. Now you get as far as inquiring whether a guy might be available and suddenly some bloke you might never have heard of pops out of the woodwork and claims responsibility for all further discussions. And they are making fortunes.

At Derby our policy is if an agent rings me up or faxes me about a player and we follow it up to the extent of wanting to sign him, we are prepared to pay a commission for an introduction. We will also look after him if he persuades somebody to buy a player we want to sell. We are not prepared to give him any money for sorting out the contract because we regard that as the player's responsibility, although they always ask for it. My chairman, Mr Pickering, has a simple philosophy on that score – 'Why should we pay him a commission to screw us?' And that's what we would be doing. But I know they get away with it at other clubs. It's as the chairman keeps saying: 'Jim, we're both in the wrong business.'

Without question the involvement of agents is the most radical change in football that I have ever experienced. And it has become a minefield. I get inundated every day with phone calls, faxes, letters and videos from people imploring me to look at their men. Most go straight into the bin but, even then, it does not stop. It often happens that when you decide to pursue one particular avenue of interest another chap will ring you and claim he is his player. On one occasion last season I had three different agents insisting I deal with them over one player. It happens often and at times like that you just do not know who is genuine, who is telling you the truth, who you have to work with. That is the murky world they operate in and sadly you have to go along with it. But if I cannot alter the status quo with players who employ agents I would prefer not to share the same breathing space with, hopefully I can influence young players in their choice of adviser. I have always told them, 'If you must have an agent make sure he has the correct professional qualifications and experience and will only look after all your interests and not regard you merely as a meal ticket.'

The fact of the matter is that anybody can be registered as a bona fide agent provided he complies with the criteria of satisfying the authorities about his character and background and is able to pay a deposit of 200,000 Swiss francs. Many footballers are advised by solicitors who do not even need to be registered and may not be qualified to act directly in transfer deals but are never far away when the big decisions are made. I would like to see a professional regulatory body set up to look at the whole question of players' representatives to sort out the good from the bad. It would benefit football greatly if we could get rid of the shady dealers.

PLAYERS

My chief scout Bobby Roberts came back from Monaco three years ago and said, 'Jim, that Emmanuel Petit is some player – get him.' I obtained Petit's mobile number and rang him, explained who I was and said, 'I understand you might be going to Glasgow Rangers but would you come to Derby

instead?' I always tell players Derby is a great place to be –
a smashing club where they will be looked after but it is not
a big city like London, Birmingham or Manchester. Petit
sounded interested. He told me he would not be going to
Rangers because he did not feel the football in Scotland was
competitive enough. We were arranging to fly to Monte Carlo
to speak to him when we heard he had gone to Arsenal for
nearly £4 million, which at the time was out of our league.
But that sort of thing will always be a problem for a club like
ours which has to sell itself in a different way to those in the
big cities, especially when we cannot compete with massive
transfer fees or wages. You use a little homespun charm and
it usually works but, at the same time, you to have to talk
straight. We tell them there is nothing we would not do to
make them comfortable; if he is a family man, we will sort
out a house in an area that will suit him best for schools.
There have been one or two who have left Derby because they
became a little too big for their shoes but no club looks after
the welfare of its playing staff more than ours.

COACHING

I drew one stark conclusion from watching Euro 2000 and
that is at international level England is well behind the best
in Europe in what I consider to be top-level coaching.
Compared to France, Italy, Holland, Portugal we looked staid
and old-fashioned. We went into the tournament with the
typical gung-ho attitude of 'let's just be strong and together
and that will carry us through'. But that is not good enough
any more because the game is advancing and we do not seem
to be advancing with it. The fluidity and pace on the ball of
other countries was totally in advance of anything we did.
We're standing still and getting left behind and something
has to be done about it to stop us becoming permanently
second-rate. But at club level we have some of the best

coaches in Europe operating in the Premiership – maybe some of them should have an input into what happens at national level.

Coaching is a fact of life in football – it is as essential as the ball itself. I have every coaching qualification that is going and it is important to keep up to date with ever changing techniques and ideas. But there is a lot of bullshit spoken in the name of coaching and holding all the badges does not necessarily make you a good coach. It's not about passing exams. The manual will help to organize your coaching but then it is up to the individual to improvise – how he does it marks the difference between those at the top of their profession and the rest. I believe some people, and I'd like to think I'm one of them, have a natural flair for it and you can put your sessions on and get your message over.

Sometimes it is hard to take some people's seriousness seriously. I remember once being involved in a general football discussion on a managers' course when somebody expounded the theory that the ball skills and superb technique of the Brazilians is due to the fact that they play a lot of football on the beaches. I stuck my hand up and inquired, 'If that is true why haven't Bournemouth won the League Championship?' And I remember taking a rather cynical attitude to the much-vaunted Pomo – Position of Maximum Opportunity – theory put forward by the FA's former Director of Coaching Charles Hughes. He once highlighted a hat-trick by one-time Italian superstar Paolo Rossi as the perfect example of his ideas put into practice. At the end of the summing up I chipped in, 'Well, I've had a call from Rossi on this and he said he had never heard of Pomo – as far as he was concerned it was all about getting to the backa sticka.' Hughes was not amused at all.

CHARACTERS

There have been many, some I have already mentioned, but

none more colourful than a director of Portsmouth called Jim Sloan, who was one of the old school who took his responsibilities really to heart. He hardly missed a game – youths and reserves, as well as the first team. Jim loved a glass of Scotch and the first time I met him was when Portsmouth played Dorchester in a pre-season friendly. After the game I went into the boardroom and he was in there with his usual whisky in his hand. His first words to me of any note were, 'Jim, I read today that some doctor said you have to have five Scotches a day for your heart – I've only had four today so I'd better have another.' Then when he finished the fifth one he turned the glass upside down as if pretending to read what was on the side and muttered quizzically, 'I wonder if these glasses were made in Poland.' It was his polite way of asking for yet another, which was duly poured. When we went to Blackburn for my first game in charge, he saw us all off on the night before the match but still got up early the next morning to go with the kit to Ewood Park. Then he got filled up again after the match and was the life and soul of any trip back until he collapsed and somebody would have to put him to bed when we got to Portsmouth. That happened after most away matches. He used to recite little rhymes like, 'Win or lose we'll have some booze, if we draw we'll have some more.' And another one went: ' 'Twas an evening in December – as well you will remember, I was walking down the street in drunken pride. When my knees came all aflutter and I lay there in the gutter and a pig came up and lay down by my side. As I lay there in the gutter, thinking thoughts I should not utter, a maiden passing by was heard to say: You tell a man who boozes by the company he chooses – and the pig got up and slowly walked away.' But Jim Gregory got fed up with his behaviour and told him in no uncertain terms he had either to stop drinking or stop travelling. I tried to warn him not to go in the boardrooms after the games but he took no notice and eventually Gregory carried out his threat to ban him. That was a pity because he was such a character and tremendous supporter – a Pompey man through and through.

HIS FAMILY

My wife Yvonne, my three daughters, Alison, Suzanne and Fiona, and now my six granddaughters and one grandson have been a constant source of love, normality and even sanity in a profession that, if I had not been short of it from an early age, could have had me tearing my hair out. We were teenagers in Sheffield when Yvonne and I met and she has shared, without complaining, the nomadic existence I led until the later years of my career. So did the kids, starting from when my first daughter, Alison, was born when I was playing for Aldershot. I remember the consternation I felt at the time with Yvonne in hospital and me sitting having a coffee in the waiting room and thinking – 'What are we doing here? He can't play cricket for Yorkshire if he is born in Hampshire.' I was no different to most Yorkshiremen – to have a son who played for the county was the dream and in those days they had to qualify by birth. Then the nurse came in and announced, 'Mr Smith, come and look at your lovely daughter.' And she was lovely . . . and all silly thoughts of playing for Yorkshire went out of the window.

The next two arrivals, when I played for Halifax, would have qualified but again we were blessed with beautiful daughters. I had just lost my dad when Suzanne was born and I felt there was a lot of him in her. Then Fiona came along – we did not have a phone at home and I went to a public box to ring the hospital. I sat Suzanne, who was crying and screaming, on the ledge, and in order to be heard over the din, ended up bawling and shouting down the line myself and could barely make out the nurse telling me I had another daughter. Every penny counted in those days – I was not able to put a deposit on our first home until I was twenty-eight, when we bought a three-bedroom semi-detached house for

£2,500. When we moved to Boston, where property was cheap, we graduated to a four-bedroom detached for £4,000.

Funnily enough it was in the summer before I went to Boston that we took our first continental holiday. I splashed out on a package trip to Cala Milor in Majorca. I couldn't believe it when I walked out of the hotel on our first day there and saw this football match going on inside the grounds. I immediately recognized many of the players on one of the sides – Kevin Hector, Alan Durban and one or two others. I found out there was a little local league in operation involving teams of waiters, hotels, lorry drivers, police, etc. I had to have a crack and finished up playing for our hotel against the waiters and scored both goals in a 2–2 draw. I also got sent off for kicking one of the opposition but it didn't spoil the celebrations. It was the first point the team had ever won and the Rioja flowed all night. I thought my next game, against a hotel full of English people, would be a good laugh but that turned out to be a kicking match as well. Things got so bad that the hotel proprietor walked on to the pitch, ordered us all off and the game was abandoned. So that was the end of my Majorcan playing career, much to the delight of Yvonne who was not too happy about me spending our first holiday abroad on the football pitch.

But travelling up and down the country seems to have done the girls no harm – they all got good jobs: Alison as a chartered account, Suzanne in her own soft furnishing business and Fiona as a personal assistant, as well as keeping up the Smith record of producing daughters. In fact we had six, including twins, in succession before Alfie was born last year. I might have had a few ups and downs as a manager but nobody has been luckier as a family man.

HIS FUTURE

During the summer I signed a new contract at Derby County which will last for another two seasons. There has been speculation about my future role at the club mainly because I am not getting any younger and last season was not the best in terms of results. Radio phone-ins give the supporters the opportunity to air their views and although there has never been a concerted demand for me to go, it has been suggested that I step sideways and allow a younger man to step in. But the chairman has always said he wanted me to be the manager. When the flak was flying a bit last season he came to me and said, 'Stick with it, Jim, because when you go – I go.' I think he enjoys talking to me on the same level; we appreciate the same things – a chat over a pint and a good laugh. We don't fall out even when we don't see eye to eye over something. I think he feels more comfortable with me than he would if a younger man was manager. It is a very close, stable relationship and I want to stay in the job as long as I am enjoying it – and I am enjoying it. The years of struggle have taught me to appreciate the finer things of life – a nice home in Oxfordshire, a place in Spain and eating at good restaurants. I was more than happy with the offer to extend my previous contract by another year because the people at Derby are not only great to work for, they are also wonderful to work with – everybody from the top administrators to the canteen staff. The place has a terrific togetherness and I like being a part of it.

I believe I have done a good job at Derby. The club was in the First Division when I took over; the chairman was down more than £10 million and it was going to take five years to complete the rebuilding of the Baseball Ground. Inside two years we were in the Premiership playing in a brand-new stadium and, from being minus a lot of money, the chairman's shares are now worth around £30 million. And it bugs me more than a little to have this popular shout of management being a young man's game being shoved down my throat. People like Bobby Robson are proving the reverse is the case and although I don't envisage being in football when I am sixty-seven like he is, I still have enthusiasm to go with experience. I think I handle problems better at my age than a younger man would. If I felt I could not do that, if I thought the job was screwing up to the point it was affecting my personality, I would turn it in tomorrow. But I am realistic enough to appreciate that I will only be in the job if we get results – the price of failure is still the sack. A club like ours is entitled to dream that one season everything could go right and we could finish at or near the top – that may be pie in the sky but a cup final is well within our capabilities . . . even if the rebuilding of Wembley will take too long for me to get there.

But after Boston United, Colchester United, Blackburn Rovers, Birmingham City, Oxford United, Queens Park Rangers, Newcastle United, Middlesbrough, Portsmouth and the League Managers' Association, for me the managerial train stops at Derby County. And, if this at last could be the right place at the right time, I think I have earned it.

CAREER FILE

JAMES MICHAEL SMITH
Born: Sheffield, 17 October 1940

Full-time playing career:
SHEFFIELD UNITED: signed January 1959
ALDERSHOT: signed July 1961
HALIFAX TOWN: signed July 1965
LINCOLN CITY: signed March 1968
BOSTON UNITED: signed June 1969
COLCHESTER UNITED: signed November 1972.

Position: wing-half
League appearances: 247
League goals: 8

Managerial career:
BOSTON UNITED: June 1969 to November 1972
COLCHESTER UNITED: November 1972 to June 1975
BLACKBURN ROVERS: June 1975 to March 1978
BIRMINGHAM CITY: March 1978 to February 1982
OXFORD UNITED: March 1982 to June 1985
QUEEN'S PARK RANGERS: June 1985 to December 1988
NEWCASTLE UNITED: December 1988 to March 1991
PORTSMOUTH: May 1991 to February 1995
DERBY COUNTY: June 1995–

Promotion:

1973–74 COLCHESTER UNITED: Division Four to Division Three.

1979–80 BIRMINGHAM CITY: Division Two to Division One.

1983–84 OXFORD UNITED: Division Three to Division Two.

1984–85 OXFORD UNITED: Division Two to Division One.

1995–96 DERBY COUNTY: Division One to Premiership.

Between March 1995 and June 1995 he was chief executive of the League Managers' Association.